"Dangerous Foreigners"

"Dangerous Foreigners"

European Immigrant Workers
and Labour Radicalism in Canada
1896-1932

Donald Avery

McCLELLAND AND STEWART

Copyright © 1979 McClelland and Stewart Limited

McClelland and Stewart Limited
The Canadian Publishers
25 Hollinger Rd.
Toronto

Printed and bound in Canada

FRONT COVER: European ''agriculturalists''
heading for railway construction work, circa 1908.
Courtesy Public Archives of Canada.

CANADIAN CATALOGUING IN PUBLICATION DATA

Avery, Donald, 1938-
  ''Dangerous foreigners''

(Canadian social history series)

ISBN 0-7710-0826-0

1. Canada – Emigration and immigration – History.
2. Labor and laboring classes – Canada – History.
3. Canada – Social conditions. 4. Radicalism –
Canada – History. 5. East Europeans in Canada.
I. Title. II. Series.

JV7225.A94 301.32'4'0971 C79-094294-1

Contents

Abbreviations

AA	Anglican Church Archives, Toronto
ADR	Annual Departmental Reports of Immigration and Colonization
APP	Alberta Provincial Police Records
BCPP	British Columbia Provincial Police Records
BP	Sir Robert Borden Papers
CAR	*Canadian Annual Review*
CNR	Canadian National Railway Colonization Records
CPC	Communist Party of Canada Records
CPR	Canadian Pacific Railway Company Records
DND	Department of National Defence Records
Glenbow	Glenbow Institute, Calgary
IB	Immigration Branch Records
IC	Immigration and Colonization
IWW	Industrial Workers of the World Records
MFP	Manitoba Free Press
OBU	One Big Union Records
PAA	Public Archives of Alberta, Edmonton. Glenbow – Glenbow Institute, Calgary
PABC	Public Archives of British Columbia, Victoria
PAC	Public Archives of Canada, Ottawa
PAM	Public Archives of Manitoba, Winnipeg
PAO	Public Archives of Ontario, Toronto
PAS	Public Archives of Saskatchewan, Regina
Queen's	Douglas Library, Queen's University, Kingston
RCMP	Royal Canadian Mounted Police Records
SP	Sessional Papers of the Dominion of Canada
UBC	University of British Columbia Archives
UCA	United Church Archives, Toronto
UMWA	Records of the United Mine Workers of America: District 18
WCOA	Western Coal Operations Collection
WFM	Western Federation of Miners Records: District 6

Introduction

This book is a study of European immigration to Canada between the years 1896 and 1931. It is not a study of the Canadian experience of particular national or ethnic groups; nor is it an examination in any great detail of the pattern of immigrant agricultural settlement. The part which European immigrant workers played in the rapidly changing economic and social life of the country is the central concern here. The value of this approach, it will be seen, lies in the challenge it offers to the notion that most of the Europeans who arrived in Canada during these years settled permanently on the land.[1]

The immigrant workers whose lives are described in this study came mainly from Eastern and Southern Europe.* Their Canadian experience had much in common with that of Oriental and Black immigrants to the country. But there were also important differences. The Canadian consensus seems to have been that Orientals and Blacks were unassimilable. Their future in the country, to the extent that they were thought to have one at all, was that of the most grinding labour. They were the Dominion's "untouchables," to be used and, if possible, discarded.[2] By con-

* This study primarily concentrates on the reaction of the English Canadian community to these European immigrant workers. There are several reasons for this approach. During this period Canadian Immigration Policy was essentially determined by English Canadians, in part, because of the fact that every minister of the Immigration Branch and virtually every major official was an Anglo-Canadian, and in part, because the strongest advocates of the "open door" policy were English Canadian businessmen. Yet another factor was that most of the Ukrainian, Finnish, and other Central European workers found employment outside Quebec. Jewish immigrants were the only exception to this migration pattern, but they gravitated towards jobs in Montreal, not to the push and rail camps of the Canadian Shield.

trast, British and English stock American immigrants were readily accorded high occupational and social status in the country.[3] But Eastern and Southern European immigrants were allowed into the country because of their brawn and industry and they were granted basic civil rights.[4] They were at once candidates for Canadianization. Yet as "foreigners" theirs was a decidedly mixed reception, the attitude of their hosts varying with time and economic circumstances. Language and culture clearly set the European immigrant apart in Canada.[5] So too, it will be shown, did occupation and place of residence. And this social distance was lengthened by the suspicion and hostility many newcomers felt when they discovered Canada could not deliver what they had come – or been led – to expect. To the immigrants who form the subject of this study, the rising Dominion both promised and threatened.[6]

That many of them should have found work as wage labourers in industry or agriculture is not surprising. Settling on the land was an expensive business in early twentieth-century Canada, and few immigrants had the capital to become full-time farmers straight away. In the critical settlement process temporary employment in railroad construction, mining, harvesting, or lumbering was for most prospective farmers an absolute necessity. For others many years of such work was necessary before a start could be made on the land at all. Nor was the ideal of the family farm necessarily the immigrant's ultimate goal; there were many who were committed to industrial employment on arriving in the country and who headed directly to the major transportation centres and company towns. Again, large numbers of immigrants regarded their Canadian residence as temporary. A man's Canadian wages might support his relatives in Europe and give him the means to improve his lot when he went back home.[7]

I

Geographical mobility and occupational pluralism typified the European immigrant experience in this period. In one year an immigrant worker might find himself cast in many roles: in February a lumber worker in Iroquois Falls, Ontario; in June a railroad navvy along the National Transcontinental; in August a harvester in Grenfell, Saskatchewan; in November a coal miner in Fernie, British Columbia. Such occupational diversity belies the simple division of the world of work into agricultural and non-agricultural categories.[8] The unskilled immigrant worker had one basic commodity to exchange – "his physical strength, his brute force, to carry, pull, push, turn, as a horse would do, or a piston or a wheel." He exchanged it from sector to sector as the demand for "human machines" shifted to a rhythm he could not but obey.[9]

Not surprisingly, Canadian immigration policy during these years was strongly influenced by spokesmen for the labour-intensive resource industries and the transportation companies. Officially, Canada wanted agriculturalists; but in practice thousands of the immigrants who came from Central and Southern Europe became either full-time or part-time industrial workers. The explanation for this dichotomy lies in the ability of industrialists and farmers to link their economic interests in demanding an "open door" immigration policy. Before 1914 the Dominion's immigration policy emphasized the recruitment of "stalwart peasants" from Europe who could both push back the frontier of settlement and provide the labour needed on a casual or seasonal basis in the country. That a large percentage of the immigrants thus recruited soon left the agricultural labour force entirely did not deflect the Dominion from its chosen course; on the contrary, it provided justification for more intensive immigrant recruitment to fill the ranks of those "agriculturalists" who had opted out. Nor did the symbiotic relationship between the industrial and agricultural sectors end in 1914. The post-war recession delayed the resumption of large-scale European immigration, but the Railway Agreement of 1925 gave the Canadian Pacific and Canadian National railway companies virtually a free hand, both ethnically and numerically, in the recruitment of European agriculturalists. This arrangement, which clearly gave priority to the imperatives of industrial capitalism and agricultural wage labour, lasted until the advent of the Great Depression of the 1930s which glutted the Canadian unskilled labour market and forced the advocates of the open door to back down.[10]

That the proponents of this policy had been so successful for so long is indicative of a larger theme: Canadian immigration policy can only be understood in terms of the country's participation in a wider transatlantic capitalist labour market. The rapid expansion of ocean and rail transportation in the late nineteenth and early twentieth centuries made it possible for European workers to hunt for jobs in North America on a mass scale.[11] Their progress through this new world of work was often presided over by ethnic intermediaries. Many of these ruthlessly exploited their fellow countrymen, but it would be misleading to dismiss the "padrone system" out of hand. It brought North American employers into easy contact with unskilled European workers; conversely, for the workers themselves, who knew nothing of the English language and North American life, it provided ready access to jobs and a means (albeit a crude one) of adjusting to a challenging new environment.[12] Kinship and ethnic connections sustained the immigrant workers both materially and psychologically and particular industries tended to attract particular ethnic groups. In some respects this homogeneity was an asset to an employer: a steady supply of labour was assured and individual worker differences minimized. On the other hand the collective strength which immigrant workers drew from these familiar ties and culture could provide an effective substitute for industrial unionism. In this way individual grievances could quickly become the basis of collective protest. Accordingly, many employers encouraged ethnic diversity and resolutely defended their right to have access to new groups of immigrant workers.[13]

Significantly, Canadian employers encountered little internal opposition in their search for unskilled immigrant workers. Occasionally native workers denounced the influx of large numbers of European agriculturalists through their unions and newspapers but they never launched a systematic campaign against the practice. Few of the English-speaking among them at least were interested in the socially undesirable jobs to be found in the mines, in the lumber camps and "at the end of steel." Nor were they particularly interested in bringing European workers into their craft unions.[14]

W.R. Böhning, one of the most eminent students of immigration, has recently noted that "the international migration of workers is characterized by essentially the same determinants the world over. The situation in traditional immigration countries like Australia or Canada differs from that of Europe only by degree."[15] Böhning's remark is very apt; indeed, his analysis of the contemporary movement of immigrant workers from the Mediterranean littoral into the highly industrialized countries of central and northern Europe might well be applied to the Canadian immigration experience from 1896 to 1931:

> Migration is a social process: a migrant leaves one social context for another on the basis of a hierarchically ordered set of values. For economic migrants the socio-economic deprivations at home are often ... a sufficient condition of his out-migration. Lured by the prospects of an El Dorado magnified through hearsay, he sees himself as a *target worker* that is,

someone who goes abroad to earn as much money as possible, in order to return home ... but in almost all cases the migrant absorbs at least superficially some of the norms and values of the host society. ... After about one year, most polyannual migrants realize that short-term participation in a high-wage economy does not once and for all eliminate their deprivation back home, however spartan their conduct in the country of employment. ... Finally this process will lead to a significant number of target workers tending to settle down in the receiving country. ... The migrant becomes an immigrant.[16]

In Böhning's scheme of things the first wave of immigrant workers consists normally of single males. These are not only the most mobile group in the emigration society, but also the closest "to the locus of the 'grapevine' which sets in motion a chain migration." Once the apparent success of a particular migration has been established more and more unaccompanied married workers join the stream, most of them intending to return to their wives and children on acquiring their "stake." In time the advantages of the host society not only delay their return but encourage them to send for their dependents. This larger pattern, it will be seen, has numerous Canadian examples in the period under review.[17]

More striking still are the similarities to be found in the Canadian and American immigration experience during these years. Before 1914 European immigrants moved back and forth across the Canada–United States border in large numbers in search of work. The two countries also shared certain exclusionist policies: mental defectives, paupers, and avowed anarchists, had to be stopped at all costs, and the numbers of Asiatic and Black immigrants had to be strictly limited.[18] After the war the two countries drifted farther apart in their policies. During the 1920s the United States government established an elaborate quota system, which sharply reduced the numbers of immigrants coming to the country from Southern and Eastern Europe. The justification for this action lay in the findings of the Immigration Commission of 1910, which made the following comparison between "new" immigrants and "old": "The old immigration movement was essentially one of permanence. The new immigration is very largely one of individuals, a considerable proportion of whom apparently have no intention of permanently changing their residence, their only purpose in coming to America being to temporarily take advantage of the greater wages paid for industrial labour in this country."[19]

Ironically, while the American Commission was strongly suggesting that the presence of vast numbers of "sojourners" was not socially wise, many Western European countries were admitting immigrants only as transients. In Germany, it was generally assumed that the importation of foreign workers would only be "a temporary expedient with which to overcome unusual demand pressures and ... that the immigrants would return home when the country returned to its normal pace." The great advantage of such a policy, it was reasoned, was that "an expendable labour force takes its problems away with it when it is re-exported." Consequently, "on the grounds of short stay, and only partial participation in the life of the society," it was possible to justify low wages, poor living conditions, and social discrimination.[20]

The Canadian authorities never formally embraced either the American quota system or the German "guest worker" (*Gastarbeiter*) policy. While Southern and Eastern Europeans certainly encountered discrimination in Canada after World War I, and found it more difficult to enter the country than did their British and American counterparts, they were never confronted with the rigidity which prevailed in the United States after 1920. Moreover, Canadian immigration authorities such as W.D. Scott, superintendent of the Immigration Branch between 1906 and 1923, time after time refused to allow industrial workers into the country on temporary permits. Officially at least prospective Canadian employers of immigrant workers from Europe had to "be able to offer steady employment throughout the year." The Dominion was still a self-proclaimed homeland for immigrants, who would shoulder the burden of its work. After three years domicile European immigrants to Canada could acquire citizenship and thereafter vote in Canadian elections.[21]

Such was the ideal; the reality of Canadian immigrant life was often very different. Even in the 1920s many of the Europeans who came to Canada were in effect guest-workers, who met the needs of Canadian agriculture and industry and then went home. Nor was the return migration confined to sojourners who had accumulated savings; it also included many who were forced out of Canada by depressed economic circumstances. The lack of unemployment benefits in the Dominion and the existence of ample means to deport public charges further swelled the ranks of the returnees.[22]

Yet European immigrant workers were by no means a docile proletariat hopelessly entrapped within the Canadian industrial system. True the power of the state was often used to repel their collective protest, but they were by no means defenceless. They fought back and made ethnicity itself a weapon in the fight. Recent studies have clearly demonstrated that modernization should not be regarded "as a linear process by which immigrant peasants, pushed through a tube, emerged as 'modern' individuals at the other end." On the contrary, newcomers to industrial society have "tended to shape the system to fit their own needs" and have "subtly exercised a collective strength in their adaptation to industrial conditions, modifying the system to fit their wants and traditions."[23] In Canada ethnic churches, fraternal societies and political organizations all contributed to the transformation of the individual immigrant's grievances into collective protest. The Ukrainian, Finnish, and Jewish immigrant communities all produced social democratic clubs and these in turn were associated with the Social Democratic Party of Canada. Nor did immigrant workers shun trade union activity; Finnish, Slavic, and other European-born workers came to the fore in many industrial unions, most notably the United Mine Workers of America (UMWA) and the Western Federation of Miners (WFM). Similarly, they were found in their hundreds in the ranks of the syndicalist Industrial Workers of the World (IWW). During the 1920s over 80 per cent of the membership of the Communist Party of Canada claimed Finnish, or Ukrainian ancestry.[24]

The involvement of immigrant workers in syndicalist, socialist, and communist activity on occasion evoked a stern response from the larger Canadian community. This was especially true in 1919 when fear of a Bolshevik revolution in Canada produced a series of repressive measures. One of these, Section 41 of the Immigration Act, gave the Dominion authorities the power to deport "dangerous" aliens. Increasingly, the Immigration Act reflected not the high ideals of a self-proclaimed homeland but the view that the "foreigner" was the agent of social and economic turmoil. Between 1929 and 1931 many "alien" radicals were cast out of the country. Following the harsh treatment accorded some immigrants during the Great War the events of the Great Depression confirmed that Canadian society harboured deep suspicions of its foreign-born, particularly of those who dared challenge the prevailing free enterprise system.[25]

II

Any study of this type inevitably involves some problems of definition. Three terms that will be used frequently here are "ethnic," "alien," and "foreigner." These terms have unpleasant connotations but the historian cannot avoid them: they were used in many ways and for many purposes in the period being studied. They are part of our history and must be accepted as such. Like many other highly emotional terms, it is impossible to give them single, simple definitions. Clearly, however, they were used to describe persons thought to lie outside the country's Anglo-Saxon Protestant and French Canadian Roman Catholic communities – persons and groups who were in the country, but not necessarily part of it. It might be argued that Scottish, Welsh, and Irish immigrants similarly stood apart in Canada, but despite their strongly felt group loyalties they were accepted as blood brothers and sisters by the larger Anglo-Canadian community and shared its majoritarian outlook. Visibly, the same could not be said of the East and South Europeans in the country. Scandinavians and Germans were a special case; many native English-speaking Canadians regarded them as close cultural relatives, although the events of the Great War brought down on German-speaking residents a fierce abuse. Scandinavians, and the war-time years excepted, Germans, fitted in easily; other Eastern and Central Europeans did not, whether the differences lay with themselves or their host society. Historical evidence from this period certainly indicates that many native-born Canadians thought of them as culturally inferior, and it was for the Central and Southern European that the lexicon of the majority – ethnic, alien, foreigner – was reserved.[26]

The historian of immigration also faces great statistical challenges. Statistically, the period of Canada's immigration history being studied here is well documented. This explains the absence of lengthy charts and tables in what follows: existing information has been used rather than duplicated. The accuracy of all that information is another matter: what Brinley Thomas has said in *Migration and Economic Growth: A Study of Great Britain and the Atlantic Community* about the quality of immigration statistics is as true of the Canadian figures as it is of those of other countries: "Immigration [records] had many inadequacies; the ignorance of port inspectors of the complex political divisions of the Old World; the dishonesty of many immigrants in dealing with alien officials; and the practice, sometimes adopted, of regarding the port of embarkation as a criterion of the nationality of the passenger."[27]

Like every study this one leaves behind it neglected themes – ideas that could have been explored in full only in a larger work.

One of these is the relationship between immigration and the business cycle. Brinley Thomas's thesis that the opening up of new regions of food and raw material production necessitates the flow of people as well as capital is here a given. The growth of staples production and population in Northern Ontario and Western Canada in the first decades of this century is a striking case in point.[28] The challenging question posed by Marcus Hansen–"who emigrated, who stayed behind, and why were choices made?"–will merely be alluded to in what follows; it must await its Canadian answers, if indeed they are possible.[29] Nor will the experience of immigrant women in early twentieth-century Canada be dealt with in any great detail here. Most immigrant wage workers were men and the extractive and construction industries they served had very few female employees. That is not to say, of course, that immigrant women did not powerfully influence the response of their communities to the challenges of Canadian life. The ability of these women to operate meagre family budgets successfully was often the condition of survival itself. Equally, in periods of industrial strife it was not uncommon for immigrant women to provide emotional support for their husbands and sons, and even to take their place on the picket line.[30]

To concentrate here on the immigrant experience in mining, lumbering, harvesting, and railroad construction is surely justified. These were the industries with the most acute labour shortages and the least appeal for the native born and the immigrant skilled. Only the European workers seemed prepared to face the irregular pay, high accident rates, crude living conditions, and isolation that characterized the world or work in these expanding parts of the Dominion's economy. In time many of the immigrants moved on from the lumber and mining camps and the railroad gangs to more stable opportunities in the steel mills and packing plants. But their passage was anguished, and the transition they made was often from manipulated foreigners to deprived Canadian working class.[31]

CHAPTER ONE

Immigrant Workers and the Canadian Economy 1896-1914

Between 1896 and 1914 Canada experienced unprecedented economic growth: railway mileage doubled, mining production tripled, and wheat and lumber production increased tenfold. This economic expansion was accompanied by dramatic population growth; in the decade 1901-11 the nation's population increased by a remarkable 34 per cent. Much of this increase was attributable to immigration; in 1914, it was estimated that three million people had entered the country since 1896. Although a substantial number of these "newcomers" settled on the land, the vast majority derived some portion of their annual income from the wage employment offered by the booming agricultural and industrial sectors of the economy whose demand for labour, both skilled and unskilled, seemed insatiable.

Led by the spokesmen for labour-intensive industries, including agriculture, Canadian public opinion came to favour an immigration policy that went beyond the traditional open-door approach to the systematic recruitment abroad of men and women who could meet the challenge of a nation freshly embarked upon great enterprise. This opinion found expression in the immigration policies of successive Dominion governments. Although the official pronouncements of the Immigration Branch in this period stressed that only farmers, farm labourers, and domestics would be recruited, exceptions were frequently made to accommodate the needs of businessmen in the expanding sectors of the economy. That Canada's search for immigrant agriculturalists was largely in the hands of steamship agents in search of bonuses further qualified official policy; many who entered the country as farmers and farm labourers quickly found their way into construction camps, mines, and factories.[1]

Ironically, agricultural immigrants were also turned towards wage employment by a settlement policy which tended to give priority to a central European peasantry too poor to establish itself directly on the land. For many who entered the country during these years the life of a yeoman farmer was either irrelevant or but a distant ideal that could be realized only through the slow accumulation of capital by wage labour. As W.F. McCreary, the Winnipeg commissioner of immigration, put it in 1897: "We have a long and wearisome task before us if we expect to settle this country with ... men with even modest means. The settlement, if, it comes at all rapidly, must come from men without means, who will earn in this territory itself the capital to enable them to homestead."[2] It was, therefore, assumed by both immigration officials and employers that many agricultural immigrants would initially, at any rate, provide a source of cheap seasonal labour. Industries such as commercial agriculture, railroad construction, mining, and lumbering all experienced peak annual work periods; their needs, and the needs of the immigrants could be harmonized – or so it appeared at the turn of the century. In the event, this arrangement was not entirely satisfactory to either party. The immigrant workers were exposed to a labour market which was both highly unstable and fraught with physical difficulties. The ideal of the Canadian developmental capitalists of this era was the sort of labour market H.C. Pentland has described in his masterful article "The Development of a Capitalistic Labour Market in Canada":

> In this market the employer is confident that workers will be available whenever he wants them; so he feels free to hire them on a short term basis, and to dismiss them whenever there is a monetary advantage in doing so ... labour to the employer is a variable cost. ... From a broader point of view, the capitalistic labour market represents a pooling of the labour supplies and labour needs of many employers, so that all may benefit by economizing on labour reserves.[3]

It was an ideal that was not fully realized. Faced with the demands of projects such as the building of two new transcontinental railways Canada's "captains of industry" required a work force that was both inexpensive and at their beck and call. To them the agricultural ideal which lay at the root of Canadian immigration policy increasingly appeared obsolete. Supply and demand should be the new governing principle of immigration policy. The best immigrants would be those willing to roam the country to take up whatever work was available – railroad construction in the Canadian Shield in the summer, harvesting in Saskatchewan in the fall, coal mining in Alberta in the winter, and lumbering in British Columbia in the spring. This view ran against the deep-seated Canadian myth of the primacy of the land but it nevertheless prevailed. By 1914 it was obvious, even to immigration officials, that Canada had joined the United States as part of a transatlantic labour market.[4]

I

Until World War I Canadian immigration policy had two determinants: the willingness of the Dominion government to give businessmen a free hand in the recruitment of the immigrants they needed for national economic development; and the determination of the Immigration Branch to recruit agriculturalists, particularly for the settlement of western Canada. The tendency to equate population growth through immigration with national prosperity was especially pronounced during the years 1896-1914. The Immigration Branch in these years was under the direction of men who reflected the expansionist outlook of western Canada: Clifford Sifton (1896-1905), Frank Oliver (1905-11), Robert Rogers (1911-12), and Dr. W.J. Roche (1912-14). In many ways Clifford Sifton established the pattern followed by his successors. The operational budget of the branch was expanded from a modest $120,100 in 1896 to a remarkable $900,000 in 1905, Sifton's last year as minister of the interior. This increase was accompanied by personnel changes which saw many of Sifton's business and political associates assume key positions. Men such as James A. Smart (deputy minister of the interior), Frank Pedley (superintendent of immigration), W.F. McCreary (Winnipeg commissioner), and W.T.R. Preston (commissioner in London, England) shared Sifton's faith that the key to Canadian prosperity was the settlement of Western Canada through expanded immigration and railroad construction. These men also accepted the notion that government officials and businessmen should work closely together to promote the opening of new agricultural regions and the development of resource industries such as lumbering and mining.[5]

Sifton and his hand-picked civil servants saw immigration in the most pragmatic terms; it didn't matter where immigrants came from as long as they could be made to fit Canada's economic priorities. Racial and cultural factors could not be ignored, but above all immigrants should be selected according to their ability to adjust to the environmental and occupational demands of the Canadian frontier. Anglo-Canadians might resent the influx of Poles, Russians, and Ukrainians with their vastly different ways, but Sifton's utilitarian approach guaranteed their entry. His attitude was summed up in one remark: "I think a stalwart peasant in a sheep-skin coat, born on the soil, whose forebearers have been farmers for ten generations, with a stout wife and half-a-dozen children, is good quality."[6] By this standard British immigrants were a doubtful quantity. Many of them not only refused to go on the land, they also refused "heavy handed work." In 1907, Dr. P.H. Bryce, the chief medical officer of the Immigration Branch, suggested that a high percentage of British immigrants were poor physical specimens, especially those from "classes which have been for several generations factory operatives and dwellers in the congested centres of large industrial populations."[7] Immigrants from the British Isles, the ancient homeland of so many English-speaking Canadians, continued to flow into the country. But for the Immigration Branch the "men in sheep-skin coats" had, for the most part, to be found elsewhere. Under Sifton's direction Canadian immigration policy acquired a vigorous continental European dimension.

Between 1896 and 1914 approximately a million immigrant farmers were found for Canada's burgeoning agricultural economy. Immigration officials were particularly anxious to maintain a steady supply of farm workers since agriculture in Canada was labour-intensive, and large numbers of men were required both during spring seeding and fall harvest. The demand for seasonal labour was most pronounced in the grain belt of Western Canada, and in the sugar beet and fruit-farming regions of Ontario, Alberta, and British Columbia. The declining number of native-born family farm workers increased the demand for immigrant farm labourers.[8] This desperate shortage of agricultural workers was vividly described by one Alberta farmer in 1907: "The government is trying to bring settlers or farmers into the west all the time. What is needed is men to work for the farmers that are already here, or those who are here will have to go out of business ... I hired a man from the Salvation Army. ... He is with me yet, but ... he knows he could get $3.00 a day if he were free, and reminds me of that fact quite often. He is the boss and I am the roust about, or chore boy."[9]

In its attempts to meet the mounting needs of Canadian farmers the Immigration Branch employed a variety of methods. The most common and traditional of these was the payment of a bonus to steamship agents and colonization organizations for each agricultural immigrant brought into the country.[10] Unfortunately, there was no way to guarantee that particular immigrants were agriculturalists, or that once in the country they would be available for farm work. Many steamship agents assumed no responsibility beyond the bonus.[11]

In 1899 an attempt was made to provide a more systematic and responsible system for the recruitment of continental European agriculturalists, particularly from Germany, the Austro-Hungarian Empire, and the Scandinavian countries. This took the form of a clandestine agreement between the Canadian government and the North Atlantic Trading Company. By 1906, when the Dominion government backed out of the arrangement, the company had directed over 70,000 immigrants to Canada, most of them from the Austrian provinces of Galicia and Bukovinia, and had been paid approximately $367,245.00.[12] The elimination of the company signalled a return of chaotic market conditions in the "immigrant" industry, though the Dominion government continued to pay bonuses to a variety of organizations and agents to bring farm workers to Canada. One of the most controversial of these "emigration" organizations was the Salvation Army. In 1903 the "Army next to God" had created a Department of Migration and Settlement for the transportation and placement of the "deserving" poor of Great Britain. The Salvation Army was able to persuade the Dominion authorities to include it in the bonus scheme for bringing agriculturalists to the country. Bonus payments to the Army rose dramatically from $500 in 1903 to $9,052 in 1907 and to $25,000 in 1914 despite continual charges from the Trades and Labour Congress of Canada that most of these "agriculturalists" soon became industrial workers.[13]

Organized labour was even more hostile towards the schemes of commercial emigration companies. One of these had at its head James A. Smart, Sifton's first deputy minister. In 1905 Smart was able to convince immigration officials to support a prepaid passage scheme whereby his agency would act simultaneously as immigrant bank, steamship agency, and labour bureau. Immigrants resident in Canada would purchase steamship and rail tickets for friends or relatives overseas through one of Smart's local offices. Those recruited in this fashion were then brought to Canada and placed in agricultural jobs by the Smart labour agency. For its efforts the company would receive both a commission on steamship tickets sold, and a bonus from the Dominion government.[14]

In 1907, the Immigration Branch itself became directly involved in the recruitment and placement of British agricultural labourers in the provinces of Ontario and Quebec. Approximately one hundred government agents were appointed, each of whom received a two-dollar bonus for every farm labourer placed. W.D. Scott, the superintendent of immigration, explained the new system in these terms: "Each agent is supposed to correspond with the [3,000] British booking agents pointing out the needs of his individual locality, the rate of wages there and to request the booking agent to direct suitable farm labourers to him. When the booking agent has succeeded in selling a ticket to an emigrant ... he immediately mails an advice form to the agent interested ... and delivers to the emigrant in question a card of introduction."[15]

In many ways this placement scheme was an attempt to attract a higher percentage of British agriculturalists to Canada. Conditions in Great Britain did not favour the emigration of such persons since agricultural wages and working conditions were often better than in Canada. Indeed, British farm labourers had little incentive to leave the Old Country for a harsh new land where irregular employment, low wages, and poor accommodation were commonplace. Nor did Canadian farmers show themselves particularly willing to make the prospect of immigration more attractive for British labourers. In 1907, the Winnipeg commissioner of immigration became so annoyed with the outlook of Prairie farmers that he suggested a reduction in the efforts being made to recruit farm labour for spring seeding.[16]

His suggestion was neither economically expedient nor politically wise. In fact the opposite occurred. Pressure from the railway companies and Prairie farmers and businessmen led the Immigration Branch into further involvement in the farm labour market in conjunction with private labour bureaus such as the Canadian Pacific Employment Agency, the Grand Trunk Pacific Employment Agency, the Canadian Northern Employment Agency, Allons Employment Agency, and Hislop Employment Agency. The phenomenal increases that were occurring in wheat production ensured that business interests recruiting farm labour would have the active co-operation of the Immigration Branch. In 1901, 20,000 harvesters had to be induced into the fields; by 1914 the number had jumped to 50,000. The movement of seasonal workers on this scale required resources which only the Dominion government and the large railway companies could supply. Immigration officials and railway agents worked together to obtain the necessary manpower. On the government side a careful estimate was made each spring of the requirements of the following harvest. The major contribution of the railway companies was the harvest excursion rates by both rail and sea. In 1907, the CPR reduced its rates for British harvesters to such an extent that it incurred the wrath of the North Atlantic Shipping Convention.[17]

Yet from the point of view of both Canadian farmers and immigration officials the British harvesters left much to be desired. A common complaint of Western farmers was large numbers of them "had no skill with the pitchfork, but great enthusiasm for the dinner fork," and that they soon abandoned farm work for easier jobs in urban centres. This in turn led to problems between organized labour and the Immigration Branch. In 1904, Arthur Puttee, the labour member of parliament for Winnipeg, charged that urban wage earners were being required "to bear the whole brunt of carrying labour on a labour market for nine months in order that farmers may use it for two or three months."[18]

Continental European immigrants proved much more malleable. Work in the grain fields of more affluent Anglo-Canadian farmers provided these men either with necessary subsistence or the means to expand existing land holdings. One survey of rural settlement in Western Canada revealed that 50 per cent of the 832 families interviewed had no money on arrival in Canada; another 42 per cent had less than $500. As a result, it was necessary for the Ukrainian settler to seek temporary employment in farm labour, railroad construction, lumbering or mining. The initial years of adaptation of one Ukrainian family in the Vonda district of Saskatchewan was typical of the experience of many continental European immigrants:

> When they arrived at Rosthern, Saskatchewan, they had not a cent left. Her husband could not get work on account of a strike of section labourers [July, 1901]. Later he managed to obtain farm work for 3 months from a German farmer near Rosthern. The month thus earned was their means of living for a whole year. They lived after this fashion for three years until they were settled on their own homestead.[19]

Steamship and railway companies assumed a central role in the recruitment and distribution of "agricultural immigrants." By 1900, the British and European had thousands of agents and subagents circulating throughout the British Isles and continental Europe advertising economic opportunities in North America and the advantages of travelling with their company.[20] At European ports such as Rotterdam, Hamburg, and Trieste steamships received their human cargo for the still difficult transatlantic crossing. Upon arrival at Halifax or Quebec City the European peasants then boarded primitive railway coaches for their journey to the Golden West. At Winnipeg and other regional centres they set out for government homesteads, or to railway land, spread throughout the prairies.[21] In *The Sowing* (Winnipeg, 1909), Emerson Hough offered this vivid account of the arrival of immigrant trains in Winnipeg:

> There is no more picturesque, albeit no more pathetic spectacle in the world than that afforded by the Canadian Pacific Railway Station in Winnipeg where most of the European immigrants make the first stop in their long journey to their chosen land. ... In this gathering ground there are to be seen Swedes, Norwegians, Germans ... numbers of Hungarians, Galicians, and others ... their striking and bright-coloured costumes of silks and skins, their strange embroidered boots and bright head coverings. ... A babel of tongues arises. Here wanders a helpless soul, with no record of any recent meal visible in his gaunt form or features, and no understandable human speech by which he may set himself right with the world.[22]

The attitude of the CPR towards immigration was typified in a comment made to Thomas Shaughnessy by Archer Baker, the European emigration manager in 1907: "We have done more in the last two years with reference to encouraging the immigration along intelligent lines from the United States, Great Britain and Europe than the whole Dominion Department of Immigration ..."[23] The company had many reasons for this level of involvement. The sale of its land was a major consideration; between 1896 and 1913 sales expanded from $216,081 to $5,795,977. The CPR also saw advantages in an arrangement whereby European immigrants would be directed by the Immigration Branch into the construction of colonization railways in the underdeveloped regions of Western Canada. Here the immigrants would satisfy several needs: they would serve as a source of cheap labour in the construction of CPR branchlines; their crops would bring further business to the company; and ultimately they could be directed into complementary resource industries like lumbering and mining. From the point of view of immigration policy, work on railroad construction gangs would be a means of initiation whereby the newcomers could adapt to

Canadian society. In 1900 the Winnipeg commissioner of immigration suggested that the presidents of the CPR and Canadian Northern should be informed that it was "their duty to employ all immigrants who have taken up land, whether they be English-speaking or foreign, in preference to importing labour of any kind."[24]

The initial response of the railway companies was favourable; settler-labourers seemed to meet their needs admirably in that they asked "no light-minded work" and were "obedient and industrious." Docility was a virtue highly prized by both the railway companies and the Immigration Branch. In 1900, James A. Smart, deputy minister of the interior, made it clear to his subordinates that Slavic navvies* should be actively discouraged from any attempt at collective bargaining: "They should be told when they need work they had better take the wages they are offered." Consideration was also given in the Immigration Branch to a system whereby time spent on railroad construction work would count towards securing a land patent.[25]

In northern Ontario immigrants were distributed throughout the Clay Belt both by private railway companies and by the provincially owned Temiskaming and Northern Ontario Railway. Here when the railway construction season ended the immigrants often found work in logging camps and sawmills. The boards of trade and municipal governments of northern Ontario pressed continually for more immigrants who would adapt to the seasonal job market of the region. In 1901, for example, the Port Arthur Board of Trade made the following appeal to the minister of the interior: "So many pulp and paper mills have been building in the northern country, which by reason of its unlimited supply of spruce timber and paper trade, that labour is becoming very scarce, and we need immigrants who, whilst making pulp wood in clearing their farms, will also help to work the mills." The arrival of Finnish and Scandinavian "agriculturalists" experi-

---

* The term "navvy" or "navigator" was derived from the British experience in railway-building during the early nineteenth century. According to one author, there were three criteria which isolated the navvy from the general body of railway workers: "Firstly, the ability to undertake heavy and difficult types of work, including blasting and tunnelling; secondly, residence in a mobile community of fellow workers; thirdly, peculiarities of diet, chiefly the consumption of vast amounts of drink and beef." In Canada the term really only described those engaged in dangerous work in the rail camps of the Canadian frontier. See D. Brooke, "Railway Navvies on the Pennines, 1841-71," *Journal of Transport History*, vol. 3 (February 1975), 41-53.

enced in "wood cutting and timber floating" and the cultivation of marginal lands soon provided an abundant source of manpower. Some of these immigrants also found their way in the winter months to the mining camps at Sudbury Cobalt, and Timmins; others drifted west and joined with homesteaders and farm labourers from the Prairies in seeking employment in a rapidly expanding Rocky Mountain coal-mining industry.[26]

II

By the turn of the century it was quite clear that a large percentage of the "poor" farmers and farm labourers recruited by the Dominion government were not becoming full-time agriculturalists. Neither seasonal employment in farm labour nor subsistence agriculture was enough to sustain life; other means had had to be found and the numerous railroad construction, lumbering, and mining camps scattered across the country provided the necessary outlets. But this adaptation of the immigrant to the Canadian environment had produced many dislocations. Commercial farmers bitterly complained about the lack of help during periods of peak production. Spokesmen for labour-intensive industries voiced a similar complaint. Occupational specialization rather than occupational pluralism was what both the established farmers and captains of industry required of the immigrant worker.[27]

The railway companies were loud in the demand that the priorities of the market place take precedence over those of immigrant adaptation. By 1900, the CPR had apparently decided that certain groups of immigrants made poor construction workers. British immigrants were especially suspect; not only were they unwilling to tolerate low wages and primitive working conditions, but they could use the English-language press to focus public attention on their grievances. In 1897, for example, the CPR was charged with gross mistreatment of Welsh and other British immigrants recruited for work on the Crow's Nest Pass Railway. The Report of Justice R.C. Clute on the matter generally confirmed the accusations which had been made, particularly those with respect to sanitary conditions in the camps.[28]

The CPR did not, however, meekly accept blame for the harsh working conditions. Instead, President Shaughnessy claimed that it was the type of worker rather than the company which was at the root of the problem:

Men who seek employment on railway construction are, as a rule, a class accustomed to roughing it. They know when they go to the work that they must put up with the most primitive kind of camp accommodation. ... I feel very strongly that it would be a huge mistake to send out any more of these men from Wales, Scotland or England. ... it is only prejudicial to the cause of immigration to import men who come here expecting to get high wages, a feather bed and a bath tub.[29]

Slavic and Scandinavian settler-labourers also became unpopular with the railway companies; their temporary commitment to railroad construction created a very unstable labour market. Many of these men were available to the companies only during the late spring and earlier part of the summer; in August they quit their jobs in order to harvest their crops. Moreover, large numbers of them were gradually able to accumulate their money and to establish themselves full-time on the land. Ironically, in 1903 James A. Smart complimented the CPR on its generosity "to foreigners coming to this country, to such an extent that hundreds and perhaps thousands of them today are living in their own homes and are practically independent."[30] But the company was not gainsaid. During the 1901 maintenance-of-way employees strike, the CPR had imported hundreds of itinerant Italian navvies from the United States, despite anguished protests from immigration officials that these workers were undesirable racially and were taking jobs from "labourers who have taken homesteads." On this occasion, Mackenzie King, deputy minister of labour, had informed the CPR president that the private employment agencies which had recruited the Italian navvies had apparently violated the Canadian Alien Labour Law. Yet no action was taken against either the agencies or the CPR itself; quite clearly the Laurier government had accepted the advice of former Winnipeg Commissioner W.F. McCreary that strained relations with the CPR "would be disastrous for Canadian immigration ventures."[31]

After 1901 the CPR systematically increased the proportion of Italian workers in its construction crews; many of these were supplied by Montreal-based labour agents such as Antonio Cordasco. Between 1901 and 1904 Cordasco had a virtual monopoly in supplying labourers to the company; for his efforts the CPR paid him a salary of five dollars a day and expenses. He was also given the right to provision the Italian rail gangs. On this particular concession Cordasco made between 60 per cent and 150 per cent profit on each item sold. What Cordasco offered the CPR was not only a regular supply of unskilled workers, but men who could be controlled either by his interpreters or by Italian foremen. The outlook of Italian navvies was greatly appreciated by CPR officials. As George Burns, the company's employment agent, put it: "Italians are the only class of labour we can employ who can live for a year on the wages they earn in six months ... if we have the Italians ... there is no danger of their jumping their jobs and leaving us in the lurch."[32]

Pressure for the recruitment of "industrial" immigrant navvies mounted after 1907 when the Canadian Pacific, Grand Trunk Pacific, and Canadian Northern were all engaged in immense construction projects. During the next seven years between 50,000 and 70,000 railroad workers were engaged annually in completing the two new transcontinental railways, in doubletracking the CPR main line, and in building numerous colonization lines. In their insatiable demand for cheap unskilled labour all three companies pressured the Immigration Branch to facilitate the entry of immigrant navvies "irrespective of nationality."[33] A survey of the labour demands of railroad contractors in 1909 revealed that the most popular immigrant workers were "non-preferred" Southern European immigrants; these, it was claimed, "were peculiarly suited for the work." Wheaton Bros. of Grand Falls, New Brunswick, reported that it "would not employ Englishmen;" the Toronto Construction Company announced that it was entirely dependent "upon Italians, Bulgarians, and that class of labour"; while the Munro Company of La Turque, Quebec, expressed a preference for "foreigners" – "Polacks, Bulgarians, Italians."[34]

There were also several schemes to import large numbers of immigrant workers from Russia. In 1907, as a mark of his goodwill towards the Canadian government, the Doukhobor leader, Peter Veregin, announced that he would recruit 10,000 Russian labourers for the building of the Grand Trunk Pacific. Nothing came of this plan, but Russian workers were brought into the country in 1909 and 1913 from Vladivostok.[35]

Dismayed at the growing percentage of "non-preferred" industrial immigrants entering the country, immigration officials embarked on a spirited defence of the settler-navvy. In 1908 they claimed that Slavic settlers were superior constuction workers since they "could be had at more reasonable figures than many others who are either in large cities or who have had past experience in railway construction work and rates of wages." This line of argument appealed to the self-interest of railroad entrpreneurs. Wages had increased appreciably from the $1.75 daily wage of 1900. By 1907 they had risen to $3.00, and by 1913 some contractors were paying as much as $5.00. But for the railway companies a return to the older settler-labourer employment pattern did not offer a realistic solution to this problem. In fact, their answer represented a further retreat from the agricultural ideal that inspired official immigration policy. What they now demanded as a solution to their problem was the flooding of the labour market with the type of Italians and other itinerant workers who would be hired cheaply and thus keep costs down. In short, the railway companies became the outstanding spokesmen for an open door immigration policy.[36]

This position was opposed by both organized labour for economic reasons, and by nativist elements for social and cultural reasons. Many of these immigrant navvies, it was charged, were nothing more than "professional vagrants" whose habits and attitudes were "repugnant to Canadian ideals." They were, in short, people who tended "to lower the Canadian standard of living." Gradually the Immigration Branch was forced into a position of reconciling the opposing demands of the railway companies and the advocates of a more selective immigration policy. The labour and nativist point of view was reflected in the introduction between 1908 and 1910 of new standards for admission to the country. Immigrants were now required to make a continuous journey to Canada and to pass a means test which required them to have an amount of money varying from $25 to $200, depending on place of origin.

Politically the Dominion government had no choice but to acknowledge the strength of nativist opinion.[37] But on balance it came down on the side of the railway companies. This was clearly revealed in 1910 when Duncan Ross, the lobbyist for the powerful construction company of Foley, Welch & Stewart, convinced Prime Minister Laurier to reverse the decision of the minister of the interior and his immigration officials to stiffen the immigrant means test. The extent of the railway victory could be seen in a circular letter sent to all immigration border inspectors in July 1912; this letter placed "railway labourers in practically the same positions as farm labourers." Moreover, railroad navvies were defined as "those who are physically able to [endure] strenuous labour and [who] ... must be able to handle a pick and shovel."[38]

The coming to power of the Conservatives in 1911 did not significantly disrupt the government-contractor relationship; indeed, the ability of the business lobby to influence immigration policy decisions was again clearly revealed in 1912. In that year Immigration officials once again attempted to limit access to the country in response to a public outcry that immigrants from southern Europe "constituted a serious menace to the community." This time they were overruled by Robert Rogers, a politician whose corporate connections were myriad.[39]

By 1913 Immigration officials were concerned that Canada was becoming increasingly committed to a guest-worker form of immigration. But the influx of itinerant immigrant workers continued: indeed, in the spring of 1913 arrangements were made to bring immigrant workers from Eastern Russia on short-term contracts which gave them a semi-indentured status. In fact, to prevent desertions both the Canadian Pacific and the Grand Trunk Pacific transported these workers from Vancouver to the Prairies in closed boxcars and with armed escorts.[40]

The mining and lumbering companies aided and abetted the efforts of the railway companies in seeking to keep the immigration door open. Corporate unity on this issue reflected economic interdependence; the transcontinental railway touched all segments of the developing resource-based industries of the "new" West and their point of view was widely shared. The movement of lumber and firewood, especially from British Columbia, provided the railways with a source of revenue which grew dramatically during this period. In 1896 the CPR moved 636,128,374 feet of lumber and 166,831 cords of firewood; by 1914 these figures were 2,953,125,699 and 287,910 respectively.[41] The rapidly developing metalliferous and coal mines of the Kootenays and Crow's Nest Pass provided an important new market for lumber. In 1910 a report of the Department of the Interior estimated that the coal mines in the Crow's Nest Pass alone were using "three million lineal feet of mining props and two and one-half million feet of board measure of lumber and dimension timber." The report also claimed that within five years this quantity would probably double, thereby requiring the product of 66,000 acres of forest. Thus the railway and mining companies had a common interest in seeing that the British Columbia forest industry had an ample supply of cheap reliable labour. The mining and lumber interests of the west interlocked with the railway companies providing the connection. The railway entrpreneur was, therefore, often the spokesman for a region whose views would be ignored by politicians at their peril.[42]

A particular concern of the transcontinental railway companies–the Canadian Pacific, Grand Trunk Pacific and Canadian Northern–was that there should be no serious work stoppages in the mining industry of the West. Coal was an indispensable source of energy; lignite coal was an essential fuel in the harsh

Prairie winter; coke was a necessary ingredient in smelting; and bituminous, or steam coal, gave motive power to the railways themselves. Hence the determination with which the railway companies attempted to guarantee a reliable mining operation, and to meet their seasonal demands for coal. They did this in two ways, by effecting a secure corporate link with the coal producers, and by going into mining themselves.[43] In 1908 the CPR opened its own mine at Hosmer, Alberta; in 1911, the Canadian Northern acquired the extensive Dunsmuir holdings on Vancouver Island. The Hosmer mine was acquired by the CPR not only to ensure coal for its locomotives during the peak harvest season, but to provide additional coke for the silver-lead-zinc smelters at Nelson, Greenwood, and Trail, British Columbia. Indeed, the previous year the company had acquired the economic leadership in this region through the formation of the Consolidated Mining and Smelting Company. Not surprisingly these corporate changes were accompanied by an intensification of the demand for an open door immigration policy.[44]

Mining promoters welcomed this initiative as the labour traditions of the Canadian mining industry were well suited to the outlook of the railway companies. During the boom years from 1896 to 1914 mining companies became even more active in the recruitment of immigrant workers. One mining authority gave this estimate of the industry's labour situation: "Canadians won't work in the mines. They are quite willing to boss the job but they are not going to do the rough work themselves. ... What we want is brawn and muscle, and we get it." The *Canadian Mining Journal*, the voice of the industry, continually maintained that the number of immigrant miners entering the country was insufficient. In 1907, the *Journal* argued that it was "quite feasible not only to select the proper class of workers across the ocean, but to place them where they are needed."[45] Although the Dominion government did not undertake the systematic recruitment of miners, it placed few obstacles in the way of the recruitment efforts of the mining companies themselves, even when strikebreaking was involved. By 1911 over 57 per cent of mine workers in Canada were immigrants; in British Columbia and Alberta the equivalent figures were 84 per cent and 88 per cent. In Ontario, only 48 per cent of the mine workers were foreign-born. But these workers were concentrated in the northern part of the province; their presence gave that region a districtively "non-Canadian–non-British" character.[46]

The Rocky Mountain coal-mining region of Western Canada

was equally polyglot. In most of the mining communities those of British stock constituted less than 50 per cent of the population; Slavic and Italian workers were in the majority. A study prepared by the Royal Commission on Coal provided the information given in Table 1 below.[47]

TABLE 1

**Ethnic Distribution in Alberta Mines
a Percentage Breakdown**

	Crow's Nest	Lethbridge	Drumheller	Mountain Park	Brazeau	Edmonton
British	44	40	61	41.5	44.5	60
American	1	2	2	1	2	1
Slavic	25	32	26	36	17.5	19
French and Belgian	7	–	–	–	5.5	–
Italian	14.5	15	3	17.5	25.5	–
Other European	8.5	8	7	4	5	18
Finnish	–	–	1	–	–	–
Oriental	–	3	–	–	–	–
	100	100	100	100	100	100

In their frantic search for immigrant unskilled labour the mining companies, in keeping with the traditions of Canadian big business, turned to private employment agencies. In 1904 there were about one hundred agencies in operation in the country; by 1913 the number had grown to over 300. Of these Ontario had the largest number (97), followed by British Columbia (45), Manitoba (36), Alberta (32), and Quebec (26). Together the agencies were placing over 200,000 workers a year, most of whom were immigrants. These agencies recruited workers not only in Europe but in the United States where they worked closely with similar labour bureaus.[48]

Agents supplying large industrial concerns often specialized in a particular ethnic group. Thus, the Dominion Coal Company of Nova Scotia was supplied with Italian workers by the Cordasco agency of Montreal, and with Armenian and Syrian workers from agencies operating in Constantinople. The approach of one of the Constantinople agencies was explained in a leading Armenian newspaper in these terms:

> The Dominion Company Ltd. of Sidney, Canada, North America, undertakes to furnish employment, which will pay you from $2.00 to $5.00 per day. Emigrants would have to go via Trieste (Austria) and there sign contracts concerning their future employment and wages. The steamship fare is $50. paid in advance. ... Come, without losing time, to our office, American Travellers' Company, No. 2, Custom House, Galata, Constantinople, which is the greatest and most important of such organizations.[49]

Many of the immigrant workers who came by this route were transported first to St. John's, Newfoundland, where there was no immigration inspection; from there they travelled on the iron-ore carriers of the Dominion Coal & Steel Company to the company's piers at South Sydney.[50]

During periods of industrial conflict the Dominion Coal Company and other mining concerns looked to the labour agencies for relief. Strike-breakers were frequently imported into the country despite the Alien Labour Act of 1897 which made it unlawful "for any person, company, partnership or corporation, in any manner to pre-pay the transportation of, or in any other way to assist or solicit the importation or immigration of any alien or foreigner into Canada under contract or agreement ... to perform labour or service of any kind in Canada."[51] During the ferocious strikes in the metalliferous regions of British Columbia between 1899 and 1901 the mining companies blatantly imported Italian and Slavic strike-breakers through labour agencies in Fernie, Spokane, and Seattle. Organized labour strongly resented the recruitment of these "foreign scabs." In July 1899, for example, the secretary of the Sandon (British Columbia) Miners' Union appealed to Prime Minister Laurier to enforce the Alien Labour Act: "1000 Canadian miners of the Slocan, with their wives and families, are being driven out of Canada by the importation of labour from the United States. ... As British subjects we naturally resent the circumstances which are driving us from our native land. Will you, as First Minister of the Crown, secure for us the protection which the Alien Labour Law provides?"[52]

The degree of support which the miners received from labour organizations across the country eventually forced the Dominion government to establish a Royal Commission under Justice R.C.

Clute of the British Columbia Supreme Court to investigate the situation. But violations of the Alien Labour Act remained a feature of life in the region. In 1901, the mining companies expanded their recruitment of alien strike-breakers, most of whom were Italians. The blunt comment of Edmund Kirby, the manager of the War Eagle Mine, showed the importance of these new industrial recruits to the position of local capital: "How to head off a strike of muckers or labourers for higher wages without the aid of Italian labour I do not know." Nor were the companies deterred either by the protests of organized labour or by warnings from Mackenzie King, the deputy minister of labour, that the Alien Labour Act would be enforced "to prevent wholesale importation of labour." Despite two convictions under the Act the mining companies achieved their goal; a sufficient number of strike-breakers were secured to re-open the mines and to crush the offending union.[53]

The events of 1901 in British Columbia revealed much about the power politics of Canadian immigration. When large industrial concerns, possessing appreciable political power, were determined to import workers, even for the purpose of strike-breaking, they would usually get their way. This principle would be demonstrated on many occasions, most notably in the metal-miners strike in Cobalt in 1907, the CPR machinist strike in 1908, in the coal-miners strike in Nova Scotia in 1909, in the dock-workers strike in Port Arthur in 1910, in the coal-miners strike in Crow's Nest Pass in 1911, in the railroad navvy strike in British Columbia in 1912, and in the coal-miners strike on Vancouver Island in 1913.[54]

III

The treatment of immigrant workers by the labour agencies and the railroad and lumber companies was a source of considerable controversy after 1896. For its part the Dominion government seemed prepared to allow the companies a free hand in the industrial use of immigrant workers, particularly in the railway camps. The rapid completion of the Grand Trunk Pacific and Canadian Northern was regarded by both the Laurier and Borden governments as a crucial economic and political priority. So great was the commitment of the government in this regard that Dominion authorities rarely questioned the characterization given by employment agencies of life in the railway work camps. In April 1910 this description of working conditions in the Grand Trunk Pacific camps appeared in the British newspaper *Answers*:

Life in the camps is strictly teetotal. ... But the feeding provided is not only unstinted, but of the best obtainable, and on a scale undreamed of by the navvy in this country ... there is an unlimited choice ... of fresh meat, fresh vegetables, groceries, butter, eggs, milk, bread and fruit. ... After work, the men amuse themselves to good purpose, with sing-songs in the shorter days of spring and autumn, and with games and sports, fishing and shooting during the long summer.[55]

The reality of immigrant life in Canada was rather different. Foreign workers were frequently cheated out of their hard-earned wages and subjected to harsh and dangerous working conditions. In the spring of 1904 the evils associated with the immigrant traffic were dramatically revealed when the Italian labour agencies of Antonio Cordasco and Alberto Dini, vying for steamship and employment commissions, lured thousands of Italian labourers to Montreal. These men soon faced unemployment and destitution; in time, their condition became so desperate that both the municipal and Dominion authorities were forced to intervene. Although a Royal Commission appointed to investigate this episode documented the many problems associated with unregulated labour agencies, and legislation was passed providing severe penalties for anyone "inducing people to come to Canada by false representations," the abuses continued.[56]

In 1907, the Austrian consul-general in Ottawa registered an official complaint about the treatment of Austrian nationals in Canada by Ukrainian and Bulgarian labour agencies operating out of Montreal, and by foremen in various railway camps. What had happened, he asserted, was so cruel and exploitative "as to make my blood curdle and ... bring shame and dishonour upon your country." His specific charge related to the recruitment by the Davis & Nagel agency of Montreal of hundreds of Ukrainian, Polish, and Hungarian immigrants for work on the construction of the Temiskaming and Northern Ontario Railway. Some of these workers had been engaged by the bureau after they had landed in Montreal; others had been sent to Montreal by labour agents in the United States. Before leaving Montreal for the construction camps in northern Ontario these immigrant workers had signed contracts with the Davis & Nagel Company.[57]

By the time they had reached the job site many of the men had already spent all their money on labour agency fees, rail fares, and hotel accommodation. The cost of these latter two items had been grossly inflated by "kick-backs" to labour agents. The situation of the workers had been made worse by the fact that the Davis & Nagel Company had misled them into believing that they would receive a refund for their transportation costs from the McRae, Chandler & McNeil Construction Company. No such refund was ever forthcoming. In addition, the construction company and the labour agency had conspired to prevent the workers from leaving the camp sites. Many of the foremen and sub-contractors had used firearms to intimidate recalcitrant workers, and most of these camps had jails where "unruly" workers had been confined after kangaroo court proceedings. Workers who had managed to escape from camp had often been tracked down by special constables and detectives engaged by their employers. These "specials" were often assisted by local police and justices of the peace. The police state tactics used in the construction of the railway had been clearly revealed in June 1907 when a group of thirty Slavic workers had been seized for violation of their labour contracts. One of the captured men described his experience as follows:

> On the 20-th inst [sic] at night, 12 men who represented themselves as policemen came again to our place and began to make a wholesale arrest, firing revolvers at the Immigrants. ... 35 men of us were arrested and packed into a fright [sic] car, for a whole long night with no water and no place to rest or even sit upon. In the morning, as they made preparations to take us away, we began shouting, whereupon said policemen entered the car and putting the muzzles of their guns to our mouths, threatened to shoot if we continued our alarm. A number of us have been beaten with sticks, ... we have obtained our release, but only after ... binding ourselves to pay each $17 for transportation and $35 for the policemen who had beaten and fired at us.[58]

The investigation conducted by the Immigration Branch provided evidence which substantiated much that the Austrian consul general had alleged. It was shown that the Nagel & Davis Company had indeed been guilty of misrepresentation, and that their agents had been guilty of physical intimidation. The quasi-judicial activities of the McRae, Chandler & McNeil Construction Company were also censured. Yet no attempt was made to prosecute either the labour agency or the construction company. Both Dominion and provincial officials argued that it was the responsibility of the victimized immigrant workers themselves to take legal action. This, of course, was impossible: the men were virtually without money and were scattered across the country.[59]

The coercive measures employed against immigrant navvies were characteristic of their harsh and dangerous lives.[60] The accident rate at "the end of steel" was particularly shocking. Between 1904 and 1911, for example, out of a total of 9,340 fatal industrial accidents in Canada, 23 per cent were related to the railway industry. But even these statistics do not tell the whole story. It was not until 1912 that the Dominion government required contractors receiving public funds to register fatalities occurring in their camps. Yet even this provision did not produce accurate statistics: "Oh, some Russian is buried there" was the passing remark that commonly designated an unkempt plot in the vicinity of an erstwhile camp.[61]

There were also numerous complaints about the level of wages and the accommodation conditions in the construction camps. Although there was an obligation on the part of the head contractor, who accepted Dominion funds to grant wages that were consistent with local standards, to maintain a reasonable level of sanitation, and to provide medical facilities, there was great difficulty in enforcing these measures.[62] It was alleged in labour circles that government inspectors visited the camps only infrequently and rarely came into contact with immigrant navvies. The foreign worker was particularly vulnerable to this type of exploitation. He was often unable to communicate in English, he was frequently manipulated by an "ethnic straw boss," and he often had a basic mistrust of state officials. For the navvies, the government inspector simply did not offer a viable channel of protest.[63]

Immigrant mine workers faced similar problems. This was especially true of the smaller mines, the so-called "gopher holes"; in these, in addition to irregular employment, it was not uncommon for the companies to declare bankruptcy and forfeit on wages. Within the mines the power of hiring and allocating contract places usually rested with the foremen and shift bosses. There were numerous allegations that these men exploited their positions and extracted bribes from desperate workers. These conditions were compounded by the danger of the working place. The reports of the Ontario, Alberta, and British Columbia Mining Inspectors throughout the period 1896-1914 were generally critical of the prevailing high accident rates, especially among the foreign workers. This criticism was most effectively stated in a 1914 Report of the Ontario Mining Inspectors:

Anyone looking over the list of mining statistics ... cannot but be struck by the large percentage of names of foreign origin. ... In part this may be due to unfamiliarity with the English language and the difficulty of comprehending quickly spoken orders in an emergency. Mental traits have also to be reckoned with, and the fact that few of these men were miners before coming to this country. ...

The report neglected to state that many mine managers were reluctant to maintain costly safety regulations. The apparent lack of solidarity among the mine employees because of ethnic differences reinforced this callous approach.[64]

The lumber companies also employed large numbers of immigrant workers, especially Scandinavians, Finns, and Slavs, most of whom were recruited by labour agencies in Vancouver, Victoria, Winnipeg, Port Arthur, Ottawa, Montreal, and Sault Ste. Marie. There were numerous complaints about the working and living conditions, especially in the "long timber" industry of British Columbia. In 1918 the *British Columbia Federationist* gave this description of a typical camp: "muzzle loading bunks ... pigs, lice and other vermin all over the place ... the stench of drying clothes and dirty socks ... enough to knock a man down."[65]

IV

Between 1896 and 1914 Canadian immigration policy served, above all else, the dictates of the capitalist labour market. Under the banner of economic growth thousands of immigrant workers were encouraged to enter the country to meet the labour needs of commercial agriculture, railroad construction, lumbering, mining, and other labour-intensive industries. Increasingly, the long-standing goal of bringing into the country only the settler-labourer type of immigrant was displaced by a policy of importing an industrial proletariat. Immigration statistics reveal that the percentage of unskilled labourers entering Canada increased from 31 per cent in 1907 to 43 per cent in 1913-14, while the percentage of agriculturalists decreased from 38 per cent to 28 per cent. This change from settler to worker immigrants was accompanied by a change in the ethnic composition of migrants. In 1907, 20 per cent of the immigrants were from central and southern Europe; by 1913, when 400,000 men and women entered the country, this figure had advanced to 48 per cent.[66]

In the minds of many Anglo-Canadians the arrival of these "hordes" of foreigners stirred deep suspicion. The immigrants posed a serious challenge to Canadian institutions, particularly in the rapidly growing urban centres of Western Canada and northern Ontario where their concentration in ethnic ghettos made them, and their manifold problems, highly visible. In 1912, Alfred Fitzpatrick, principal of Frontier College, posed this problem to his countrymen: "We must either meet the foreigner at the camp – his first point of contact with our civilization – interest him in our homestead regulations, assist him ... care for and educate him ... or submit to one of two alternatives. Either we shall see him go back to his native land, take our money with him, or worse, drift into the saloons, shacks and already overcrowded tenement houses of our towns and cities."[67] It was a problem that they would not soon solve.

CHAPTER TWO

Immigrant Workers and Labour Radicalism in Canada 1896-1914

The transatlantic migration of thousands of immigrant workers between 1896 and 1914 greatly altered the social and economic fabric of Canada and the United States. In both countries much of the rapid economic progress in railway construction, mining, lumbering, and secondary manufacturing that occurred during this time can be attributed to immigrant manpower. Yet the immigrants themselves paid a high price for North American economic gains.[1] In her book *Men in Sheepskin Coats* (Toronto, 1947), Vera Lysenko has graphically described the plight of these foreign workers: "they were systematically underpaid ... tortured by physical labour, torn by nostalgia for the old country, crushed by loneliness in a strange land, and by the fear of death which [they] often looked in the face. ..." This theme of exploitation and alienation has fascinated many historians of immigration.[2]

Another problem which has preoccupied scholars is the apparent docility with which these workers responded to the North American working place: this found its most dramatic expression in their seeming reluctance to support North American working-class organizations. It has been argued that the docility of these immigrant workers can largely be explained by the fact that they participated only marginally in the North American "way of life." Immigrant workers were essentially sojourners who cast lingering backward glances. Their wages flowed in part to dependents in Europe while they thought of their savings as a means of upward social mobility in their old European homelands. Because of their economic priorities immigrant workers were prepared to accept low pay and to tolerate abominable working conditions, at least by North American standards. They were also anxious to avoid any action which might affect their chances of steady employment.[3] Even when immigrant workers remained in North America, so the argument has it, they remained remarkably docile. Residing in their ethnic enclaves, highly ethnocentric in their orientation, they were indifferent to organizations such as the Knights of Labour, the Western Federation of Miners (WFM), and the Industrial Workers of the World (IWW) which challenged the evolving pattern of industrialization.[4]

How valid is this theme of alienation and docility to the understanding of the Canadian experience of European immigrant workers in the period 1896-1914? To what extent was the attachment of the immigrant workers to Canadian society an alienating experience? And did the thousands of immigrant workers really prevent the emergence of working-class movements in Canada which could challenge the power of the country's industrial capitalists? The consideration of these important questions will be the subject of this chapter.

I

The inferior occupational positions and the low social status afforded European immigrant workers in Canada prior to the Great War were essentially functions of Anglo-Canadian immigration priorities. As John Porter has so persuasively argued in *The Vertical Mosaic* (Toronto, 1966), the most important factor in determining entrance status for immigrant groups is "the evaluations of the 'charter' members of the society of the jobs to be filled and the 'right' kind of immigrants to fill them."[5] Quite clearly in this period most Anglo-Canadians recognized the importance of having an available source of cheap unskilled labour for use in both the agricultural and industrial sectors of the economy. Combined with this, however, were a number of reservations about the movement of immigrant workers within Canadian society. Throughout the latter part of the nineteenth century Canadian politicians and immigration officials had assured the public that Canada's recruitment of immigrants would be confined to Great Britain and to Northwestern Europe, a selective policy which would be greatly superior to the American open door.[6] In 1891 Sir John A. Macdonald had deplored the influx of millions of Slavic and Southern European immigrants into the United States: "It is a great country, but it will have its vicissitudes and revolutions. Look at that mass of foreign ignorance and vice which has flooded that country with socialism, atheism and all other isms."[7] In contrast, Canada would seek only those vigorous northern races who were culturally sound and who could quickly conform to the norms of Anglo-Canadian life.

The employment boom at the turn of the century, with its insistent demand for Slavic and Italian workers, shattered this vision of a culturally harmonious Canada. Not surprisingly, the Anglo-Canadian response to these new immigrants from Central and Southern Europe was initially hostile. The Toronto *Mail and Empire* set the tone in 1899 when it branded Clifford Sifton's immigration policy as "an attempt to make of the North-West a sort of anthropological garden ... to pick up the waifs and strays of Europe, the lost tribes of mankind, and the freaks of creation."[8] Organized labour had particular fears; as the guardian of the rights of the Canadian working men it stood squarely against the importation of cheap labour. The fears, prejudices, and emotions of Canadian trade unionists were epitomized in an 1904 article of *The Independent*, a Vancouver labour newspaper: "This question of alien immigration ... strikes at the foundation of every labour organization in the Country ... This labour is generally garnered from the slums of Europe and Asia, and thus thrown into direct competition with all kinds of Canadian labour. The immigrants having been brought up under conditions which no Canadian ... (would) tolerate – work for wages upon which no Canadian could ... exist."[9]

Many Anglo-Canadians were also disturbed by evidence of social deviance among immigrant workers. The ethnic ghettos, which quickly sprang up in the major Canadian cities and almost all single-enterprise communities west of the Ottawa River, were increasingly thought of as a breeding ground for "filth, immorality and crime."[10] The reports of the Royal North-West Mounted Police (RNWMP) from Western Canada frequently stressed the tendency of foreign workers to take the law into their own hands; according to these accounts the prevalence of knives and guns could turn even minor disagreements into violent confrontations. When the foreign worker was brought into contact with liquor, especially at festive occasions, social anarchy ensued.[11] This situation was vividly described by the Reverend C.W. Gordon (Ralph Connor) in his famous novel *The Foreigner*:

> In the main room dance and song reeled on in uproarious hilarity. In the basement below, foul and fetid, men stood packed close drinking while they could. ... In the dim light of a smoky lantern, the swaying crowd, here singing in maudlin chorus, there fighting savagely to pay off old scores or to avenge new insults, presented a nauseating spectacle.[12]

The 1914 convention of the Port Arthur Finnish Social Democratic Party. Courtesy of the Robert Kenny Collection, University of Toronto.

Outraged by these conditions Gordon and other Anglo-Canadian reformers such as J.S. Woodsworth sought to alleviate the lot of the immigrant workers. Their vision of immigrant life accords well with the notions of the historian Oscar Handlin who has written of the period: "Immigration had transformed the entire ... world within which the peasants had formerly lived. From surface forms to inmost functioning, the change was complete. ... In the process, they became, in their own eyes, less worthy as men. They felt a sense of degradation that raised a most insistent question: Why had this happened?"[13] That the lives of immigrant workers had been seriously disrupted cannot be doubted, but was the transformation as complete as reformers such as Gordon and Woodsworth and historians such as Handlin would have it? Any attempt to answer this question in the Canadian context must of necessity take account of the reasons why emigrants left Europe for Canada, and of the social and economic adaptation which they made on Canadian soil.

II

The vast majority of European immigrant workers who came to Canada between 1896 and 1914 were of peasant background. Generally speaking they came from regions where agricultural technology was primitive, crop productivity low, and landholding minute; for many, emigration was "an alternative to the restrictive opportunities of [their] traditional agrarian societies." In the case of immigrants from the Austro-Hungarian Empire about 60 per cent were Slavs from the provinces of Galicia and Bukovinia, regions where most of the landholdings were below the five hectares necessary for subsistence. A similar situation prevailed in other areas of high emigration most notably in Southern Italy, Slavonia, and the coastal regions of Sicily.[14]

The peasant face of all these societies belies the true nature of their employment patterns. Thus while the traditional life of the land was the focus of work, economic circumstances forced many peasants to become migratory industrial workers for at least part of the year. The produce of the land and the industrial wage had for some formed the economic package by which they and their families were sustained. Modernization had intruded on these societies, and there existed within them rural proletarians who could "feed themselves from their own soil for only a few months, and for the rest of the year ... worked as hired labour for 'others'."[15] In their search for casual employment these peasant workers had considerable geographical mobility both within their own and neigbouring countries. In 1908 alone some 300,000 Slavic workers from the Austro-Hungarian Empire crossed into Germany seeking short-term employment in the Junker farms of East Prussia and in the coal-mining and steel-producing regions of the Ruhr and Saar. Such labour mobility had transformed traditional peasant life in many parts of Central and Southern Europe. By 1900 the closed nucleated village of the nineteenth century had been replaced by a relatively open community whose residents "continuously interacted with the outside world and tied their future to its demands." In time, this "outside world" became transatlantic as well as continental.[16]

Returned sojourners acted as a source of information about economic conditions in North America and were of great importance in chain migrations whereby prospective migrants learned of job opportunities, were provided with transportation, and had initial accommodation in North America arranged for them. This adaption of "familial and dyadic patronage" significantly influenced immigrant behaviour across the Atlantic. One familiar aspect of this was the creation of a series of "Little Italies" and "Slavtowns" in the towns and cities of the United States and Canada; another less well explored aspect was the carving out of ethnic niches within the North American job market.[17] *The Social Survey of Ukrainian Rural Settlement in Western Canada* (Winnipeg, 1917), showed that the kinship and village patterns of the Old World clearly influenced settlement patterns in the New. Similarly, Reino Kero's study of Finnish immigrants from the province of Karvia has revealed that the majority gravitated towards three communities: Port Arthur and Nipigon in Ontario and Covington in Minnesota. Close familial and fraternal connections persisted among these immigrants, the international boundary notwithstanding.[18]

The role of the ethnic intermediary or go-between, whether *padrone*, steamship agent, employment agent, or village sponsor, was also important in the movement of migrants from Southern and Eastern Europe to Canada. The revelations of both the *Royal Commission to Inquire into the Immigration of Italian Labourers to Montreal, and Alleged Fraudulent Practices of Employment Agencies* (Ottawa, 1904), and investigations by the Immigration Branch showed that labour and steamship agencies annually facilitated the movement of thousands of immigrant workers to Canada through the issuance of prepaid tickets, and the arrangement of jobs.[19] Nor did the relationship between the intermediary and the immigrant end with the latter's arrival in Canada; the intermediary, whether agency or individual, provided a variety of services for the migrant in the old homeland. In 1907, for instance, 55.3 million dollars was received in the Austro-Hungarian Empire from immigrant banks located in North America, while another six million dollars was paid in postal money orders. The intermediary also facilitated departure from North America both for those who had satisfied their economic ambitions, and for those who were forced back across the Atlantic either by unemployment or infirmity.[20]

Going home was one method of dealing with economic exploitation and social discrimination. Seeking the protection of national consulates was another; thus, there were numerous incidents of complaints to consuls resulting in investigations by Dominion and provincial authorities. Of even greater importance to the migrant was the companionship and mutual assistance offered within the evolving ethnic communities of both single-enterprise towns and large urban centres. Prior to 1914 the North End of Winnipeg was the most famous of these immigrant neighbourhoods from which the immigrants could derive social, economic, and psychological sustenance.[21] To Canadians at large the North End was best known for its crowded housing, and for the unsanitary and unhealthy conditions which characterized so many of the ethnic neighbourhoods across the country.[22] But what even reformers such as J.S. Woodsworth missed in their preoccupation with sanitation levels and social pathology was the extent to which institutions such as the ethnic boardinghouse were providing a sense of stability in an alien world.[23]

Beyond the boardinghouse stood the ethnic church, "the first and most easily understood form of oranization" immigrants brought from the Old World to the New. In major regional centres, such as Montreal, Toronto, Hamilton, and Sault Ste. Marie, Italian parishes were formed in the first decade of the twentieth century. Finnish churches appeared in both Port Arthur and Sudbury; indeed, in Port Arthur three rival Lutheran churches established themselves.[24] The Ukrainian communities in Western Canada also exhibited a religious factionalism; here the Uniate, Greek Orthodox, Ukrainian Baptist, and Independent Greek churches all vied for the souls of the Ukrainian workers. All of these ethnic churches faced formidable problems in reaching and holding the immigrant workers. There was a continual shortage of both priests and money, with the result that formal church organization lagged behind the felt needs of the immigrants. In the case of the Uniate church, for example, it was not until Bishop Budka arrived in Winnipeg in 1912 that the needs of Ukrainian immigrants in Canada received systematic attention. Ukrainian workers in rail and mining camps were, however, almost totally neglected by the church except for the communication which existed through the Uniate newspaper *Canadian Ruthenian*.[25]

The churches also faced from some a degree of indifference and hostility which went beyond what they had known in the conservative world of the European village. Some immigrant workers thought of the clergy as agents of an exploitative land-holding class in Europe – in short men whose talents could be easily adapted to the needs of North American capitalists. Some other immigrants, such as the southern Italian *contadini* (peasants), were only nominally Roman Catholics: "theirs was a folk of religion, a fusion of ... animism, polytheism, and sorcery with the sacraments of the church." Finally, the churches encountered serious competition from other Old Country institutions, particularly the secular and sometimes socialist mutual benefit and cultural organizations. But these considerations notwithstanding, the churches were still the Old World institution to which immigrant workers were most likely to turn in the first instance in an alien environment.[26]

A second European peasant and working-class organization which caught hold in North America, particularly among Italian, Finnish, and Ukrainian emigrants, was the mutual aid society. In 1885 there had been about 4,896 of these organizations in Italy with an estimated membership of 791,296. In *Italy: School for Awakening Countries* (New York, 1961) Maurice Neufeld makes this comment about the role of mutual aid societies in the development of Italian working-class consciousness: "They served the cause of later, more militant unionism by tiding artisans, mechanics and skilled workmen over difficult years of trial and error while at the same time ... provided aid to the sick and disabled members, pensions to the aged, subventions to the unemployed, as well as education to brother workers and their families."[27]

An example of such a society is the Cristoforo Colombo Association which was established in 1905 by a group of Italian immigrants in the mining community of Trail, British Columbia. This association worked "to solidify the bond of brotherhood." Its meetings provided an opportunity for companionship and a chance to hear news from Italy. Such gatherings also provided a sympathetic forum for the discussion of both individual and collective problems. Indeed, one of the main functions of the society was "to protect members against future misfortune ... without resorting to cold public charity." In the event of sickness or accident each member could collect between one and two dollars a week.[28]

Many of these mutual aid organizations also had important cultural and educational functions. The Taras Shevchenko Reading Association established in Winnipeg in 1899 maintained a hall in the North End stocked with numerous Ukrainian books and newspapers; this hall was also used for cultural events and festivals. Among Finnish immigrants various temperance societies such as the Uusi Yritys ("New Attempt") of Port Arthur provided a similar outlet.[29]

All of this suggests a revision of the view of the immigrant worker held by most Anglo-Canadian contemporary writers and later historians. In this view the immigrant workers were hopelessly divided and vulnerable, swept along willy-nilly by the demands of the capitalist labour market. No doubt the immigrants were subjected to powerful forces of alienation and assimilation, but family ties, and ethnic organizations provided a countervailing influence. The factors of collective identity and individual pride are, therefore, crucial to an understanding of the latent power of immigrant workers in the Canadian industrial system and their willingness to join other workers in union and political activity.

III

Any attempt to understand the collective actions of European immigrant workers in Canada must take into account both existing explanations of working-class behaviour and empirical evidence. Thus, many concepts which sociologists, anthropologists, and other social scientists have derived from their research can be usefully applied here. Of particular importance are those studies which have analyzed the causes of collective protest, especially those common to industrial and industrializing societies. E.P. Thompson and Neil Smelser, among others, have examined the impact of industrialization on workers drawn from premodern societies, with special reference to the alteration of traditional values and behaviour patterns. Their studies have focused in particular on the altered nature of work and living standards; in case after case, they argue that the cumulative effect of such change has been alienation and that workers caught in this maelstrom sought to ameliorate their condition through collective action and violence. Severe economic and social deprivation has often been accepted as another explanation for collective protest in both the short and long runs. Adherents of this theory have suggested that sustained deprivation can produce a shift "from the individual protest experienced through strike or boycott over immediate dissatisfaction to permanently organized economic or political action." Protest, in their view, is evolutionary – moving inevitably from primitive to structured.[30]

Other scholars have pointed out, however, that it is quite possible to examine "questions of strikes and trade unions as avenues of protest without assuming the inevitable progression from inchoate outbursts to a class conscious militant labour union supported by a socialist party." In this view even primitive protest has great political significance.[31] Edward Shorter and Charles Tilly for example, have asserted that "at all periods in the course of industrialization the working class movement has been politically organized for the explicit sake of obtaining advantages for the working classes through access to the polity."[32]

Quite clearly it is not a simple matter to analyze either collective protest or collective violence, and in the case of European immigrant workers in Canada the task is complicated by ethnic diversity and geographical division. The spectrum of protest among groups of railroad navvies, miners, and lumber workers in Canada ran from primitive and clannish to highly sophisticated and intensely ideological. On the other hand it is readily apparent that some occupations fostered working-class self-consciousness more than others. It has been said that miners everywhere have "a pre-existing tradition of conflict" and that their work by its very nature "gives them a powerful capacity for collective enterprise".[33] This thesis was certainly borne out in the mine fields of Cape Breton Island, northern Ontario, Alberta, and Vancouver Island. But the response of miners to the Canadian working environment was by no means uniform. Cultural factors were also to the fore – above all the extent to which communal values in the Old European homelands had been affected by industrial capitalism.

Many Italian, Slavic, and Finnish immigrant workers came from societies where collective action against economic and social exploitation was an established fact. During the 1890s there had been a series of peasant uprisings in Sicily and Northern Italy and in at least two instances martial law had been required to curb the unrest. Again, both agricultural and industrial workers had been mobilized by the Italian Socialist Party despite strenuous opposition from that country's business community and landed gentry. At the turn of the century Italy was rocked by a series of strikes, including a five-day general strike in 1904.[34] Many immigrant workers from the Austro-Hungarian and Russian Empires had also been exposed to movements of social protest. By 1900 thousands of the Slav agricultural workers and small farmers who had moved to the industrial cities of Galicia and Bohemia had become members of benevolent societies, trade unions, and socialist organizations. Although activism by workers in Russia was a much more difficult undertaking, secret Workers' Clubs and Social Democratic organizations had by 1900 become a significant feature of that country's social landscape.[35] In Finland the labour and socialist movements had both class and national characteristics. Indeed, the 1901 conscription riots and the 1905 general strike in that country were as much directed against Russification as against capitalism. After the 1905 upheaval Finnish intellectuals, such as the utopian socialist Matti Kurikka and the syndicalist Leo Laukki, were forced to flee to North America, and thus strengthened the already well-established radical point of view among Canadian Finns.[36]

It must be remembered, however, that not all European immigrants brought to Canada the same level of working-class consciousness. Indeed, most of those who came would have been more attuned to rural peasant than to urban industrial values. Richard Pipe's description of Russian Workers' protest movements would probably apply equally to their Italian, Austro-Hungarian, and Finnish counterparts: "... their sporadic outbursts of protest resembled less industrial strikes than rebellions similar in their motives and manifestations to the peasant *bunty* of the same time. It was a relatively undifferentiated mass of frightfully exploited, illiterate labourers, cut off from the world, and to a large extent still rooted in the village."[37]

Yet despite their limited world view such people might constitute the suitable raw material for a militant working class. In some instances the Canadian job market provided the catalyst that produced such a transformation. Many of the immigrant workers who came to Canada as sojourners, and were not prepared to support actions which limited employment opportunities. This did not mean, however, that there were no tensions between them, and their employers. Seasonal fluctuations in labour demand, and the tendency of most mining, lumbering, and railway companies during slack periods to discharge temporarily their unskilled employees, produced deep hostility among immigrant workers. Those periods of idleness not only prevented the accumulation of funds, but actually depleted accumulated sav-ngs, thereby postponing a profitable return to the Old Country. Immigrant resentment over this cyclical employment pattern often expressed itself in militant demands for higher wages and better working conditions. When these methods failed at least some immigrant workers were not adverse to collective action, and, in some cases, outright violence.[38]

Numerous incidents could be cited from the period 1896 to 1914 of immigrant workers in the rail, mine, and lumber camps resorting to collective action to remedy specific grievances. In many cases worker demands were accompanied by violence or the threat of violence. Action was directed against employers and ethnic intermediaries alike. A 1908 report of the Dominion Police gives this account of the response of Bulgarian navvies to an attempt by a Sava Angeloff, a labour agent, to extract an additional commission from them:

> Last week he [Angeloff] went down to La Turque to collect some board money owing him by some of the Bulgarians and they got after him to mob him, but he drew a revolver and kept them off, and while he was at the camp the men poured coal-oil all about the place with a view to setting fire to it and burning him up, but on a promise to refund from $5.00 to $10.00 to each man, which he did, they let him go back to Montreal.[39]

In September 1907 a group of forty Italian navvies at Nanton, Alberta, went on strike against unsatisfactory conditions in the CPR camps.[40] They also threatened to use violence unless the company complied with their demands.[41] After consultations with the local RNWMP officers, the company eventually made the necessary concessions; at the same time, however, the CPR roadmaster indicated that "he would at once transfer some of the discontented men in the Gang to other parts of the Division so as not to have them all together in case of further trouble."[42]

Ethnic group loyalty was also a factor in larger confrontations between capital and labour. During the maintenance-of-way employees strike of 1901 the CPR attempted to displace striking Italian workers with other Italians brought from Montreal. This plan collapsed when the potential strike-breakers kicked over the traces on recognizing ties of kin and region with those who had walked out. It was only when the labour agent Antonio Cordasco imported hundreds of Italian workers from New York, who had no particular links with those on strike, that the CPR was able to get its way.[43]

This and other incidents revealed that regional and kinship loyalties carried from the Old World could work as much against as for working class unity. Of course this was nothing new in Canadian history. Irish canal workers in the 1840s had been deeply divided into rival Protestant and Catholic camps, while bloody clashes between competing groups of navvies from the regions of Munster and Connaught had been even more commonplace "to obtain work for themselves by driving off the other party."[44] Ethnic and regional rivalries were often taken advantage of by employers to keep wages low. The pattern of the 1840s was repeated on a grander scale in the period 1896-1914. In the Rocky Mountain coal-mining district, for example, immigrants were generally relegated to inferior positions in the mines, and were housed in ethnic ghettos and shack towns.[45] Ethnic hostility in these communities could at times be very intense, a characteristic described by Magdelana Eggleston in her book *Mountain Shadows*: "Why do people behave the way they do? Everyone at each other's throats. The English detesting the foreigners, as they call them contemptuously. ... The Europeans flying at each others throats, scared each will get ahead of the other. And you call that a melting pot?"[46]

Yet there were other factors which tended to allay this ethnic hostility and suspicion, and produce a sense of worker solidarity against outside forces. In their article "The Inter-Industry Propensity to Strike: An International Comparison," C. Kerr and A. Siegel have argued that collective action can often emanate from single-enterprise communities where miners, loggers, and navvies "form a largely homogeneous ... isolated mass [engaged] in a kind of colonial revolt against far removed authority"; this collective action, they argue, was also "an outlet for accumulated tensions and a substitute for occupational or social mobility."[47] Another factor which operated among immigrant workers was that a common sense of peasant folk culture often provided a basis for communication between different linguistic and ethnic groups. This growth of worker comradeship has been vividly described by Vera Lysenko:

> In the evenings, the men smoked, chewed gum, told jokes at the expense of the foreman, went for joyrides with hand cars, read newspapers, wrote letters to their families, played poker with matches ... there were always a few musicians among them (and) the men joined in singing in a mixture of many languages ... the Hungarians sang their wild Magyar songs, the Roumanians and Ukrainians sang theirs in turn.[48]

The development of a broader sense of class consciousness and the consequent decline of ethnic hostility among Canadian immigrant workers can be traced in a variety of ways. The series of bitter strikes on the docks of Fort William and Port Arthur afford one of the best illustrations of this shift. Conditions in this region hardly seemed favourable to the development of working-class unity. Both cities had heterogeneous populations with hundreds of Finns, Italians, and Slavs competing for unskilled jobs. The major employers in the area were the Canadian Pacific and the Canadian Northern, companies well versed in the techniques of corporate coercion, and the exploitation of ethnic rivalries. Set against this were extremely alienating working conditions: wages were low, employment irregular, and work arduous. Moreover, neighbourhood competed with ethnicity for the loyalty of immigrant workers.[49]

Common occupational and residential experiences could, however, reduce ethnic differences, as the experience of the Lakehead region during periods of industrial conflict showed.[50] In 1903 the first major protest against the railway companies occurred when a group of Italian freight handlers struck the CNR. The corporate and civic response was quick and decisive; the Italian workers were dismissed from their jobs and their leaders arrested. Coercion was justified in the local newspapers by reference to the latent criminality of Italian immigrants; nefarious secret organizations such as the Black Hand, it was alleged, were behind the disturbance. This was the reaction of "respectable" society; there is no evidence that it was shared by other ethnic workers.

Indeed, in 1906 another strike involving Italian, Greek, Finnish, Hungarian, Slavic, and English-speaking workers occurred on both the CNR and CPR docks. The strike was spontaneous, but before long it was being directed by an inter-ethnic committee. Ethnic loyalty worked for and not against labour in this instance. Thus, when the CNR imported Italian strike-breakers they refused to work in the freight sheds, and marched into the Port Arthur Italian community "to the resounding cheers of the strikers." When the companies refused to negotiate violence ensued. On October 2, a gun battle occurred between the strikers and the CPR and Fort William police: one police constable and three strikers were seriously injured. Eventually the strikers gained concessions, but their victory was dearly bought.[51] The strike had produced a strong anti-alien sentiment in the local Anglo-Canadian community. In a 1906 editorial the Port Arthur

Daily News made this forthright comment: "for a community of British citizens to have to submit to the obloquy of insults and armed defiance from a disorganized horde of ignorant and low-down swashbucklers and peanut vendors is making a demand upon national pride which has no excuse."[52] During the 1907 shipping season the CPR decided to punish some of the ethnic workers involved in the strike of the previous year; all Italian and Greek workers were excluded from the CPR freight sheds and their places given to recent immigrants from Poland and Hungary. These new ethnic workers, however, proved to be equally rebellious and in 1909 it was necessary to bring troops from Winnipeg to suppress a violent uprising on the CPR docks.[53]

The most spectacular attempts to organize unskilled immigrant workers in Canada were undoubtedly those made by the Industrial Workers of the World (IWW), the famous American-based syndicalist union. In this work the "Wobblies" had a number of advantages. In the first place, their approach was entirely class-oriented; unlike the situation in most craft unions there was little Anglo-Saxon hostility in their ranks towards ethnic workers. As one Prince Rupert Wobbly exclaimed "when the factory whistle blows it does not call us to work as Irishmen, Germans, Americans, Russians, Greeks, Poles, Negroes or Mexicans. It calls us to work as wage workers, regardless of the country in which we were born or color of our skins. Why not get together then ... as wage workers, just as we are compelled to do in the shop?" The second great advantage of the IWW was the extent to which its organization was geared to the migratory work patterns of the foreign worker: its initiation fees and dues were low, the membership cards were transferable and the camp-delegate system of union democracy made it possible for an immigrant worker to become a "full time organizer while he wandered." Nor did the IWW waste time in sterile ideological controversy; despite their syndicalist underpinnings their attention was focused on specific grievances. Moreover, IWW organizers usually waited until a labour disturbance erupted before launching a recruiting drive. Finally, many European workers, particularly those from France and Italy, had previously been exposed to syndicalist methods and accepted the view that the only way to attack the Canadian capitalist system "was by economic rather than political means, notably a great general strike"; in their view the local strike was seen "as a forerunner of, a kind of primary school training for, the general strike."[54]

The IWW entered the hard-rock mining regions of the Kootenays in 1907, but it was their involvement in the spectacular Canadian Northern strike of March 1912 which put them in the front lines of Canadian labour. The situation in the numerous and isolated railway camps of the Canadian Northern and Grand Trunk Pacific offered the IWW a great opportunity. Indeed, in October 1909 the Edmonton Trades and Labour Council had made representation to the Dominion minister of labour about the improper treatment of construction workers employed by the Grand Trunk Pacific. The council had pointed out the disgraceful condition of the company camps; the prevalence of typhoid fever within the camps; the inadequacy of the food and accommodation supplied to the men while en route to the job site; and the delays which were occurring in the payment of wages. A subsequent government investigation exonerated the company and its leading contractor Foley, Welch & Stewart. But the workers had remained restless.[55]

In the spring of 1912 Joe Hill "the Wobbly Warbler," Joe Biscay, Louis Moureau, and other IWW organizers entered the camps to assume leadership of the mounting labour unrest. A bitter strike ensued with over seven thousand navvies laying down their tools. This massive confrontation was to test severely the IWW's ability to organize unskilled labour in Western Canada. Initially the IWW seemed to stand a reasonable chance of victory thanks to a remarkable degree of labour solidarity. An article in the *British Columbia Federationist* of April 5, 1912, hailed the walkout as "an object lesson as to what a movement animated by an uncompromising spirit of revolt ... can accomplish among the most heterogenous army of slaves that any system of production ever assembled together." In a later edition, the *Federationist* noted that the ethnic antagonism which had previously allowed the railway contractors to divide the men had been laid aside: "Canadians, Americans, Italians, Austrians, Swedes, Norwegians, French and Old Countrymen all on strike ... a hint to King Capital to look for some other country more healthy for him to exploit labourers in than this country."[56]

To maintain labour solidarity on the railroad frontier was a formidable task. Strikers were responding to specific grievances and few had any real knowledge of unionism; they were, in the words of one IWW organizer "a mass of undisciplined bundle stiffs who ... were only held by the food that we provided." Despite the generous financial assistance from IWW headquarters, various socialist organizations, and even the American Federation of Labour, the strikers were soon on the verge of destitution.[57] Nor did this situation escape the attention of Canadian Northern owners Sir William McKenzie and Sir Donald Mann. In a candid interview with the Montreal *Witness* McKenzie confidently predicted a quick victory: "We can afford to wait ... and they cannot. A month or two does not make any difference in the construction of a transcontinental." Mann's private actions, however, presented a different aspect. In an interview with Robert Rogers, the minister of the interior, he claimed that unless navvies could be imported from the United States the completion of the Canadian Northern would be seriously delayed.[58] Immigration regulations were immediately altered in the company's favour, while the Dominion government refused to consider a request from the IWW to appoint a conciliation board.[59]

Newspaper reaction in Western Canada towards the strike reflected the business outlook. The Calgary *Herald* referred to the IWW actions as "incipient outlawry," while the Edmonton *Journal* charged that Martin Welch and other prominent contractors had received threats that "they would be blown up unless they granted the demands of the IWW." The Vancouver *Sun* echoed this theme asserting that the entry of IWW represented "an invasion of the most despicable scum of humanity," and it called upon the McBride government "to drive these people out of the country."[60] The provincial government did not need much persuading, the more so since it had received a confidential report that the IWW was engaged in "a stupendous scheme for tying up the leading industries of the Pacific coast." Squads of provincial police were rushed to the railway camps where they assumed a major role in escorting strike-breakers, closing the IWW camps and intimidating union organizers. By the end of May there were over 250 Wobblies in provincial jails, and scores had been deported.[61] These repressive measures taken against the IWW organizers and the destitution of the navvies eventually broke the strike.

The IWW did not, however, abandon its attempts to organize the railway workers and in July about 2,000 navvies struck the contractors of the Grand Trunk Pacific. But this strike was short-lived. By the middle of August 1912 the IWW railway strikes were finished, leaving little gain for either the navvies or the IWW.[62] While working conditions had been marginally improved wages remained the same and the iniquitous sub-contracting system still reigned supreme. The IWW had failed, but the memory of its involvement and the syndicalist creed of industrial sabotage cast a long shadow over future industrial relations in Western Canada.

Not least among its effects was the legacy of paranoia which it left in the minds of public officials and industrialists in the region.[63]

The most successful attempts to organize immigrant workers into lasting industrial unions were made by the Western Federation of Miners (WFM) and the United Mine Workers of America (UMWA). Their activities centred on the Rocky Mountain mining regions where immigrant workers were in the majority. The WFM entered the region at the turn of the century, led by the British and native-born. The Western Federation did not, however, adopt the racial exclusiveness of the craft unions associated with the American Federation of Labour; indeed, the union had a concerted effort to recruit immigrant mine workers. In 1903, for example, the ritual and constitution of the union were translated into Italian, Finnish, and Russian. With their pronounced class appeal and active organizational work, the Western Federation of Miners made appreciable headway in both the metalliferous and coal mines of Alberta and British Columbia. But the combined power of the mining companies and the British Columbia and Dominion governments was sufficient to drive the union out of the region. By 1903 the Western Federation of Miners had vacated the coal mining fields to their rival industrial union, the United Mine Workers of America (UMWA).[64]

The spectacular growth of the UMWA from a membership of about 10,000 in 1897 to over 400,000 in 1913 was directly attributable to the ability of this union to attract the immigrant miner. According to the labour historian Victor Greene the heterogeneity of the UMWA effectively refutes the allegation that immigrant workers obstructed the development of militant industrial unions in the coal-mining districts of Pennsylvania. By 1910 the international leadership of the UMWA recognized the enormous importance of appealing to the foreign miners. As Thomas Lewis, a prominent official of the union stated at the binational conference of that year: "The foreign speaking mine workers have the same interests in the UMWA as all others who are members. ... It is our duty to give them every reasonable opportunity of understanding the mission of the union."[65] The UMWA adopted the practice of distributing union literature in Italian, Finnish, and certain Slavic languages. Moreover, Italian and Slavic-speaking organizers were appointed to a number of Canadian districts, most notably District 18, which encompassed the Rocky Mountain coal-mining region.[66]

The ethnic character of the mines in this region changed appreciably between 1899 and 1912. In 1899 the Royal Commission on

Coal Mining Conditions in British Columbia described the labour force of the Crow's Nest Coal Mining Company, the largest concern in the region; it was stated that "nearly all are British subjects ... except perhaps one or two foreigners".[67] By contrast, in 1912 most of the miners were foreign workers with "a majority of Slavonians in one camp, and a majority of Italians in another, and so on throughout the District." In the meantime the membership of the UMWA realized that unless they successfully appealed to the immigrant workers they would "go out of existence."[68] The concern of the union for the foreign miners extended from the workplace to the ethnic neighbourhoods. At one annual convention after another, the district delegates denounced sanitation conditions in the company towns, particularly in the areas inhabited by immigrant workers.[69]

The union also provided sickness and funeral benefits for foreign brothers and sought to secure workmen's compensation for the accident victims. The latter cause acquired great urgency after the Bellevue disaster of December 1910 in which twenty-seven of the twenty-nine men killed were non-Anglo-Saxon. At the 1911 Convention of District 18 the following resolution was passed:

> We Seven Thousand United Mine Workers in District 18 one and all of us, must make it our business to find out the names of the Insurance Companies that these Coal Operators do business with, so that we may be in a position to denounce them in the street, on the platform, in the press, and if possible in the pulpit for their cruel, heartless cheating of the poor widows and orphans, especially those of our foreign brother."[70]

Thereafter the UMWA and the WFM combined their resources to fight a test case through the courts; the Krzus v. Crow's Nest Pass Coal Company eventually reached the Judicial Committee of the Privy Council where a favourable decision was rendered.[71]

Environmental factors also facilitated the growth of class consciousness among foreign mine workers. In his article "Sociological Models of the Mining Community," M.I.A. Blumer has argued that "mine workers constitute a group of workers who ... experience exploitation in an extreme form through performing alienating labour the surplus value of which is enjoyed by the capitalist entrepreneur." Blumer also maintains that mining towns develop a sense of occupational community in which "the social relations of work ... carry over into nonwork activity."[72] The mining towns of the Rocky Mountain region almost invariably conform to this pattern. Most of the companies had their head offices in either central Canada or the United States, while the mine managers were frequently American or British. In many towns the power of the company was absolute. The corporate autocracy was vividly demonstrated during a district-wide strike in 1911 when wholesale evictions of strikers and their families were threatened during the middle of winter. In the mind of capital little distinction seemed to be made in industrial conflict between job and home; it is not surprising that unions and miners should have taken the same view.[73]

The effort to bring the foreign workers into the UMWA met with great success. Indeed, between 1906 and 1911 immigrant miners assumed a major role in the many ferocious and sustained strikes which occurred in District 18 over union recognition and the "closed shop." Here the ability of the foreign worker to subsist on meagre funds and to secure alternate employment was revealed to full advantage. Of perhaps equal importance was the fierce resistance which these workers displayed towards strikebreakers. The turbulence of this period was more than a mere disagreement between capital and labour; it was a life-and-death struggle and any deviance from the group action was branded as traitorous.[74] The following letter sent to a Hungarian strikebreaker reveals the emotional intensity of the situation:

> Judas, in the bible, is a true man compared to you. Judas sold Christ, but Judas had no family so he brought shame on himself alone. But you Joseph Cros, and especially your two sons ... betraying now, not only yourself and family but the whole of the American Hungarians. You must know that the soldiers will guard you forever, but if those 500 strikers get mad at you those 12 soldiers could not be of any use in guarding you.[75]

When quiet persuasion failed, the property of the "scabs" was dynamited, and they themselves were assaulted by mobs composed not only of workers but their wives and children. Even the protective cordon of Royal North West Mounted Police (RNWMP) stationed to protect company property and maintain order, did not intimidate the foreign community. Many an officer had his shins kicked, face scratched, or nose punched in mob action. Not surprisingly, district superintendents usually insisted upon the maximum deployment of police units on the grounds that "these people have been ruled by force for generations [and] ... in consequence, it now requires force to keep them in order."[76]

Following the 1911 strike a foreign worker, Nick Thachuk, was elected to represent Canmore at the District 18 Annual Convention. At this gathering Tachuk enthusiastically endorsed the notions of a One Big Union and a General Strike. In the aftermath of the 1911 strike there had been wholesale blacklistings and the level of bitterness on the union side was extremely high. Capital was victorious but at the price of drawing the WFM, the IWW and the UMWA towards a common front.[77] The case for such a regional industrial union was put by James Roberts of the WFM: "There is no longer any room for sectionalism or small units amongst the Workers. The introduction of modern machinery is levelling things up; the skilled mechanic of yesterday, becomes the ordinary labourer of tomorrow, therefore the need of more harmony and solidarity, and the adoption of a Universal Working Card."[78] For the moment the movement he represented did not succeed, but the bitter harvest of industrial conflict in the Canadian West would be realized in 1919.[79]

Beyond the unions were the various socialist parties which actively operated among immigrant workers, especially in Western Canada and northern Ontario. The most successful of these organizations were usually located in single-enterprise communities or major urban centres, drawing much of their support from ethnic ghettos. This was especially true of regions where there were large numbers of Ukrainian and Finnish immigrants.

The first major organizational effort of immigrant socialists occurred in 1907 when the Ukrainian Socialist Labour Committee was formed in Winnipeg. This Committee attempted to link Ukrainian socialists across the country through its newspaper *Chervony Prapor* ("Red Flag"). The paper was "printed for that section of the Canadian proletariat which speaks the Ukrainian language." Its purpose was "to help this section in awareness, education and organization, and towards a clear understanding of the international idea of socialism." *Chervony Prapor* proposed to lead "the working masses in the fight against lawlessness, exploitation and slavery."[80]

That is not to say, however, that all Canadian Ukrainian workers were sympathetic to industrial unionism and socialist ideas. Indeed, the parent Ukrainian Social Democratic Party (RSDRP), originally founded in Galicia in 1890, experienced considerable difficulty in its recruitment campaigns. This was partly because the leadership of the party was dominated by Great Russians and Jews, and partly because the organization was reluctant to consider Ukrainian autonomy "either within the party or within the future socialist state." It was not until about 1910, when Lenin and other Social Democratic leaders recognized the strength of "Ukrainian nationalism and agrarian socialism," that the RSDRP began to make appreciable headway in the Russian Ukraine and in the Austro-Hungarian provinces of Galicia and Bukovinia. Although Lenin was careful not to promise the establishment of a Ukrainian national state, he did write in *Pravda* ("Truth") that the future Soviet Republic would be based on "full equality of all peoples and languages."[81]

The Old World experience of Ukrainian socialists considerably influenced their behaviour in Canada. Initially they seemed prepared to work within the confines of the Socialist Party of Canada, accepting the notion that this organization was dedicated to uniting "workers of all nations and faiths." But even at this early stage Ukrainian socialists argued that the education and mobilization of the "100,000 Ukrainian proletarians" in the three Prairie provinces required a Ukrainian Socialist Union within the Socialist Party of Canada (SPC). The emphasis which Ukrainian socialists placed on cultural and ethnic values enabled them to secure considerable popular support; thus the socialist hall was not only a political but a social institution.[82]

On the negative side the ethnocentric appeal of the Ukrainian socialists often brought them into conflict with the Anglo-Saxon leadership of the Socialist Party of Canada. Although the platform of the SPC had been translated into Ukrainian, and the *Red Flag* had received a degree of financial support, by 1910 the differences between Anglo-Saxon and Ukrainian socialists, both in Winnipeg and in the Dominion as a whole, had become irreconcilable. Hence, in February 1910, a Ukrainian Social Democratic Federation was established with headquarters in Winnipeg. Ukrainian socialists also played a major role, later that year, in the formation of the Canadian Social Democratic Party (SDP). In contrast to the SPC this was a loose federation which united Eastern European and English-speaking socialists. Between 1910 and 1914 the Ukrainian Social Democrats launched an ambitious organizational campaign which effectively utilized their militant newspaper *Robochny Narod* ("Working People").[83]

Written in simple and colourful language, this newspaper was highly ideological in content. Frequent reference was made in it to the depravity of Canadian politicians, Ukrainian priests, and Ukrainian national democrats. A 1914 issue, for example, provided the following account of the way of life which Ukrainian immigrants could expect in Canada:

Canada is one large country of literate illiteracy. ... There are mostly Englishmen in Canada. All of them are literate, that is true, but after scrutiny, they are worse than illiterate. They aren't interested in a single progressive thought – the only thing they know is the dollar. ... They are hardly interested in politics, except when it is a matter of how many dollars it will bring them ... when one considers the English [Canadian] working class ... they have no class consciousness and their social democratic movement is very weak, greatly weaker than the Ukrainian. In truth, the greater part of them are organized into unions, but these unions are not interested in anything. Each of them belongs to a union because the union assures him of higher pay. He doesn't think of anything but his pay.[84]

The *Robochny Narod* also attempted to recruit Ukrainian workers into the Ukrainian Social Democratic Party by promoting a system of social security; if a worker joined he was assured of a twenty-dollar lump sum payment in event of sickness or unemployment unless these resulted from drunkenness. In their recruitment campaigns the Ukrainian Social Democrats were fortunate in having in their ranks experienced socialists like Timothy Koreichuk, Hoyhorg Tkachuk, Matthew Popovich, and Savva Federenko. The careers of these four men illustrate the extent to which Ukrainian socialism had been transmitted to Western Canada. Koreichuk had previously worked with poor Ukrainian peasants and workers in Bukovinia, where he had run as a Social Democratic candidate before going to the Western Canadian mining districts in 1912. Tkachuk and Popovich had both been active Social Democratic organizers among Ukrainian peasants in Galicia; in 1912 they both settled in Winnipeg's North End ethnic ghetto and quickly emerged as leading socialists.[85] These men brought to Canada organizational skills that were variously employed in the establishment of workers' mutual aid societies, in socialist newspapers and in direct political action. The *massovka*, or workers' picnic, was but one example of the transfer of working-class customs from Russia to Canada. At this event politics and pleasure were served up in equal portions. Fortified with ample supplies of food and drink the participants would "listen to poetry or sing revolutionary songs until late into the night."[86]

Ukrainian Social Democrats in Canada were also able to get support by appealing to Ukrainian nationalism and by denouncing the Tsar. In 1910, Canadian Ukrainians were stirred into action by the attempt of the Russian government to have Savva Federenko, a participant in the 1905 Russian revolution, extradited from the country. Significantly, the USD defence of Ferenko was given vocal support by prominent members of the Anglo-Canadian community who recoiled at the prospect of their government being "an ally of Russian autocracy."[87] The successful defence of Federenko's right to remain in Canada was illustrative of the growing strength of the Ukrainian socialists. By 1914 the USD had eighteen branches, five of them in Manitoba. Though the number of party members was still small, their level of dedication was high.[88]

The links between nationalism and socialism were equally visible elsewhere. Finnish Social Democrats appealed just as strongly to their countrymen's sense of ethnic consciousness and nationalist aspiration. Moreover, the high level of Finnish involvement in socialist and syndicalist organizations was partly because they arrived in North America with a "higher level of literacy" and educational aspiration. Nor was this involvement confined to males. Within the Finnish immigrant community women were afforded unusually high status. In Finland itself, women were granted the franchise in 1905, approximately eleven years before their Canadian counterparts. For Finnish women, therefore, removal to Canada meant a frustrating loss of electoral privilege. Unlike other immigrant groups the Finns did not benefit greatly from religious leadership.[89] The Finnish churches were deeply divided and offered little social leadership at home, and even less in North America. Cast adrift in this fashion Finnish workers increasingly turned to the socialist *emigré* intellectuals for guidance, men such as Matti Kurikka, Martin Hendrickson, Antero Tanner, Leo Laukki. "In Marxism they found an ideology which seemed to explain the condition of their lives and offer a means by which these conditions could be transformed and a better world created."[90]

IV

There were many occasions between 1896 and 1914 when European immigrant workers showed that they were prepared to resist forcibly the demands of exploitative capitalism in Canada. Their resistance ranged from spontaneous uprisings to systematic support of industrial unions and socialist organizations.[91] It has been argued, however, that their day-to-day influence did not rival that of skilled workers, most of whom were English-speaking. Equally, it has been argued that even syndicalist organizations such as the IWW were dominated by "native Americans, or the most Americanized immigrants." These arguments lead to the conclusion that immigrant workers, though not docile, were marginal to working-class organization.[92]

No doubt, there is substance in this point of view. The collective protest of immigrant workers was often sporadic and temporary. But British- and native-born workers could just as well be accused of vacillation in their commitment to working-class goals. In Toronto, for example, the advent of the depression of 1907 brought about the collapse of some fifty-six craft locals, while another forty-seven were dissolved during the 1913-1914 recession. Quite clearly, the stereotype of the European immigrant worker, with no interest in militant class action, leaves as much to be desired as the stereotype of the British worker as "practical and tolerant, content with piecemeal causes and nonviolent."[93] Sustained membership in a trade union must not be regarded as the *sine qua non* of working-class protest. Studies such as Tamara Haraven's "The Laborers of Manchester, New Hampshire, 1912-1922: the Role of Family and Ethnicity in Adjustment to Industrial Life" have demonstrated that familial and ethnic ties could often provide a substitute for industrial unionism. The ability of immigrant groups to maintain job control through slow-downs and other measures cannot be overlooked; ethnicity could provide a "major organizational framework for workers' adjustment to the pressures of factory labor."[94]

Of course ethnicity must not be confused with class solidarity. Sometimes there was greater hostility between competing ethnic groups than between worker and boss. Yet the experience of immigrant dockworkers in the Lakehead, foreign navvies in the railway camps of British Columbia and of Italian and Slavic mine workers of the Rocky Mountain coal region shows that ethnicity could be a potent stimulant to a broader working-class consciousness. This trend was associated not only with the presence of ethnic mutual aid societies and socialist clubs but a frontier work setting. Economic exploitation in an isolated and dangerous work-place could produce frustrations which overcame all national and linguistic differences.[95]

Certainly Anglo-Canadian politicians and industrialists recognized a growing assertiveness on the part of immigrant workers; indeed, there were increasing public pronouncements from prominent citizens which warned that the continual influx of European immigrants would threaten the stability of Canadian society.[96] This alarmist news was clearly revealed in 1908 when strenuous efforts were made by Winnipeg civic officials to prevent the famous anarchist Emma Goldman from visiting the city. Mayor J.H. Ashdown, a prominent local businessman, articulated the view of the city's Anglo-Canadian elite when he criticized the Immigration Branch for not excluding such "professional agitators":

> ... we have a very large foreign population in this City, it consists approximately of 15,000 Galicians, 11,000 Germans, 10,000 Jews, 2,000 Hungarians and 5,000 Russians and other Slavs and Bohemians. Many of these people have had trouble in their own country with their Governments and come to the new land to get away from it, but have all the undesirable elements in their character that created the trouble for them before. They are just the right crowd for Emma Goldman or persons of her character to sow seeds which are bound to cause most undesirable growths in the future. ...[97]

Emma Goldman was eventually allowed into the country but this incident cleared the way for a 1910 amendment to the Immigration Act which provided for the exclusion and deportation of those professing anarchist views. The amendment was a portent of what was to follow in 1919.

CHAPTER THREE

Enemy Aliens and "Foreign" Bolsheviks, 1914-1919

The economic status of immigrant workers on the eve of the war was not favourable. By 1912 the unsettled state of European affairs had helped produce a prolonged economic slump in the transatlantic economy. This recession was particularly felt in Western Canada, a region which was very dependent on foreign capital for its continued prosperity. By the summer of 1914 there was widespread unemployment in the area, the more so since over 400,000 immigrants had arrived in the previous year.[1] Before long many Prairie and west coast communities were providing relief to unemployed workers. Most of the men laid off in the railroad, lumbering, and mining camps made their way to the major transportation centres of Vancouver, Edmonton, and Winnipeg hoping to find there either new jobs or government assistance. They were frequently disappointed; urban jobs were scarce and most municipal government denied relief to persons who were "not entitled to claim domicile."[2] For the immigrant worker the new situation was particularly bleak; he could either use his hard-earned savings to maintain himself in Canada or return to Europe. Many chose the long journey across the Atlantic. The plight of the foreign workers who remained was described by *Robotchny Narod* as follows: "Hundreds of unemployed Ukrainian workers groan from the blow of hunger, and those who have luckily found work suffer unheard of cruel treatment and mockery from their employer benefactors."[3] But worse was to follow – especially for those immigrants unlucky enough to have been born in those countries which took up arms against the British Empire.

I

The outbreak of war in August 1914 forced the Dominion government to adopt a comprehensive set of guidelines for dealing with the enemy alien resident of the country. Of the persons classified as enemy aliens there were 393,320 of German origin, 129,103 from the Austro-Hungarian Empire, 3,880 from the Turkish Empire, and several thousands from Bulgaria.[4] The Dominion government's position was set forth in a series of acts and proclamations, the most important being the War Measures Act of August 1914. This measure specified that during a "state of war, invasion, or insurrection ... the Governor in Council may do and authorize such acts ... orders and regulations, as he may ... deem necessary or advisable for the security, defence, order and welfare of Canada. ..." Specific reference was made to the following powers: censorship on all forms of communication and the arrest, detention and deportation of dangerous enemy aliens. Subsequent Orders-in-Council in October 1914 and September 1916 prohibited enemy aliens from possessing firearms and instituted a system of police and military registration.[5] By end of the war over 80,000 enemy aliens had been registered, though only 8,579 of these were actually interned. This number included: 2,009 Germans, 5,954 Austro-Hungarians, 205 Turks, 99 Bulgarians, and 312 classified as miscellaneous. These 8,579 prisoners of war were located in some twenty-four different camps, although most were placed in either Kapuskasing (Ont.) or Vernon (B.C.).[6]

Although there were very few incidents of sabotage or espionage on the home front during the war, enemy aliens soon became the object of intense Anglo-Canadian hostility. This was particularly true of those enemy aliens categorized as Austrians since most of them were immigrants of military age who retained the status of reservists in their old homeland.[7] The spectacular intervention of Bishop Nykyta Budka did not help the Austrian reservist position in Canada. On July 27, while the world waited breathlessly for the Austrian reaction to the assassination of the Archduke Francis Ferdinand, Bishop Budka issued a pastoral letter calling upon his Ukrainian parishioners to remember their duty to the Austro-Hungarian Empire if war should occur:

> The Canadian Ruthenian Ukrainians ... make evident their sentiments in church services for the assassinated ones, and in their prayers for the fate of their native land. ...
>
> All Austrian subjects must be at home in positions to defend our native land, our dear brothers and sisters, our Nation. Whoever should receive the call should feel obligated to go to the defence of our threatened Fatherland.[8]

In a hastily prepared second pastoral letter Budka affirmed his loyalty to the British Empire, but his initial statement was not soon forgotten and during the early months of the war there was pressure for his internment. Anglo-Canadian concern over the activities of the bishop and his party were compounded by rumours of seemingly related Austrian and German activities in the United States. Throughout the fall of 1914 there were alarming reports about what was afoot in the German-American communities of several American cities; one agent reported from Chicago that "should the Germans achieve a single success I believe that we in Canada are in danger of a repetition of the invasion of 1866 on a larger scale. What made the threat from the United States even more ominous was the steady flow of migrant labourers across a virtually unpatrolled border; many of those on the move were either enemy aliens or members of alleged pro-German groups such as Finns.[9]

The fear of a fifth column among unemployed and impoverished enemy alien workers was also widespread.[10] Conversely, their strong support for the nation that enemy aliens who had jobs should be turned out of them; in 1915 there were many dismissals for "patriotic" reasons. This policy was popular both among Anglo-Canadian workers and immigrants from countries, such as Italy and Russia, now allied with the British Empire. Some labour intensive corporations, however, held a different point of view.[11] The Dominion Iron and Steel Company, for example, resisted the pressure to dismiss their enemy alien employees on the grounds that Nova Scotia workers "would not undertake the rough, dirty jobs." It was only when the company obtained an understanding from the Dominion Immigration Branch that it could import even more pliable workers from Newfoundland that it agreed to join temporarily in the patriotic crusade.[12] Elsewhere corporate resistance was even stronger. In June 1915 English-speaking and allied miners threatened strike action at Fernie (B.C.) and Hillcrest (Alta.) unless all enemy alien miners were dismissed. The situation was particularly tense at Fernie where the giant Crow's Nest Coal Company initially balked at this demand. Eventually a compromise was achieved: all naturalized married enemy alien miners were retained; naturalized unmarried enemy aliens were promised work when it was available; the remainder of the enemy alien work force, some 300 in number, were temporarily interned. Within two months, however, all but the "most dangerous" had been released by Dominion authorities.[13]

This action indicated that, despite severe local and provincial pressure, the Borden government was not prepared to implement a mass internment policy. The enormous expense in operating the camps and an antipathy to adopting "police state" tactics partly explain the Dominion government's reluctance. There was also a suspicion in Ottawa that many municipalities wanted to take advantage of internment camps to get rid of their unemployed. Arthur Meighen articulated the view of the majority of the Cabinet when he argued that instead of being interned, unemployed aliens should each be granted forty acres of land which could be cultivated under government supervision; he concluded his case with the observation that "these Austrians ... can live on very little."[14] By the spring of 1916 even the British Columbia authorities had come around to this point of view. One provincial police report gave this account of how much things had quieted down: "From a police point of view, there has been less trouble amongst them [aliens] since the beginning of the war than previously, the fact that several of them were sent to internment camps at the beginning of the war seemed to have a good effect on the remainder ... In my opinion, if there is ever any trouble over the employment of enemy aliens, it will be after the war is over and our people have returned."[15]

But the changed attitude in British Columbia also reflected a dramatically altered labour market. As the war progressed serious labour shortages developed in both the province and in the country. In the summer of 1915 there was a demand for about 10,000 harvest labourers in the Prairie provinces. Many of those who came to do the harvesting were unemployed enemy alien workers from the slums of Vancouver and Winnipeg who had their transportation subsidized by the Dominion and Western provincial governments.[16] Government involved in the recruitment of such workers was increased in 1916 when it became apparent that the supply of labour available on the Prairies would again be insufficient to meet the harvest demands. The Dominion Immigration Branch now began placing advertisements in United States newspapers urging Americans to look northward for employment. Instructions were also issued to the agents of the branch that the money qualifications of the Immigration Act were to be relaxed. By the end of September 1916, over 5,000 harvesters had crossed the international border attracted by generous wages ($3.50 a day) and cheap (1¢ a mile) rail fares from border points.[17]

Increasingly, the practice of securing industrial workers from the United States was also regarded as essential to the maintenance of the Canadian war economy. By an Order-in-Council of August 1916 the Alien Labour Act was temporarily shelved in order to facilitate the movement of industrial labour northward. Thousands of American residents were soon streaming into Canadian industrial communities.[18] But with the entry of the United States into the war in 1917 this source of labour supply was abruptly cut off. Of necessity the focus of Canadian recruitment efforts now shifted overseas, most notably towards the Orient and the West Indies. The most ambitious proposal called for the importation of thousands of Chinese coolies on a temporary basis.[19] But this solution met with the same violent objections it had always encountered from organized labour and nativist opinion, and was ultimately rejected by the Dominion government.

With an overseas solution seemingly impossible, the new labour situation put a premium on the surplus manpower available in the country. This made the alien worker, whether of enemy extraction or not, a very desirable quantity indeed. The implementation of conscription in the summer of 1917 only aggravated an already difficult situation; by the end of the year it was estimated that the country faced a shortage of 100,000 workers. From the spring of 1917 onwards foreign workers found themselves not only wanted by Canadian employers, but actually being "drafted" into the industrial labour force by the Dominion government.[20] As of August 1916 all men and women over the age of sixteen were required to register with the Canadian Registration Board, and in April 1918 the so-called "anti-loafing act" provided that "every male person residing in the Dominion of Canada should be regularly engaged in some useful occupation."[21]

As early as 1916, the Dominion government had adopted the practice of releasing non-dangerous interned prisoners of war (POW's) under contract to selected mining and railway companies both to minimize the costs of operating the camps, and to cope with labour shortages. Not surprisingly this policy was welcomed by Canadian industrialists since these enemy alien workers received only $1.10 a day, and were not susceptible to trade union influence.[22] One of the mining companies most enthusiastic about securing large numbers of the POW workers was the Dominion Iron and Steel Corporation. In the fall of 1917 the president of the company, Mark Workman, suggested that his operation be allocated both interned and "troublesome" aliens since "there is no better way of handling aliens than to keep them employed in productive labour." In December 1917 Workman approached Borden, before the latter left for England, with the proposal that the POW's interned in Great Britain be transferred to the mines of Cape Breton Island. Unfortunately for the Dominion Steel Company the scheme was rejected by British officials.[23]

The railway companies, particularly the Canadian Pacific, also received large numbers of POW workers. The reception of these workers harked back to some of the worst aspects of the immigrant navvy tradition of these companies. During 1916 and 1917 there was a series of complaints from POW workers, and on one occasion thirty-two Austrian workers went on strike in the North Bay district to protest dangerous working conditions and unsanitary living conditions. Neither the civil nor military authorities gave any countenance to these complaints; the ultimate fate of these workers was to be sentenced to six months imprisonment at the Burwash prison farm "for breach of contract."[24]

This coercion was symptomatic of a growing concern among both Anglo-Canadian businessmen and Dominion security officials about alien labour radicalism. Not surprisingly, a 65 per cent increase in food prices between August 1914 and December 1917 created considerable industrial unrest, and the labour shortages which began developing in 1916 provided the trade unions with a superb opportunity to strike back. In 1917 there were a record number of strikes and more than one million man days were lost. Immigrant workers were caught up in the general labour unrest and in numerous industrial centres in northern Ontario and Western Canada they demonstrated a capacity for effective collective action, and a willingness to defy both the power of management and the state. The coming of the Russian Revolution in 1917 added to the tension in Canada by breathing new life into a number of ethnic socialist organizations.[25]

These organizations, particularly among the Ukrainians and the Finns, had been greatly affected by the outbreak of the war. The Ukrainian Social Democratic Party (USDP) had opposed the war in an August 19 editorial: "It wasn't enough for the capitalists to spill the blood of the proletariat in the mines and the factories. There wasn't enough blood flowing in the Balkan wars. And though the tears haven't dried in the eyes of mothers, fathers, orphans and sons, now the capitalists have decided on new sacrifices of flesh and blood." In April 1915 the USDP helped organize a demonstration of unemployed Ukrainian workers in Winnipeg; in its account of the event the *Robotchny Narod* charged that the city police had "pushed the crowd aside in a brutal manner."[26]

The paper put a bold front on the strength of the party, but there was little doubt that both the economic recession and the security regulations had severely disrupted the Ukrainian socialist movement. *Robotchny Narod* itself reported not only substantial drops in local members, but the forced departure of many organizers from the country. Other Ukrainian political and labour activists were included in the roundups of enemy aliens which occurred in the spring of 1915. The problems of the party were highly visible in the Rocky Mountain mining region where the hysteria directed at enemy aliens had shattered the working-class solidarity that the UMWA had achieved before the war. Events in this region drew a mixed reaction from *Robotchy Narod*. On the one hand the paper saw what was happening as a plot by English-speaking capitalists to encourage racial chauvinism in order to weaken industrial unions like the UMWA and "to sow among the working class discord for the future." On the other hand it was contemptuous of those Anglo-Canadian and Italian miners "who gave over to be arrested 300 of their brothers in order to increase their shifts by four hours." An exception was made for UMWA organizers who, it was claimed "had used all their strength to pacify the 'black hundreds' and prevent outrages from the hooligans."[27]

Despite the extreme provocation, *Robotchny Narod* called upon all Ukrainian miners to avoid falling into the pit of ethnic conflict which the capitalists had dug: "Let the inflated English chauvinistic miners run our brothers out of Nanaimo, Fernie & other places; let them put them in camps. We will survive this misfortune and not only will we remain faithful anti-militarists but we will try to teach those workers who have gone crazy over chauvinism."[28]

With the return of more favourable economic conditions in 1916 and 1917 the party quickly recovered. In the spring of 1917 the Ukrainian socialists launched a major campaign to enlist all Ukrainian workers in industrial unions and in the Ukrainian Social Democratic Party. The leading figures in this campaign were Matthew Popovich, John Navis, N.D. Thachuk, V.N. Kolisnyk, John Boychuk, and Timothy Koreichuk; their organizational efforts were directed primarily at Western Canada and northern Ontario. The basis of their appeal was the need for working-class solidarity in mining and other mass production industries:

> We must join the union and the social democratic party, for the past has shown us that in organization is strength. Comrades, don't be afraid to belong to an economic or political

organization. ... This one dollar, comrades you give every month for your organization is like driving one nail into the capitalist heart every month. ... THERE SHOULD NOT BE A SINGLE UKRAINIAN WORKER WHO DOES NOT BELONG TO THE MINERS' ORGANIZATION.[29]

News of the Russian Revolution spurred Ukrainian organizers to even greater activity. Earlier Ukrainian socialists such as Paul Krat had argued that workers should be "like wood worms gnawing at the capitalist oak at its roots"; these gradualists now gave way to a revolutionary element exemplified by Matthew Popovich, who became the editor of the *Robotchny Narod* in 1917.[30] At a rally in Winnipeg on March 25, 1917 Popovich proposed this resolution:

"We Ukrainian workers assembled at a massive meeting in Winnipeg send fraternal greetings to the Russian revolutionary workers with the arrival of a shining revolutionary triumph over the autocratic Czar and the destruction of the prison of the peoples from which will also come forth thirty million Ukrainians. We are convinced that the Russian comrades will not stop at the complete overthrow of the political structure of Russia but will carry forth the struggle of the working people to full victory over its enemies."[31]

In June 1917 Ukrainian socialists were involved in a major strike of unskilled construction workers in Winnipeg over the issue of collective bargaining. The strike erupted in violence and twenty-three foreign strikers were arrested. The unnaturalized enemy aliens among those arrested were sent to an internment camp at Cochrane, Ontario; the rest were charged in the Winnipeg courts. But despite this repression, and further attempts by the Builders' Exchange to recruit strike-breakers, the workers won a limited victory. The construction workers' union was recognized, and working conditions in the industry gradually improved. Significantly, at a rally of the jubilant strikers a motion was passed thanking Matthew Popovich "for his help in the organization of the union ... and in aiding the families of the arrested strikers."[32]

The *Robotchny Narod* was now also stridently critical of the policies of the Dominion government, particularly of the decision to implement compulsory military service. The Dominion censorship authorities soon responded in kind, and in the fall of 1917 there were various suggestions that both *Robotchny Narod* and its Russian language twin *Rabotchny Narod*, should be suppressed. The position of the papers was further imperilled when it was reported that the editor of *Rabotchny Narod*, Michael Charitinoff, a Russian Jew, was "the ambassador of the Bolsheviks in Western Canada" and that he was in constant communication with Bolshevik elements in the United States.[33] The Borden government held back, however, because it did not wish to antagonize the new Soviet government by implementing a full-scale purge of Slavic socialists in Canada. But this moderate approach did not long survive. The proliferation of strikes in essential war industries, and the widespread rumours that the IWW was bent on seizing control of industrial communities in Western Canada and northern Ontario.[34]

Increasingly in 1916 and 1917 Anglo-Canadian businessmen and Dominion security officials came to believe that the American-based IWW posed the greatest threat to industrial harmony in Canada. This problem was compounded by the need to recruit both industrial and agricultural workers in the United States; this dependency, it was thought, gave the IWW an opportunity to extend its activities northward once more, and in particular to dominate those industries where foreign workers were concentrated. Nor were Canadian fears about the IWW restricted to the industrial sector of the economy. The rapid growth of the Agricultural Workers' Association (AWO), an offshoot of the IWW, in the American Northwest in 1915 posed a threat that migrant farm labourers on the Canadian Prairies would also be radicalized.[35] The IWW problem acquired a new dimension in the spring of 1917 when the American authorities began to prosecute many of the Wobbly leaders; there were now reports that IWW organizers were "flocking in by the hundreds to Canada." This "invasion," however, was greatly exaggerated; an investigation by the Dominion police during the summer of 1917 revealed "no trace ... of any activity on the part of the IWW in the country."[36] Yet industrialists who believed that "ninety percent of the ... labour trouble [was] engineered by the IWW kept up the flow of complaints to Ottawa.[37]

No doubt the growing militancy of alien workers accounted for the continuing fear of the IWW. In September 1917 it was reported that foreign miners were joining the IWW in droves in the northern Ontario communities of Cobalt and Timmins.[38] Syndicalism was also said to have caught hold in the Finnish communities of Port Arthur and Sudbury. One Anglo-Canadian resident of Port Arthur described the Finnish population there to the Dominion Police as "anarchists pure and simple;" he urged that his letter be kept confidential "as this would be a perfectly justifiable excuse, according to the Finlander's way of thinking, for sticking a knife between my ribs on the first dark night." That violence was indeed close to the surface at the Lakehead would be borne out during the dock strike of October 1917.[39]

The fear of social anarchy was also evident in the Rocky Mountain coal mining region where the militant UMWA had staged a series of strikes. The coal operators now attempted to enlist the Dominion authorities against the UMWA alleging that the union was dominated by irresponsible and dangerous aliens whose wage demands were "absolutely insatiable." RNWMP reports also stressed the unreliability of alien unionists in the region, their impatience with prolonged bargaining procedures, and their tendency to resort to drastic action. It was also claimed that the radical leaders of the UMWA owed their positions to their alien constituents who voted en bloc. The District President was referred to as being "dishonest and an agitator ... otherwise he would not have been elected ... and supported by the foreigners."[40]

By the spring of 1918 the Dominion government was under great pressure to place all foreign workers under supervision, and, if necessary, to make them "work at the point of a bayonet." The large-scale internment of radical aliens and the suppression of seditious foreign-language newspapers and organizations were also now widely advocated. Winnipeg exhibited all the strains of the anti-alien cause. There, a construction strike in June 1917 was followed by an even more spectacular general strike in May 1918. Enemy aliens were once again singled out by spokesmen for the local business community as the instigators of the continuing unrest. A representative of the Manitoba Gypsum Company, one of the firms affected by the strikes, charged that "all of the men who have gone out are of alien nationality, many of them not naturalized."[41] Local military officials supported this view. Thus the register of enemy aliens informed Colonel Sherwood, the commissioner of the Dominion Police, that many prominent Anglo-Canadians were becoming impatient about the "lenience with which these Alien Enemies are treated." The registrar recommended stronger measures, including the internment of enemy alien strike leaders. This, he argued, "would have a very beneficial effect upon the labour situation."[42]

In point of fact, the Dominion government, alarmed by the reports of IWW and socialist activity among the foreign-born population, had already acted. In June 1918 C.H. Cahan, a wealthy Montreal lawyer, had been appointed to conduct a special investigation into the matter. In the course of his inquiry Cahan solicited information from businessmen, "respectable" labour leaders, police officials in both Canada and the United States, and various members of the immigrant community in Canada.[43] One of those interviewed was the redoubtable Bishop Budka—himself once a security risk. According to Budka there was a "distinct and well-organized Bolsheviki movement in Canada" directed by those associated with *Robotchny Narod*.[44] The report which Cahan submitted to the Cabinet in September 1918 confirmed the existence of such a conspiracy among "Russians, Ukrainians and Finns, employed in the mines, factories and other industries." These workers were "being thoroughly saturated with the Socialistic doctrines which have been proclaimed by the Bolsheviki faction of Russia." Cahan further alleged that delegates from Bolshevik organizations in Russia had recently come "to the United States, and no doubt to Canada to organize and inflame their comrades in America. ..." On the basis of his report, the Borden government implemented a series of coercive measures; by two Orders-in-Council (PD 2381 and PC 2384) the foreign-language press was suppressed, and a number of socialist and anarchist organizations were outlawed.[45]

The newspapers most affected by the censorship regulations were those which published in the languages categorized as "enemy alien": German, Bulgarian, Ukrainian, Estonian, Ruthenian, Hungarian, Turkish, Russian, Finnish, Croatian, and Livonian. Not suprisingly, therefore, almost all of the organizations categorized as unlawful under PC 2384 were composed of ethnic workers; the most prominent were the Ukrainian Social Democratic Party, the Russian Social Democratic Party, and the Finnish Social Democratic Party. Significantly, Jewish, Italian, and Scandinavian organizations and newspapers were not directly affected by the legislation; there was, however, some pressure from Dominion security officials to outlaw the Jewish Social Democratic Party and to supervise closely the Yiddish publications *The Israelite* (Winnipeg) and *The Eagle* (Montreal).[46]

The penalties for possession of prohibited literature, and continued membership in any of these outlawed organizations were extremely severe: fines of up to $5,000 or a maximum prison term of five years could be imposed. In October 1918 a Public Safety Branch under the Department of Justice was created in order to enforce the new regulations; not unexpectedly, C.H. Cahan was appointed director of the branch.[47] The full powers of censorship and police harassment were now directed against the alien radical. A case involving Michael Charitinoff, the former editor of *Rabotchny Narod*, clearly revealed this tendency. In October 1918 Charitinoff was arrested and charged with the possession of prohibited literature. Judge Hugh John Macdonald, a prominent member of Winnipeg's Anglo-Canadian community, sentenced the young Ukrainian socialist to three years' imprisonment and a fine of $1,000.[48]

Yet Charitinoff was surely more than an "ethnic figure"; his case was taken up by Anglo-Canadian socialists first in Winnipeg and then throughout Western Canada. The support he received was illustrative of a growing solidarity between Anglo-Canadian and alien radicals in the region – a connection that belied the notion that the foreigner was at the root of Canada's labour ills.[49] Nor was admiration of the Russian Revolution confined to the alien community; utopian ideas were also current among English-speaking labour leaders. In the words of William Yates, a Western Canadian unionist, the time had perhaps come "to adopt the tactics of the IWW or the Russian Revolution."[50]

III

The hatreds and fear stirred up by World War I did not end with the Armistice of 1918; instead social tension spread in ever-widening circles. Anglo-Canadians who had learned to despise the Germans and the Austro-Hungarians had little difficulty transferring their aroused passions to the Bolsheviks. Though the guns were silent on the Western Front, Canadian troops were now being sent to Siberia "to strangle the infant Bolshevism in its cradle."[51] Within Canada, there was widespread agitation against potentially disloyal aliens and those involved in socialist organizations. An editorial in the *Winnipeg Telegram* summed up these sentiments: "Let every hostile alien be deported from this country, the privileges of which ... he does not appreciate."[52]

In the early months of 1919 the Borden government was deluged by a great wave of petitions demanding the mass deportation of enemy aliens. Inquiries were actually made by the Dominion government concerning the possible implementation of a policy of mass expulsion. Surveys by the Department of Justice revealed that there were over 88,000 enemy aliens registered, 2,222 of whom were located in internment camps. There were also 63,784 Russian subjects in Canada, many of whom officials in Ottawa believed to be potentially hostile.[53] The policy of mass deportation was rejected, however, both because of its likely international repercussions, and the demands it would make on the country's transportation facilities at a time when the troops were returning from Europe.[54]

The need to find jobs quickly for the returning soldier also affected the situation of the foreign worker. Both politicians and businessmen faced a powerful argument in the claim that all enemy aliens should be turned out of their jobs to make way for Canada's 'heroes;' but their actions were also motivated by the fear that the veterans would be radicalized and lured into socialist organizations if their economic needs were not immediately satisfied.[55] By February 1919 the British Columbia Employers' Association, the British Columbia Manufacturers' Association and the British Columbia Loggers' Association had all announced that their memberships were prepared to offer employment to returned soldiers by dismissing alien enemies. This pattern was repeated in the mining region of northern Ontario where in the early months of 1919 the International Nickel Company, for instance, dismissed 2,200 of their 3,200 employees, the vast majority of whom were foreigners.[56] Even the CPR joined the "patriotic crusade" of dismissals. As Vice-President D.C. Coleman put it, "The aliens who had been on the land when the war broke out and who went to work in the cities and towns, taking the jobs of the men who went to the front ... [should] go back to their old jobs on the land."[57]

But not even the land of the "men in sheepskin coats" was now safe for the immigrant worker; rumours were abroad that the Dominion government intended to cancel large numbers of homestead patents, and assaults on aliens by returned soldiers were commonplace.[58] Even the usually passive *Canadian Ruthenian* denounced the harsh treatment which Ukrainians and other foreigners were receiving from the Anglo-Canadian community and the Dominion government:

> The Ukrainians were invited to Canada and promised liberty, and a kind of paradise. Instead of the latter they found woods and rocks, which had to be cut down to make the land fit to work on. They were given farms far from the railroads, which they so much helped in building – but still they worked hard ... and came to love Canada. But ... liberty did not last long. First, they were called 'Galicians' in mockery. Secondly, preachers were sent amongst them, as if they were savages, to preach Protestantism. And thirdly, they were deprived of the right to elect their representatives in Parliament. They are now uncertain about their future in Canada. Probably, their [property] so bitterly earned in the sweat of their brow will be confiscated.[59]

By the spring of 1919 the Borden government had received a number of petitions from ethnic organizations demanding either British justice or the right to leave Canada. The *Toronto Telegram* estimated that as many as 150,000 Europeans were preparing to leave the country. Some Anglo-Canadian observers warned, however, that mass emigration might relieve the employment problems of the moment but in the long run leave "a hopeless dearth of labour for certain kinds of work which Anglo-Saxons will not undertake."[60]

Concern about the status of the alien worker led directly to the appointment by the Dominion government of the Royal Commission on Industrial Relations on April 4, 1919. The members of the Commission travelled from Sydney to Victoria, and held hearings in some twenty-eight industrial centres. The testimony of industrialists who appeared before the commission reveals an ambivalent attitude towards the alien worker. Some industrialists argued that the alien was usually doing work "that white men don't want," and that it would "be a shame to make the returned soldier work at that job." But in those regions where there was high unemployment among returned soldiers, and where alien workers had been organized by radical trade unions, management took a strikingly different view. William Henderson, a coal-mine operator at Drumheller, Alberta, informed the commission that the unstable industrial climate of that region could only be reversed by hiring more Anglo-Canadian workers, "men that we could talk to ... men that would come in with us and co-operate with us. ..." Many mining representatives also indicated that their companies had released large numbers of aliens who had shown radical tendencies; there were numerous suggestions that these aliens should not only be removed from the mining districts, but actually deported from Canada.[61]

The fears of businessmen like Henderson were compounded by alarming reports of an international Bolshevik conspiracy. Throughout the early months of 1919 Canadian security officials submitted report after report implicating alien workers in Bolshevik subversion. The dangers to the traditional Canadian way of life were manifest. One report that was widely circulated described how the Bolsheviks had implemented the practice of nationalizing women. Clearly personal property, religious principles, and the sanctity of the family unit would all be destroyed if the Bolsheviks gained power in Canada.[62] The gradual dismantling by the Unionist government of the wartime security apparatus was strongly resisted by those caught up in the "Red Scare."

Both C.H. Cahan, the director of public safety, and Major General Gwatkin, the chief of the general staff, deplored the restoration of civil liberties to "dangerous" individuals and groups. Gwatkin was particularly critical of the politicians for catering to the demands of organized labour on this matter and predicted that "one day they will regret that, adopting the tactics of the ostrich, they took no measure for their own protection."[63]

No doubt Cahan and Gwatkin had in mind the revival of radical ethnic organizations. Finnish, Ukrainian, and Russian socialist organizations had survived the period of repression. Persecution had, however, forced upon them a number of important structural changes. In the case of the Finns the Social Democratic Party had been replaced by the Finnish Socialist Organization of Canada (FO); by the spring of 1919 this body was involved in a variety of activities. In Port Arthur, for example, it established a co-operative restaurant and assisted in the formation of an IWW Lumber Workers local in the camps of the region. The assertiveness of the FO was further demonstrated in its campaign to end censorship of the foreign-language press. In March 1919 the secretary of the organization requested the help of the Trades and Labor Congress of Canada, claiming that foreign workers were greatly handicapped "in their efforts at education and self-protection against unjust exploitation."[64] In Ahlqvist's view labour solidarity could be best presented through ethnic organizations.

Ukrainian socialists were also on the march under the leadership of the Winnipeg-based Ukrainian Labour Temple Association which Matthew Popovich and other Ukrainian socialists had formed in 1917. Throughout the spring of 1919 the ULTA established a series of branches in northern Ontario and the West; but it was the Rocky Mountain mining region and in urban centres such as Winnipeg and Edmonton that the ULTA influence was most pervasive. The *Ukrainian Labour News*, which had succeeded *Robotchny Narod*, facilitated the work of the new organization although the paper was somewhat hampered by censorship regulations.[65]

Another new radical organization was the Russian Workers' Party, which had its greatest influence in Montreal and Vancouver. This party had first attracted the interest of Dominion security officials in the spring of 1918 when large numbers of its members had assembled in Vancouver with the purpose of returning assisting the Bolshevik faction in the Russian Civil War.[66] In May 1919 an RNWMP report indicated that those members of the party who had remained on the west coast were "spreading a spirit of unrest among the foreign element in Vancouver ... the majority ... of the ignorant class. ..." Jews were said to occupy leading positions in this and other radical organizations. Jewish radicals were thought to be especially dangerous not only because of their prominence within the Soviet Bolshevik leadership, but also because they represented a cultural minority which manifested "the bitterest hostility" towards Anglo-Canadians.[67]

Despite the Red Scare the growth of working-class unity was impressive; District 18 was a case in point. At the February 1919 convention almost one-third of the delegates were foreigners, the most notable being Sam Susnar and Steve Begalla, both of whom held executive positions in the UMWA. Indeed, discussion of the role of the alien worker in the Rocky Mountain mining region dominated the proceedings. The gathering represented a notable attempt to reconcile the interests of alien workers and returned soldiers. In the presence of five representatives from the Great War Veterans' Association Sam Susnar argued that the foreign miner had been the victim rather than the beneficiary of Canadian capitalism: "I know when I came to Canada I had a few dollars in my pocket and today I am three or four hundred dollars in the hole. After spending eighteen years in the country ... and no money." Another speaker, David Rees, the district organizer of the union, charged that Canadian businessmen were attempting to categorize enemy aliens to include all those who threatened their power, a trend which was particularly pronounced "since the Seattle strike" of February 1919.[68]

Co-operation between English-speaking and foreign workers reached a higher level of achievement in March 1919 with the formation of the One Big Union (OBU), "the first large scale Canadian experiment in 'industrial unionism.'" At the founding convention in Calgary reference was made to the goal of worker control over essential industries, and to the use of the general strike as a means of achieving social and economic reform. OBU spokesmen appealed directly to the foreign workers. A resolution was passed declaring that "the interests of all members of the international working class being identical that this body of workers recognize no alien but the capitalist."[69] Nor was this empty rhetoric. In their campaign to displace the faltering UMWA in District 18 the OBU organizers paid special attention to the alien miners. Foreign-language organizers were appointed and the *District Ledger* stressed the common class goals of all workers. Their strategy worked. By the middle of May 1919 not only had the District Executive Board endorsed the OBU, but every local of the UMWA in District 18, save one, had affiliated with the OBU. There seems little doubt that the foreign mine-workers of the region, because of their numbers alone, were crucial to the triumph of revolutionary industrial unionism. Indeed, analysis of the contributors from local #4070 of the UMWA in Cumberstone, Alberta, to the OBU reveals that thirty-seven of the fifty-three names were non-British.[70] Significantly, on May 10, 1919, the *Ukrainian Labor News*, strongly urged "Ukrainian workers to support wholeheartedly the One Big Union."[71]

In the event the OBU needed all the help it could get. Ranged against it were the combined forces of management, the conservative craft unions and the Dominion government. Yet initially its prospects appeared favourable. OBU organizers met with an enthusiastic response in many parts of the country, and by May 1919 the union had been endorsed by many local trades councils as well as by powerful trade unions such as the UMWA, Mine, Mill & Smelter Workers and the B.C. Loggers' Union. Victor Midgely, the organizing secretary, caught the elan of the movement when he confidently predicted that "the success of the One Big Union [was] absolutely assured."[72]

The advance of the union evoked a quick response from the Dominion government. For some time the RNWMP had been preparing for a major confrontation with the Canadian Bolsheviks: socialist meetings were being carefully monitored, particularly in such volatile centres as Winnipeg, Edmonton, and Vancouver, and secret agents were at work in the radical organizations.[73] The RNWMP and other Dominion security agencies were also resorting with increasing frequency to the weapon of deportation. At the end of the war enemy alien internees had been summarily "repatriated" to Europe. Then, between February and May 1919, the Winnipeg-based Alien Investigation Board ordered a further series of deportations.[74] Security officials in Vancouver, Fernie, and other industrial centres also looked to deportation to weaken radical organizations by eliminating "clever and dangerous" leaders. Significantly, British-born radicals like R.B. Russell and W.A. Pritchard were now included in the undesirable category.[75] Yet it was the "foreigner" who bore the brunt of the attack, in part, because of his greater vulnerability, and, in part, because of the nativism of the militant veterans' organizations. To keep the veterans on the side of established authority was an important part of the strategy of the Dominion officials. As Major Jukes, the Military Intelligence Officer for British Columbia put it, "if the extremists should really start any trouble, their only allies would be the Aliens, the returned soldier would be the asset of the Government to clean up the situation at home."[76] Events in Winnipeg would soon test these views.

IV

In the spring of 1919 Winnipeg was a city of many solitudes. Within its boundaries rich and poor, Anglo-Saxon and foreigner lived in isolation. The vast majority of the white-collar Anglo-Saxon population was to be found in the south and west of the city; the continental Europeans were hived in the north end. This ethno-class division was also reflected in the disparity between the distribution of social services and the incidence of disease. Infant mortality in the North End, for example, was usually twice the rate in the Anglo-Saxon South End. The disastrous influenza epidemic which struck the city during the winter of 1918-19 further demonstrated the high cost of being poor and foreign.[77]

Not surprisingly, foreign workers often struck out against their alleged oppressors. The strikes of 1917 and 1918 had been more than mere economic struggles; for many in the North End these had been the first battles in a war against a capitalist system which spoke with an English tongue.[78] Nor was the Anglo-Canadian establishment of the city unaware of the hostility emanating from the foreign workers and their English-speaking allies. In March 1919 there were RNWMP reports that some of the "better" classes were considering the establishment of a Citizen's Protective Association which would help the civil authorities "in suppressing any incipient riots;" it was also reported that this vigilante organization was considering direct action against "leading socialists" and foreigners.[79]

During January and February 1919 there were a series of anti-alien incidents in the city. One of the worst occurred on January 28 when a mob of returned soldiers attacked scores of foreigners and wrecked the German club, the offices of the Socialist Party of Canada, and the business establishment of Sam Blumenberg, a prominent Jewish socialist. Reports of the event in the *Winnipeg Telegram* illustrate the attitude adopted by many Anglo-Canadian residents of the city towards the aliens. The *Telegram* made no apologies for the violence; instead, the newspaper contrasted the manly traits of the Anglo-Canadian veterans to the cowardly and furtive behaviour of the aliens: "It was typical of all who were assaulted, that they hit out for home or the nearest hiding place after the battle. ..."[80] Clearly, many Anglo-Canadians in the city were prepared to accept mob justice. R.B. Russell reported that the rioting veterans had committed their worst excesses when "smartly dressed officers ... [and] prominent members of the Board of Trade" had urged them on. Nor had the local police or military security officials made any attempt to protect the foreigners from the mob.[81]

At the provincial level Premier Norris's response to the violence was not to punish the rioters, but to establish an Alien Investigation Board which issued registration cards only to "loyal" aliens. Without these cards foreign workers were not only denied employment, but were actually scheduled for deportation.[82] Indeed, the local pressure for more extensive deportation of radical aliens increased during the spring of 1919, especially after D.A. Ross, the provincial member for Springfield, publicly charged that both Ukrainian socialists and religious nationalists were armed with "machine guns, rifles and ammunition to start a revolution in May."[83] The stage was now set for the Red Scare of 1919.

The Winnipeg General Strike of May 15 to June 28, 1919 brought the elements of class and ethnic conflict together in a massive confrontation. The growing hysteria in the city brought with it renewed alien propaganda, a close co-operation between security forces and the local political and economic elite, and finally, attempts to use the immigration machinery to deport not only alien agitators but also British-born radicals. The sequence of events associated with the Winnipeg Strike has been well documented: the breakdown of negotiations between management and labour in the building and the metal trades was followed by the decision of the Winnipeg Trades and Labor Council to call a general strike for May 15. The response was dramatic; between 25,000 and 30,000 workers left their jobs. Overnight the city was divided into two camps.[84]

On one side stood the Citizens' Committee of One Thousand, a group of Anglo-Canadian businessmen and professionals who viewed themselves as the defenders of the Canadian way of life on the Prairies. Their purpose was clear: to crush the radical labour movement in Winnipeg. In their pursuit of this goal the Citizens' Committee engaged in a ferocious propaganda campaign against the opposing Central Strike Comittee, both through its own newspaper *The Citizen*, and through the enthusiastic support it received from the *Telegram* and the *Manitoba Free Press*. The committee's propaganda was aimed specifically at veterans, and the strike was portrayed as the work of enemy aliens and a few irresponsible Anglo-Saxon agitators.[85] John W. Dafoe, the influential editor of the *Free Press*, informed his readers that the five members of the Central Strike Committee – Russell, Ivens, Veitch, Robinson, and Winning – had been rejected by the intelligent and skilled Anglo-Saxon workers, and had gained power only through "the fanatical allegiance of the Germans, Austrians, Huns and Russians. ..." Dafoe advised that the best way of undermining the control which the "Red Five" exercised over the Winnipeg labour movement was "to clean the aliens out of this community and ship them back to their happy homes in Europe which vomited them forth a decade ago."[86]

That some veterans, perhaps a majority, were sympathetic to the strike only intensified this kind of propaganda. The enlistment of veterans to the ranks of the strikers can be attributed to the active educational campaign launched by local socialists such as R.B. Russell, and, in part, to the growing resentment of the returned soldiers about the failure both of government authorities and business leaders to resolve their social and economic problems. On the opening day of the General Strike the major veterans' organizations in the city endorsed the demands of the strikers; they also accepted the pledge of the Central Strike Committee that law and order would be maintained. The *Western Labor News*, the official publication of the Winnipeg Trades Council, continually reminded the returned soldiers that the enemy aliens had been brought to the Dominion "by the men who are now prominent in the 1,000 Committees across Canada." The paper also charged that the current anti-alien campaign was directed against all workers: "so long as they were ... abject slaves, they were desirables; now that they have become a little better off and a little better informed they are aliens."[87] By early June security officials and members of the Citizen's Committee were alarmed by the success which strike leaders like R.E. Bray were having in establishing links between the strikers, ethnic organizations, and the veterans.[88]

Dominion security officials were equally alarmed and were now convinced that the time had come for the use of extraordinary powers. Sympathetic strikes had been started in other cities, most notably Vancouver and Calgary, while OBU organizers like W.A. Pritchard and R.J. Johns seemed to be trying to build the Winnipeg upheaval into a national movement.[89] Moreover, a major strike had developed in District 18 where almost 6,000 miners put down their tools.[90] More menacing still was the possibility of a nation-wide railway strike, a prospect which Labour Minister Gideon Robertson blamed on a "Red element," who were "persistently working among the railway men."[91]

Robertson's solution to the Bolshevik threat was the one favoured by many businessmen and security officials: the stern use of the recently enacted Section 41 of the Immigration Act to deport "anarchists and Bolsheviks" from the country. On June 15 the commissioner of the RNWMP indicated that one hundred aliens had been marked for deportation, of whom thirty-six were in Winnipeg. The following day RNWMP commanding officers across the country were given the special authority to effect these deportations. As a first step the deportees were to be brought to the internment camp at Kapuskasing.[92] In the early hours of June 17 officers of the force descended on the residences of ten Winnipegers: six Anglo-Saxon labour leaders and four "foreigners." The Anglo-Saxons arrested, were as follows: R.B. Russell, William Ivens, R.E. Bray, A.A. Heaps, John Queen, and George Armstrong. The four foreigners seized were Michael Charitinoff, Samuel Blumenberg, Moses Almazoff and Oscar Schoppelrie, all of whom had been considered dangerous and had been placed under police surveillance weeks before the strike.[93]

Ultimately none of these men was summarily deported. In the case of the Anglo-Saxon strike leaders an immediate protest was registered by numerous labour organizations across the country, including the conservative Executive of the Trades and Labor Congress.[94] In Winnipeg itself even John W. Dafoe deplored the government's action arguing that the arrest of the strike leaders would "enable them to pose as martyrs in the cause of the working-men." Alarmed by this uproar, the Borden government announced that it did not intend to employ Section 41 against the British-born agitators either in Winnipeg or any other centre. Of equal significance was the decision on June 21 to release on bail the Anglo-Saxon Winnipeg strike leaders, a gesture which was not extended to the four foreign radicals who remained lodged in the Stoney Mountain penitentiary.[95] The same day there was a violent confrontation between the strikers and the RNWMP. In the melee scores were injured on both sides and two foreigners were killed by gunfire. During this clash members of the special police and the RNWMP and special police forces associated with the Citizen's Committee arrested some thirty-one "foreign rioters."[96] Other police action soon followed. On July 1 a series of raids was carried out across the country on the homes of known agitators and the offices of radical organizations. These RNWMP forays resulted in the seizure of a great mass of "incriminating" material. In Winnipeg, the Ukrainian Labor Temple and the homes of thirty socialists were ransacked.[97]

The stage was now set for the Dominion government to initiate legal action against those accused of radical activity. At this moment, the Dominion authorities appear to have decided on two separate courses of action in dealing with the detained radicals: Anglo-Saxons would be given jury trials; aliens would be subject to deportation hearings before a Board of Inquiry. Samuel Blumenberg, Michael Charitinoff, Solomon Almazoff, and Oscar Schoppelrie appeared before an Immigration Board of Inquiry presided over by Judge R.M. Noble. Crown council was A.J. Andrews, one of the leading members of the Citizens' Committee of One Thousand, and a confidant of Arthur Meighen; the defence was conducted by three lawyers – T.J. Murray, Marcus Hyman, and E.J. McMurray – appointed by the Winnipeg Trades and Labor Council.[98] More than the fate of the accused was at stake at these hearings. If Section 41 could be made to stand up to the requirements of this situation, the way would be cleared for the deportation of hundreds of other immigrant agitators across the country. Moreover, the fate of the foreign strike leaders would obviously influence the outcome of the trial of their Anglo-Saxon counterparts which was to follow. Section 41 was tested and found wanting. Only Schoppelrie was deported – and not for having violated Section 41 but for having crossed the border illegally three years before.[99]

The aliens arrested in Winnipeg on June 21 were not as fortunate. Most of these men were denied the formal deportation proceedings specified under Section 41. Instead, they appeared before Winnipeg Magistrate Hugh John Macdonald who ordered them sent to the internment camp at Kapuskasing for "safe-keeping." Despite the angry protests of the defence council appointed by Winnipeg Trades and Labor Council, these men were subsequently deported in secret.[100]

In time the repression of radical aliens took many different forms. In combatting the woodworkers unions the British Columbia Loggers' Association established a central employment agency and began to import workers from Central Canada. In addition, an extensive blacklisting system was implemented. The eighty firms associated with the association placed some 256 woodworkers on a blacklist; most of these men were alleged to be either foreigners or IWW organizers. Further blacklists were established during the December 1919 loggers' strike. At that time the association agreed to dismiss all members of the IWW, and the OBU, as well as those "known to have seditious, radical or disloyal leanings."[101]

In District 18 the coal operators were able successfully to with-
stand a lengthy strike and to purge local radicals. In this effort
both the International headquarters of the UMWA, now concerned over the number of wild-cat strikes and the growing radicalism of District 18, and the Dominion government provided
assistance. In July 1919 the International Executive of the UMWA
suspended the charter of the District. The International, the coal
operators, and the commissioner of coal operations engineered a
closed shop. Subsequently, only members of the UMWA were eligible for employment and for the substantial wage increase which
was added as a sweetener. All members of the policy committee
of the OBU were automatically rejected for employment, while
the political record of the remainder of the mining population
was thoroughly investigated.[102] An appeal for reinstatement by F.
Scaltritti, an Italian-born miner at Coalhurst, is quite representative of the anguish and confusion of many blacklisted alien
workers:

> I was one of the men which was refused work by the North
> American Collieries here. ... I voted for the One Big Union
> along with the rest of the boys because I thought it would be
> welcomed by the Canadian Government but when the govern-
> ment denounced it as an ellegal [sic] organization I stood up in
> Local here and told them I was done with it. I have come from
> Italy six years ago and have no intention of breaking the Cana-
> dian law. I will support the agreement and constitution of the
> United Mine Workers of America.

His appeal was summarily dismissed by the Manager of the
North American Collieries who claimed that Scaltritti was no
mere peasant worker, but "a very active agent of the OBU ... the
recognized leader of that movement among the Italians here."[103]

A considerable number of alien workers in this region were
also placed in internment camps. One of these, Timothy Koreichuk, a leading organizer for the Ukrainian Social Democrats in
District 18, died while interned at Vernon, British Columbia. To
the *Ukrainian Labor News* Koreichuk was a heroic victim of capitalist oppression: "Sleep and dream martyr! Your fervour for the
struggle which you have placed in the hearts of all Ukrainian
workers will remain forever."[104]

In their attempts to deport the approximately two hundred
"anarchists and revolutionaries" rounded up in the summer raids
of 1919 the Immigration Branch worked very closely with United
States immigration authorities. This co-operation was indicative of

a link which was being forged between Canadian and American security agencies; the formation of the Communist Labor Party of America and the Communist Party of America in the fall of 1919 further strengthened this connection.[105] The RNWMP and Military Intelligence also maintained close contact with the British Secret Service. Lists of undesirable immigrants and known communists were transmitted from London to Ottawa. Indeed, the Immigration Branch had now evolved from a recruitment agency to a security service.[106]

By the winter of 1919 the region of greatest radical activity within Canada shifted towards the central part of the country. After the collapse of the Winnipeg Strike a number of prominent socialists drifted eastward to pursue their organizing work there. The working-class districts of Toronto and other Ontario industrial centres were soon the subject of concern among security officials.[107] There were also reports that Bolsheviks were active among Jews and Slavs in Montreal; Becky and Michael Buhay, both members of the Jewish Social Democratic Party, were cited as being "the cleverest and most outspoken" of the radicals in the city.[108]

Nativist sentiment among Anglo-Canadians, especially in heterogenous communities, was kept alive by this continuing radical ferment. In November 1919, for example, the Grand Jury of Port Arthur issued the following resolution during the fall assizes: "we notice with regret that so many of our foreign population seem to consider it their duty to endeavour to destroy all constituted authority in this county and we would suggest that the proper course is to deport all foreigners who are not willing to live peacefully and abide by the laws of the country." Nor would the bogey of the radical alien disappear after 1919; with the advent of the Great Depression in 1929 shrill demands to deport the foreigner would once again be heard across the land.[109]

V

The events of 1919 produced a spirited national debate on whether Canada should continue to maintain an open door immigration policy. Since many Anglo-Canadians equated Bolshevism with the recent immigration from Eastern Europe, support grew for policies similar to the quota system under discussion in the United States.[110] The Winnipeg Strike, the surplus of labour, and a short but sharp dip in the stock market removed some of the incentive for industrialists to lobby for the continued importation of alien workers. Even the Canadian Manufacturers' Association, the long-time advocate of the open door immigration policy, sounded a cautious note: "Canada should not encourage the immigration of those whose political and social beliefs unfit them for assimilation with Canadians. While a great country such as Canada possessing millions of vacant acres needs population, it is wiser to go slowly and secure the right sort of citizens."[111] Ethnic, cutural, and ideological acceptability had temporarily triumphed over economic considerations. Whether Canada was prepared to accept a slower rate of economic growth in order to ensure its survival as a predominantly Anglo-Canadian nation now became a matter of pressing importance.

Among the European workers themselves the enemy alien hysteria and the Red Scare produced great bitterness. This was especially true for Ukrainian, Finnish, and Russian immigrants, many of whom had considered returning to Europe in the spring of 1919. The unsettled economic and political conditions in their homelands had, however, ultimately prevented their exodus. But their future prospects in Canada looked anything but promising. Certainly there seemed little reason to believe that they could ever become part of the mainstream of Canadian life. In these circumstances Ukrainian, Finnish, and Russian organizations offered an alternative to the "Canadian Way of Life" – an alternative that found sustenance in the achievements of Soviet communism.[112] The distinctive outlook of Slavic and Finnish socialists in Canada was described as follows in a 1921 RCMP intelligence report:

> If in earlier years they came sick of Europe, ready to turn their backs on their homelands, and full of admiration for the native Canadian and Canadian civilization, they have changed their point of view. The war and revolution have roused their intense interest in Central Europe. They belong almost wholly to the poorest element in the community, and it is highly exciting to them to see the class from which they come, composed in effect of their own relatives, seize control of all power and acquire all property.[113]

Such was the legacy of the year 1919 – the floodtide of radical labour politics in Canada.

CHAPTER FOUR

Post-war Adjustments and the Resumption of European Immigration, 1919-1931

In June 1919 Canadian immigration policy was dramatically revised. Whereas before 1914 economic considerations had been paramount, now the principal criteria became political and cultural acceptability. Previously acceptable ethnic groups, most notably Germans, Ukrainians, Russians, and Finns were either barred from the country or had stringent entrance requirements placed on them. [1] The prevailing view of those who designed immigration policy was that sufficient numbers of Anglo-Saxon agriculturalists and industrial workers could now be secured either within the country or from the United States and Great Britain. This notion assumed a new role for the Dominion government in both land settlement and in the distribution of labour; the instruments of this new role were to be the Soldier Settlement Branch of the Department of Reconstruction and the Employment Service of Canada which fell under the Department of Labour.

The high hopes of an ethnically pure Canada were soon dashed. In the immediate postwar period the urbanization of native-born Canadians continued at an accelerated rate, and relatively few entered the country from the Anglo-Saxon homelands of Great Britain and the United States. Indeed, thousands of Canadian workers, both rural and urban, abandoned the country and its mounting economic problems for the United States. In time these developments strengthened the position of the old open door lobby of transportation, and resource-based industries. By 1925 spokesmen for these interests had managed to achieve the removal of all disabilities from Germany and its wartime allies. In September of that year the Dominion government entered into an agreement with the Canadian Pacific Railway and the newly formed Canadian National Railways which allowed these companies a free hand in the selection and distribution of Central European agricultural immigrants. In the next six years more than 369,905 continental European immigrants entered the country.[2]

The arrival of thousands of continental European workers between 1925 and 1930 had significant economic and social ramifications. Resource-based labour intensive industries were once more allowed access to cheap unskilled labour. The price of this free hand for business was partly paid by Canadian workers who were already facing the challenges of technological change and scientific management. But, as before 1914, the interests of the immigrant workers themselves were the first consideration to be swept aside in the name of Canadian economic progress. Immigrant workers drifted across the country in a desperate search for jobs. Many searched in vain, unable to accumulate enough money either to settle on the land or to return to Europe. These "New Canadians" also encountered a notable hostility on the part of some Anglo-Canadian trade unionists and farmers who joined forces with nativists organizations to lobby against the railway agreement. The ideological garb of this new agitation was racial: Canada's Anglo-Saxon character, it was claimed, was being destroyed. That the percentage of people of European origin in Western Canada had increased from approximately 29 per cent in 1921 to 35 per cent in 1931 only led credence to the exclusionist argument.[3] Since Yugoslavs, Czechoslovaks, and Hungarians had followed the earlier practice of Ukrainians and Russians in forming communities within communities, whether in town or country, the threat seemed visible enough.

Not surprisingly, the advent of the Great Depression intensified the existing fear of the foreigner, the more so since unemployed alien workers seemed to be the natural constituency of the Communist Party of Canada and other radical organizations. Between 1929 and 1931 the Dominion government once more reversed its immigration policy. In 1931 the Railway Agreement was cancelled, and only bona fide farmers with ample capital were allowed into the country. Simultaneously a programme was implemented to deport thousands of indigent immigrants back to their European homelands. This was accompanied by an expanded use of Section 41 of the Immigration Act, especially against those alien radicals associated with the Communist Party. By 1931 it was evident that Canada had not only closed its doors to the foreigner, but that the social and political rights of non-British immigrants were in jeopardy.

I

That Section 41 should have become so much to the fore in the
1930s reflected its central importance in the changes made in the
Immigration Act in 1919. Under the terms of this Section "any
person other than Canadian citizen [who] advocates ... the overthrow by force ... of constituted law and authority" could be deported from the country.[4] This sweeping provision reinforced
Section 38 of the Act which gave the governor general in council
authority "to prohibit or limit ... for a stated period or permanently the landing ... of immigrants belonging to any nationality
or race deemed unsuitable." It was this section which had been
invoked consistently to exclude either U.S. or West Indian Blacks
from the country.[5] In 1919 Section 38 was also used to exclude
various European immigrants. By Order-in-Council PC 1203,
Germans, Austrians, Hungarians, Bulgarians, and Turks were
excluded because of their wartime associations; by Order-in-
Council PC 1204 Doukhobors, Mennonites, and Hutterites were
excluded because of "their peculiar customs, habits, modes of
living and methods of holding property."[6]

These measures reflected prevailing Anglo-Canadian opinions.
Pejorative terms such as "Bohunks," "Huns," and "Dagos"
abounded in the popular writing of the time. One very successful
work, *Breaking Prairie Sod*, by the Reverend Wellington Bridgman, even went so far as to charge that all Germans and Austrians
were capable of "unnameable treachery and crime." Bridgman
also attributed the industrial unrest of 1919 to the foreign workers,
and predicted that Canada would never achieve industrial stability
until they were swept from the country.[7] Nor was this an isolated
outburst. In the fall of 1919 *Maclean's Magazine* ran a series of
articles exposing the evil associations of alien radicals, especially
those of Finnish, Ukrainian, and Russian background.[8] The same
spirit prevailed in the Department of Immigration and Colonization. F.C. Blair, the departmental secretary, wrote that immigration from Finland was being discouraged because "a number of
Finnish people seem to be very busy spreading IWW propaganda
and occasionally one is found doing something worse." Ukrainians and Russians, especially those who lived in Soviet-controlled
territory, were seen in a similar light.[9] Even Italians were now suspect, not only for an alleged propensity for crime, but also because
the Bolshevik menace had spread to their homeland. In September
1920 F.C. Blair informed the president of the Algoma Steel Corporation that "hundreds of industries have been seized in Italy by
workers and there is a good deal of unrest in that country at the
present time." In future, he warned, Italian immigrants would "be

carefully examined regarding their attitude towards organized government."[10]

Yet the flow to Canada from Central and Southern Europe was not stopped completely. During the war the European inspection offices of the Immigration Branch had been closed. Hence the Dominion government lacked even information about the departure of immigrant workers. Undesirable immigrants could, of course, be rejected at Canadian ports of entry; but in this regard the Dominion government proved highly susceptible to the pressure tactics of both big business and ethnic organizations.[11] In October 1919, for example, despite the opposition of Immigration officials, the Shepard & Morse Company of Ottawa was able to secure the services of Finnish immigrant workers by arguing that they could not obtain the workers they needed in Canada.[12] Mining companies were even more aggressive in their search for cheap and malleable labour. In September 1919, the Dominion Coal Company requested the admission of large numbers of continental European miners into Cape Breton. These men were needed not only because of labour shortages of cheap unskilled labour, but because many of them came from allied counties and had lived in the region during the war. The company got its way despite the protests of the miners' union and local immigration officials.[13]

Similar pressure tactics were employed by mining companies in northern Ontario, both through direct lobbying in Ottawa and Toronto, and in the pages of the *Canadian Mining Journal*. In February 1920 the *Journal* claimed that unless the immigration doors were opened wider the mining and metallurgical industries of northern Ontario would be seriously disrupted.[14] Significantly, this grim prediction was supported by published reports of the Ontario Department of Labour indicating that one-third of the mines of northeastern Ontario were operating below peak capacity both because of the shortage of unskilled labour and their high turn-over rate. According to the deputy minister of labour, the province's solution to this problem was "to get a steady class ... of foreigners," especially Italians. These, he described, as ideal mine-workers, because of their great physical strength and deep commitment to occupational mobility within the industry. They are quite capable, he wrote, of "advancing themselves from jobs as muckers to the high positions of machine runners, joistmen, cage tenders etc." In October 1920 this same official recommended that 2,000 European miners should be brought into northern Ontario.[15]

The railway companies were equally insistent. In the spring of

1920 the Railway Association of Canada petitioned the Dominion government for the immediate admission of 20,000 Italian navvies: "Canadian Railways are rapidly approaching a very serious situation ... of obtaining an adequate supply of track labour to carry out the heavy maintenance and improvement work. ... The difficulty arises out of the steady exodus to Europe of those classes of foreign-born persons upon whom the railways have long been dependent for track work ... and the aversion of the native-born and other Canadians toward this class of work."[16] Another industry petition suggested that the Russians, Czechs, and Poles, who had served with the "White Armies" in Vladivostok, and were now retreating homeward across Canada, also be drawn into the railroad construction labour market.[17]

The immediate response of the Dominion government to these proposals was quite favourable; but the strenuous opposition from organized labour and Great War Veterans and other patriotic organizations soon forced a change of heart.[18] In November 1920 the *Labour Gazette* reported that 10.2 per cent of organized workers in Canada were unemployed; by April 1921 this percentage had increased to 16.3 per cent.[19] This was clearly a time for caution in immigration policy, and the strict application of existing regulations. In January 1921 an Order-in-Council was passed which required even a British immigrant arriving in Canada to have at least two hundred and fifty dollars in his possession.[20] Two years later, faced with an even more severe domestic economic situation, the Dominion government, through Order-in-Council PC 183, established firm occupational guidelines to restrict further the entry of European immigrants. Only the following would be admitted into the country.[21]

(1) A bona fide agriculturalist ... [with] sufficient means ...
(2) A bona fide farm labourer entering Canada to follow that occupation and has reasonable assurance of employment.
(3) A United States citizen entering Canada from the United States provided it is shown to the satisfaction of Immigration Officer in Charge, that his labour is required in Canada.
(6) Any British subject entering Canada directly or indirectly from Great Britain, or Ireland, Newfoundland, the United States of America, New Zealand, Australia or the Union of South Africa who shall satisfy the Immigration Officer in Charge at the port of entry that he has sufficient means to maintain himself until employment is secured.

Asiatics were specifically excluded from the provisions of this arrangement, and in the same year a Chinese Immigration Act was passed which virtually stopped all immigration from that source.[22]

The entry of the Dominion government into programmes of direct unemployment relief both through the Employment Service of Canada, established in 1918, and other means gave Dominion officials a greater awareness of the economic repercussions of large-scale immigration than they had before 1914. Between 1920 and 1929 the Dominion government assumed the burden of one-third of a municipality's costs for the relief of the unemployed. This was, however, said to be a temporary measure and the theory of the system remained that unemployment was "fundamentally a municipal responsibility."[23] That a high percentage of the unemployed were immigrants placed the Dominion government in an awkward position in the matter. Traditionally the welfare of immigrants had been its responsibility and this matter could not now be disentangled from these questions. During the 1920s the Dominion government continued to place immigrant agriculturalists on Canadian farms and to house them in the twelve immigration halls located in Western Canada.[24]

The Dominion government was also deeply involved, through the Employment Service of Canada, in the problems of economic adaptability being faced by immigrant workers. In the prewar years some Immigration officials tried to protect European workers from unscrupulous employment agents and employers, a paternalism exemplified by the passage of Order-in-Council PC 1028 in May, 1913. This Order-in-Council had required all employment agencies dealing with immigrant workers to obtain a licence from the superintendent of immigration. Such agencies also had to keep an accurate record of the workers registered with them, and could not charge a labour placement fee of more than one dollar. A further requirement forbade the dispatching of workers until there was written proof that the jobs to which they were being sent actually existed. Violations of these guidelines could result in the loss of an agency's licence and fines for its owners.[25] During the war the Dominion government had gone farther in asserting its control over the recruitment and placement of immigrant workers, most notably with the National Registration Act of 1916 and the so-called "Anti-Loafing Law" of 1918 which required all adult males residing in Canada to be gainfully employed.[26] Another Order-in-Council, issued in 1918, provided for the establishment of public employment offices on a Dominion-provincial basis. According to T.W. Crothers, the minister of labour, it was in the national interest that the existing labour exchanges of Quebec, Ontario, Manitoba, Saskatchewan, and British Columbia "be linked up with a clearing house in Ottawa," and that the Dominion government "should contribute to the expense of establishing and maintaining them." Under the new legislation funds were provided on a graduated scale: $50,000 in 1918-19; $100,000 in 1919-20; and $150,000 in each succeeding year to the end of the decade. Between 1924 and 1930 the Employment Service of Canada provided jobs for over 1,879,791 male workers.[27]

Incidentally, this new government initiative in the labour market provided for a more systematic and equitable method of placing immigrant workers. It did not, however, remove many of the major problems of the prewar years, especially the seasonal nature of employment available to unskilled workers. During the 1920s about 25 per cent of those workers placed by the Employment Service held their jobs for less than one week. Nor did the advent of national employment planning mark the downfall of the private employment agency, although initially many of the smaller agencies were forced out of business by the new government regulations and the competition offered by the public system.[28]

The immediate post-war years did not favour the old free enterprise immigrant labour traffic. Between 1919 and 1925 Canadian immigration policy discouraged the entry of both European workers and agriculturalists. The purpose of the Dominion government now was to re-establish the Anglo-Saxon character of the country. What this meant in immigration terms was selective recruitment in Great Britain and in the United States. British immigrants it was felt could be attracted in large numbers: Canada offered them superior economic opportunities and an attractive geographical and social milieu.[29] In the event this expectation was not realized; indeed, during the 1920s British immigration only amounted to about 50,000 a year or about 45 per cent of prewar levels.

The pessimistic viewpoint towards British immigration in the interwar years was perhaps most forcefully stated by former Minister of Immigration Clifford Sifton in a letter to John W. Dafoe in November 1920:

> The farmer class in England will not emigrate; they are doing too well. ... There is left only the Agricultural labourer; they [sic] are a diminishing quantity. Their wages have lately doubled and they are going to stay up. They will not emigrate.

There remains only the mechanic, the artisan, and the drifter in the Southern towns. These are the people that Frank Oliver got in by the thousand and which flooded Canada and would have precipitated a crisis in labour if it had not been for the war. The worst blunder on earth would be to encourage their immigration. They are hopelessly incapable of going on farms and succeeding. Pretty nearly all the Great War Veterans Associations that are making trouble are composed of these fellows who enlisted in the Canadian Army when the war came and want the country to support them for the rest of their lives.[30]

Because of the difficulty of placing British immigrants in agricultural regions the Imperial and Dominion governments agreed in the Empire Settlement Act of 1922 to co-operate in a variety of colonization programmes. By 1931 about 127,654 had come to Canada under these schemes; most of these received reduced transportation fares, agricultural training, and placement on Canadian farms. The effect of this imperial legislation on the transportation fare was particularly dramatic; the Liverpool to Winnipeg fare was reduced from $120 to $30. Yet cheap transportation was not sufficient to guarantee that those who left Great Britain would become Canadian farmers and farm labourers. In the 1931 Census it was observed that immigrants from the British Possessions showed the least inclination to go into agriculture ... [and] less than 10 p.c. were found to be farmers." In the 1920s British immigrants also shied away from railway construction, mining, lumbering, and unskilled labour in the cities; in Montreal, for example, the percentage of British workers in the construction industry fell from 20 per cent in 1920 to 12 per cent in 1931.[31]

The situation was worsened by the population movement to the United States. The flow of people across the Canadian-American border in the 1920s was affected by changes in American Immigration legislation in 1921 and 1924. These changes, which drastically reduced the numbers of immigrants who could enter the United States from continental Europe while placing no quotas on immigration from North American countries, ensured that the north-south movement of people would be much greater.[32] This exodus of Canadian agricultural and industrial workers alarmed Canadian employers and patriotic organizations. Sir Joseph Flavelle, a prominent Anglo-Canadian businessman, correctly analyzed the situation in a letter to an English banker in December 1924: "Until the United States adopted the policy of strict limitation of immigration of all except native born Canadians, we always welcomed the promise of great activity in the United States because it was followed some months later by somewhat similar conditions in Canada. During the last two or three years, however, ... with increasing activity, and sectional or general shortages of labour, important numbers of Canadians are attracted to the United States. The trouble is, our loss is chiefly in men between twenty-five and thirty years of age." *Industrial Canada*, the organ of the Canadian Manufacturer's Association went one step further, blaming the loss of Canadian workers on the failure of the King government to support Canadian industry either through tariff protection or an active immigration policy.[33]

The failure of the Dominion government's Anglo-Saxon immigration strategy to satisfy the labour requirements of the country produced renewed agitation from Canadian farmers and businessmen to open the immigration door wider. Farmers and businessmen were not, however, united on the question of the long-term effect of immigration from Continental Europe. The United Farmers of Manitoba and the United Farmers of Alberta, both Anglo-Saxon to the core, enthusiastically endorsed the efforts of the Western Canada Colonization Association to attract American farmers despite the WCCA's being "composed chiefly of large corporations and wealthy individuals."[34] The *Grain Growers' Guide*, the official voice of the UFM, continually called upon the Dominion government to expand the British harvester scheme of 1923 into an annual event.[35] Neither of these plans was, however, able to supply a steady source of Anglo-Saxon farm labour. The British hired hand was in great demand, but despite every exhortation Central Europeans continued to form the bulk of the farm labourers in Western Canada, cultural antipathies not withstanding.[36]

If some farmers were still troubled by the social and cultural implications of such a policy, few spokesmen for the transportation companies and the labour-intensive industries shared their concern. On the business front the tone was set in 1922 when Clifford Sifton made his famous speech to the Canadian Club in Toronto in which he claimed that Western Canada needed another 500,000 "stalwart peasants." These people, he argued, should be immediately brought from "Central Europe, particularly Hungary and Galicia." Sifton's opinions were strongly endorsed by Sir Thomas Shaughnessy, chairman of the CPR

Board of Directors; in his view continental Europe could supply Canada with "thousands of rugged, splendid people."[37] If anything, the mining companies were even more confident than Shaughnessy of this result. In the words of the *Canadian Mining Journal*: "We want to see the doors opened not only to farmers and farm labourers, but also to such an extent in other directions as will enable our manufacturers and businessmen to secure the skilled workers and other help they require in their industries. At present they cannot get these. Nor will they early be able to do so, if the Labour unions in this country can work their sweet will. We have a shrewd idea that it is the fear of these Labour unions that has been responsible for the lethargy and the laxity that the Government has so long displayed in this matter of immigration."[38]

Although the "immigration boosters" did not immediately gain their objective, they did force the King government to remove gradually most of the barriers against large-scale European immigration. In 1923 PC 1203, which restricted the entry of immigrants from Germany and its wartime allies, was repealed. More significant still were the modifications of PC 183; the regulations under this order were now interpreted to allow the entry of more immigrants from continental Europe. In 1924 the Dominion government entered into a number of agreements with the railway companies to facilitate the recruitment of immigrants from the source. A joint farm-labour scheme brought 6,727 farm labourers to Canada "under the auspices of the Canadian National Railways and Canadian Pacific Railway Company." Various ethnic organizations within Canada were also used as recruitment agencies, most notably the Lutheran Immigration Board, the Canadian Mennonite Board and the Association of German Catholics and the St. Raphael Ukrainian Society. This was considerable change, but the appetite of the transportation companies remained unsatisfied.[39]

In February 1925 Edward Beatty and Sir Henry Thornton sent Prime Minister Mackenzie King a joint letter urging the Dominion government to assist their companies in developing the millions of acres of unused land in Canada. This development, they asserted, required large-scale recruitment of continental European farmers and farm labourers, and they volunteered their services in a new colonization undertaking. Specifically, the companies proposed that the overseas officials of the Colonization Departments of the CPR and CNR be granted the authority to issue certificates showing that prospective immigrants met the occupational and guaranteed employment requirements of PC 183. The government's own immigration officers would henceforth restrict their activity to the issuance of medical certificates and visas.[40]

The initial response of the Dominion government to this bold initative was negative, largely because the officials of the Department of Immigration and Colonization resented the prospect of losing some of their administrative prerogatives. The railway presidents, Beatty especially, were not easily deterred. In August 1925 the latter warned King that unless the Liberal government made "a vigorous declaration" in favour of expanded immigration the two major railway companies would be forced to dismantle their colonization departments, a development which "would be disastrous to Canada." Implicit in his message was the warning that with an election campaign in progress the Liberal Party could not afford to alienate the transportation giants and thei corporate allies.[41] Mackenzie King's reply of August 7 was most conciliatory: "I agree entirely with both views ... With respect to immigration, I have in mind making a vigorous declaration on the first occasion I speak in public and shall indeed be pleased if it serves to further the efforts of agencies at present involved in colonization and help to remove some of the obstacles you are meeting at present."[42]

On September 5, 1925, the Dominion government and the two transcontinental railway companies signed an agreement giving the CPR and CNR control over the recruitment of "bona fide" European agriculturalists until September 1928, at which time the agreement could be renewed. Under this arrangement the representatives of the transportation companies could now issue occupational certificates to immigrants from those countries which had previously been designated "non-preferred" by the Department of Immigration and Colonization. As a result of these changes prospective immigrants from Estonia, Latvia, Lithuania, Russia, Poland, Czechoslovakia, Yugoslavia, Austria, Hungary, Romania, and Germany were now on the same footing as those in Western Europe.[43]

The railway companies had made an important gain, but the Immigration Branch, fighting a rearguard action, was still able to impose certain restrictions on them. The companies were instructed to recruit only from those nationalities, races and modes of life ... "readily assimilable into the population and citizenship of Canada." Another memorandum was even more blunt. "From Russia, Mennonites and German Russians and from Romania, the German and Hungarian types are the only ones desired." Immigrants recruited by the companies could also be deported if they did not secure farm employment or settle on the land within one year of their arrival. In such cases the cost associated with their deportation would be assumed by the railway companies.[44]

Public reaction to the Railway Agreement varied. On the one hand there was substantial support for it for it from pro-business newspapers, boards of trade, and leading industrialists. In Western Canada newspapers such as the Edmonton *Journal* and the Calgary *Herald* applauded the new immigration policy.[45] On the other hand many Canadians regarded the agreement as a sell-out to the transportation interests and predicted dire consequences for their country. Organized labour was especially critical of the agreement. Throughout the early 1920s Tom Moore, the president of the Trades and Labor Congress, had warned that any attempt to recruit large numbers of agriculturalists from Central Europe would be in effect a conspiracy "to rush in a heterogeneous conglomeration of people to furnish cheap labour for the farms, coal mines, railway construction and other industrial activities."[46]

Labour's opposition found many echoes in cultural and religious institutions. The newly formed United Church of Canada publicly criticized "the handing over of the promotion of immigrations from the British Isles and European countries to the transportation companies." Nor did all agrarian organizations welcome the change. The *Grain Growers' Guide* criticized the extent of power given to the railway companies, and claimed that a massive influx of Central European peasant farmers would not improve agricultural productivity in Western Canada. Such immigrants, it asserted, could only adapt to agriculture of "a crude nature, and on a small scale."[47] Most critical of all were the reactions of immigration officials such as Deputy Minister W.J. Egan who saw the agreement as a "pernicious attempt to destroy the selective immigration policy, and to return to the chaotic labour market which existed in the pre-war years."[48] The next five years were to provide ample evidence to support this gloomy analysis.

III

Between 1925 and 1930 about 185,000 Central European immigrants entered the country under the terms of the Railway Agreement. In most respects the CPR and CNR adopted similar tactics in their immigration work. Prospective immigrants were initially approached by representatives of the railway companies, normally steamship agents who were paid five dollars for each bona fide agriculturalist. The prospective immigrants then proceeded to the major European ports, primarily Danzig, Riga, and Hamburg, where they were screened by officials of the railway companies who had the responsibility of issuing occupational certificates. They were then checked by Canadian immigration officials to ensure that they were medically sound and their passports were in order. They were transported to a Canadian port on either CPR steamships or on vessels of steamship companies associated with the CNR.[49] They then travelled by rail to the major transportation centres of Western Canada to be met by representatives of the railway colonization departments, and, if possible, placed on the land. Some found their way into the employment of Western farmers who had previously requested agricultural workers; in these requests, or nomination certificates, the farmer described the location of his farm, the wage he proposed to pay, and the type of accomodation he could provide. The farmer could also specify preference for farm workers of a specific ethnic or national background.[50] Religious, ethnic, and local organizations often acted as intermediaries between farmers, employers, transportation companies and European workers. The CPR worked closely with organizations such as the Lutheran Colonization Board, the Hungarian Slovak Colonization Board, and the Ukrainian Colonization Board, while the CNR, for its part, established close working relations with the Lutheran Immigration Board and the German Catholic Immigration Board.[51]

Perhaps the most extensive fusion of transportation, agricultural, and ethnic interests developed in the sugar beet region of southern Alberta. In order to secure the necessary immigrant labour the CPR, sugar beet growers, boards of trade, and the Hungarian Colonization Board established the Colonist Placement Service Association (CPSA). This was a multipurpose organization, but it was above all else an extension of the CPR's Colonization Department. Significantly, it was the CPR which co-ordinated the recruitment and selection of immigrant workers, and which provided financial support for the Hungarian Colonization Board.[52] The CPR also made use of this board to secure unskilled workers for its own section gangs, as the following extract from an 1927 report of the Dominion Land Settlement Branch reveals:

Those arriving under the Canadian Pacific are met on Train No. 1 arriving at four o'clock in the morning by a Mr. Schwartz, Manager of the Calgary Hungarian Colonization Board. They are directed by him to rooming houses and they are invited to register with him for ultimate naturalization. These people "mill" around Mr. Schwartz' office and the streets until they are placed. ...

Mr. O. Hanson, who keeps the Canadian Pacific Employment Office one block away, whenever he requires men for Extra Gangs, telephones over to Mr. Schwartz who sends him the number of men required.

The report also indicated that Schwartz gave preferential treatment to Hungarians, Poles, and Slovaks in distributing CPR jobs; in return for such favours the men were required to pay a labour placement fee, and to buy their provisions through Schwartz's store at greatly inflated prices.[53]

The CPR had a particular interest in this type of recruitment because it wanted to avoid having to return its clients to Europe since the return passage would be paid by the company. In May 1927 the Land Settlement Branch indicated that 75 per cent of the continental European immigrants who had arrived in Calgary under the terms of the railway agreement had obtained jobs with the company. Another report of the branch pointed out that companies which did business with the CPR were expected "to give new immigrants the first chance of jobs"; this was especially true for immigrants who had "come in on CPR ships."[54] The CPR's anxiety not to give the impression of exacerbating the country's unemployment situation by flooding the country with immigrant workers created severe problems within the immigrant community itself.[55] Thus when the CPR dumped large numbers of new immigrants in the lumber camps of northern Saskatchewan it not only depressed local wages but also displaced an earlier wave of immigrant workers who were attempting to open up the land of the region: "these settlers rely solely on bush work during the winter to enable them to carry on for the first few years of settlement. If this work is not available for them, lack of capital will force the relinquishing of their holdings and mean that they must seek other work on which they can support their families."[56] The CPR's immigration strategy also meant that there was an ample supply of poor foreign workers in the country who could be used as strike-breakers. In 1926, for example, large numbers of recent Hungarian immigrants were said to have taken the place of striking miners in the Nordegg Mines in Alberta.[57]

The influx of immigrant workers seems to have made the employment situation in the Rocky Mountain Coal Mining region particularly volatile. In March 1927 the Alberta Department of Labour reported on the depressed condition of the numerous coal towns in the region as follows:

> Recently a number of immigrants from Europe, just arrived have come to The Pass Camps seeking employment. The argument is that if the natural production of The Pass Coal Camps was mined by the men who are making their homes in The Pass, and not by temporary or non-resident men, then there would be ample employment and reasonably good conditions in The Pass Towns, instead of frequent periods of slack work in the Mines, with consequent hard times and requests for relief from the Government.[58]

Canada's employers also had access to cheap immigrant labour outside the terms of the Railway Agreement. In 1926 an amendment to PC 183 provided for the admission under permit of any immigrant "whose labour or service was required in Canada." In the period 1926 and 1929 thousands of immigrant workers entered the country by this means.[59] General Hervey, an influential Ontario railway contractor made 300 requests for the necessary permits, many of which were endorsed by representatives of the CNR and CPR. In June 1926 W.J. Black wrote as follows to the Immigration Branch on behalf of both General Hervey and the Morrow & Beatty railway construction company:

> The applications are apparently not in any way identified with the project of any steamship line or other agency to secure immigration for the benefits which accrue in transportation.
>
> With these two contractors we have the opportunity of placing a total of 500 workers to be made up of Poles, Czechs, Slovakians, Yugo Slavs and Ukrainians. We have assurances that the conditions of employment are satisfactory and are, therefore, prepared to give to you our assurances that the number mentioned will be placed by use with these contractors under conditions such as usually prevail in the business of railway building.[60]

As was so often the case, however, the reality of the employment situation was so much different. The immigrant workers who were permitted into the country as a result of this appeal were charged excessively for their transportation, paid well below the advertised wage level and given only eight days' work. Destitute and unemployed they soon became dependent on municipal charity.[61] Imigration officials such as F.C. Blair were shocked by such blatant disregard for the immigration standards the government was trying to maintain: "The Permit business still flourishes. If there is any present day desire close to my heart, it is the desire to wipe out this cursed business at one strike. ... With unemployment ... it seems a terrible thing to have to issue Permits day after day for the admission of Italians, Greeks, Jews and others of the less desirable classes of immigrants, and merely because some Member of Parliament or other influential gentleman demands that it be done."[62]

Dissatisfaction with the permit system and railway agreement intensified during the spring of 1927. Immigrant workers, it was argued, were not only displacing established labourers in resource industries, but also in the manufacturing sector. In Oshawa it was reported that some companies had dismissed half of their labour force in order to secure cheap immigrant replacements. In Winnipeg some immigrant workers were so destitute that they were even working below "the minimum wage for women" in the garment industry.[63]

Such accusations strengthened the hand of the Immigration Branch vis-à-vis the transportation companies. In June 1927 F.C. Blair told his deputy minister that public opinion was once again insistent on a more selective immigration policy and that instead of fighting with our backs to the wall "the moment had now come to carry" the war into the other camp." Blair even suggested that the Immigration Branch launch a campaign to have the railway agreement terminated: "There will be a terrific outcry from the Railway Companies if the thing is cancelled. On the other hand there is bound to be a worse situation created by public opinion in Canada if the present conditions are allowed to continue." Ultimately, however, a prosperous economy permitted the transportation companies at least for the moment, to weather this particular storm; in September 1928 the Railway Agreement was renewed for another two years.[64]

In the spring of 1926 the CPR, CNR, and the Canadian Bankers' Association had launched their own campaign "to endeavour to overcome the opposition of farmers and farmers organizations to an active and aggressive immigration policy." The purpose of such publicity was "to influence Western Dailies by various means to refrain from featuring unemployment stories, local crop inquiries etc. which find their way into the European press and neutralize propaganda overseas." Another approach was "to interest Western provincial governments through pressure of public opinion in constructive co-operation regarding colonization." Local boards of trade could help matters by fostering "a more tolerant attitude towards supporting unemployed immigrants," and pushing the view that "unemployment was a more or less temporary by-product of active immigration efforts."[65]

The central figure in this publicity campaign was C.W. Peterson, editor of the Calgary-based *Farm and Ranch Review*. Peterson distributed the news releases, arranged speaking tours for the immigration booster lobby. By December 1926 he had distributed articles to 216 dailies with a circulation of 1,112,234, and to 126 weeklies with a circulation of 848,489. The funds for this activity were provided by the transportation companies and the Bankers' Association through a discrete account with the Royal Trust in Calgary. In this regard Colonel Dennis of the CPR issued instructions that the funds were to be handled in such a manner that it could never be claimed that "payments are being made by either of the railway companies or the Bankers' Association directly to Peterson."[66]

One of the most spectacular initiatives by the immigration boosters occurred during the summer of 1928 when the transportation companies, agrarian organizations, and Imperial Settlement officials proposed that some 10,000 unemployed British coal miners be transported to the harvest fields of Western Canada. This scheme went ahead despite the strenuous opposition of immigration officials such as F.C. Blair who argued that "it was folly" to bring in a lot of green Britishers with the hope of getting five or six weeks of harvest work." The opposition of the civil servants was once more overcome. Between August and September 1928 about 8,499 British harvest-miners came to Canada. Half the transportation costs of these workers was paid by the Overseas Settlement Branch, while the Canadian Land Settlement and Employment Service committed themselves to finding them jobs with farmers in Western Canada.[67] Not surprisingly, the scheme was hailed as a great imperial undertaking, and patriotic organizations like the Orange Lodge calld upon their members to assist these harvesters in every possible way. The United Farmers of Manitoba also endorsed the scheme while the *Grain Growers' Guide* enthusiastically declared that these harvest excursions from Great Britain would soon become "an annual event with ever increasing success."[68]

There was, however, evidence which indicated that the harvest excursions had not been such an unqualified success. The Trades and Labor Congress claimed that the economy of the country could not "absorb these workers after the harvest had been garnered," and that the manpower needs of prairie farmers could be met from within the country.[69] There were also reports that the British harvesters had faced numerous problems in adjusting to the living and working conditions in rural regions of Western Canada. Increased use of combines and threshers had substantially reduced the demand for harvesters; but even in areas where more traditional methods were employed these British harvesters were said to have suffered from a lack of suitable work experience.[70] Finally, it was charged, that British workers had been discriminated against in areas dominated by Central Europeans. As one disgruntled harvester put it: "we were engaged by a German farmer or a Polack but the minute one of their own people could be secured, we were fired and our jobs taken by those who could speak the language of this bunch." The *Toronto Telegram* went one step further and claimed that there was a conspiracy against the British harvester scheme in order "to make it that much easier for the European hordes to fill jobs and desirable farms in Saskatchewan." The fact that about 75 per cent of the harvesters returned to England tended to give credence to these charges.[71]

These observations were indicative of a growing anti-alien sentiment which had developed among many Anglo-Canadians, especially in Western Canada. In 1928 various patriotic and religious organizations launched a new assault against the Railway Agreement; in the forefront of this campaign was George Lloyd, the Anglican bishop of Saskatoon. One of Lloyd's persistent charges was echoed by organized labour: it was that the existing immigration policy created "a great deal of unemployment among our British friends due to the low wages the foreigner will work for."[72] The same view was dressed up in scholarly clothes by Professor A.R.M. Lower of Wesley College, in a series of articles. Applying Sir Thomas Gresham's monetary theory to Canadian Immigration policy, Lower came to this conclusion:

"cheap men" will always drive out "dear" men. The men with the higher standard of living cannot compete with the man with the lower. Broadly speaking, all immigrants are "cheap" men in this sense, for it is noticeable that a man arriving in the country should take what he can get in the way of a job. ...

The gradual displacement of the English speaking farmers from the small farms and soils by Central Europeans who demand less from life is an illustration of the principle of the "cheap" and "dear" man.

In the sphere of labour ... the immigrant's handicap is the employer's advantage, for the employer gets a man who must at all costs hold his job. Wholesale immigration productive as it is simply turns us into a training ground for American citizens. The time has come for us to sit down and think over the terms of our national future. What more likely to determine that future than the policy which will decide who should be our citizens?[73]

Canadian citizenship was also much to the fore with the nativist organizations. The National Association of Canada (NAC) charged that thousands of Canadian workers had been forced "to seek employment under the Stars and Stripes while the CPR & CNR Railways flooded the country with the riff-raff of Europe." The Native Sons of Canada called for a stop to any immigration which tended "to make Canadians a mixed or coloured race or lower the standards of living, education or morals."[74] In a class by themselves were the statements of the Ku Klux Klan of Kanada. Between 1927 and 1929 a number of Klan locals were organized in Canada. The Klan had its greatest success in Saskatchewan where it was estimated that it had a membership of 10,000. According to one study of this phenomena "joining the Klan gave hundreds a vent for ingrained prejudice in the semblance of safeguarding all that was admirable in British institutions, Protestantism and the Canadian Way of Life."[75] J.H. Maloney, one of the most successful Canadian Klan organizers, offered this account of his views on Central European immigrants:

I am loyal to Canada and the British Crown – a Canada composed of those strong virile men of the north, the Nordic or Anglo-Saxon race ... men whose forefathers fought for this country by expenditure of British blood and treasure, whose sons died on Flanders field. ... but I am not loyal to a Canada composed of men who jabber all the tongues that destroyed the tower of Babel, men who tighten their bellyband for breakfast, eat spaghetti and hot dog and rye bread for lunch and suck in his [sic] limburger cheese for supper – men who crowd our own people out as the example at Yorkton by offering to work for ten cents an hour, men who come to Canada with tags on them telling you their destination. ... we are a great melting pot, but let us see what that the slag and scum that refuse to assimilate and become 100 percent Canadian citizens is skimmed off and thrown away.[76]

Charges of a Catholic conspiracy also found a receptive audience where the separate school issues were ever-virulent. The Klan did not hesitate to draw connections between the increasing militancy of Catholic separate schools in Saskatchewan and the massive influx of Central European Catholics; this movement was, in fact, part "of their world-wide Romanization campaign." The immigrant assault was also held responsible for rising crime rates and the growing power of the Bolshevik elements. The conviction of the Finnish Communist, Arvo Vaara, in December of 1928 for blasphemous references to the British monarchy was regarded as symptomatic of the type of "disloyalty and sedition" which was being fostered across the country.[77]

The nativist campaign against the Railway Agreement intensified during 1928. At the 1928 annual convention of the Trades and Labor Congress of Canada there was considerable discussion about the increasing encroachment "of non-English speaking immigrants ... a majority of whom seek employment in urban centres and industrial activities, which [was] in violation of the agreement." The problem was there for all to see; solving it was another matter. On one hand there were those at the convention who proposed that the congress bring pressure to bear on the Dominion government to adjust its policies so as to ensure "that not less than 75 per cent of immigrants coming into Canada shall be English speaking." Some of the restrictionists went even further and advocated the enactment of a measure by which immigrants who had not been naturalized after five years in the country would be deported. On the other hand, there were many delegates who did not wish to stand in the way of workers from other countries "bettering their lot in life." They tended to see quota systems and deportation procedures as reactionary. Ultimately the restrictionists were defeated at the convention, though they remained a strong grass roots minority.[78]

The 1928 convention also went on record against the recommendations of the chiefs of police of Canada that all European immigrants be finger-printed on entering the country. Moreover, the convention reaffirmed labour's belief that those who induced immigration into the country should be responsible for their welfare. Two resolutions were passed in this regard: one recommended that "any company, society or individual bringing settlers to this country for gain shall be answerable for the maintenance of the immigrant or immigrants for a period of twelve months." The other demanded "that the Federal Government or the railways or shipping companies be made responsible for the support of all immigrants brought in by them for a term of not less than two years."[79]

In a similar vein the 1928 convention of the United Farmers of Alberta recommended that all future farm labourers admitted to the country have "a knowledge of the English language." William Brownlee, premier of Alberta, publicly criticized the Dominion immigration policy for being "overwhelming in favour of the middle European races."[80] In Ontario, Premier Ferguson indicated his displeasure over the railway agreement when he openly criticized the transportation companies for bringing out immigrants "without due regard to the Provinces."[81] In Ottawa, R.B. Bennett, the new leader of the Conservative Party, warned that continuing Central European immigration would seriously threaten the Anglo-Saxon character of the country: "we must still maintain that measure of British civilization which will enable us to assimilate these people to British institutions, rather than assimilate our civilization to theirs."[82] The chorus of complaint was completed by the representatives in Canada of a variety of European countries. They spoke disparagingly of a system which left immigration to private enterprise claiming that many of their nationals who had come to Canada under the Railway Agreement had experienced unnecessary hardship and exploitation.[83]

In the face of all this pressure the King government decided in the beginning of 1928 to have the subject of immigration policy examined by the Select Committee on Agriculture and Colonization. Between February 29 and May 22, 1928 some twenty-nine representatives of the transportation companies, patriotic organizations, churches, and other groups appeared before the committee. Not surprisingly there were sharp differences of opinion about the national implications of the Railway Agreement. Edward Beatty claimed that "the country had not erred in free immigration; ... we have been careful; we have made it as selective as possible and we have proceeded on the assumption ... that if we have more people ... the prosperity of Canada will be increased."[84] By contrast, Canon C.W. Vernon, general secretary of the Council for Social Services of the Church of England in Canada, referred to the alarming increase in the percentage of immigrants other than British stock; this group he claimed, had risen from 22 per cent in 1923 to 50 per cent in 1927. Vernon warned the committee that unless immediate steps were taken to reverse this trend Canada would find herself in the same dilemma as the United States: "In the neighboring Republic, where the preponderating proportion in immigration from central Europe has already become a most serious problem ... [there are] warnings that we should profit from their experience and not flood the country with immigrants who will produce the puzzling problems with which they are already confronted."[85] In the course of its work the committee also investigated the charges made by Alderman M.J. Coldwell of Regina that "a regular traffic was carried on at Ottawa of the sale of permits to admit men who were not ordinarily eligible for entry into Canada ... for a sum of $100. each." No charges were ever laid in this regard, but the evidence before the committee had a decided effect on its findings.[86]

On June 6, 1928 the committee submitted its final report to the House of Commons. It made two major recommendations: the first called for the modification of the Railway Agreement; the second for stricter control over the issuance of permits or letters of assurance of employment.[87] Anticipating this recommendation the Department of Immigration and Colonization had already curtailed the numbers of European workers entering the country. In January 1929 the transportation companies were informed that they would have to reduce by 30 per cent the numbers of immigrants they had recruited in 1928. In the case of the Prairie provinces the transportation companies were issued more specific guidelines.[88]

In October 1929 in a deteriorating employment situation, the railway quota was reduced another 25 per cent, and instructions were issued cancelling all visas in the hands of prospective European immigrants.[89] During the 1930 Dominion election campaign the Conservatives strongly attacked the Liberal immigration policy as being too lax. As prime minister, R.B. Bennett now had to make good on this criticism. In October 1930 the railway companies were informed that the Dominion government was cancelling its agreement with them. W.A. Gordon, the new minister of immigration and colonization offered this defence of government policy in a joint letter to Beatty and Thornton: "Analysis showed that of the total immigration of 221,561 people admitted to Canada in the sixteen months ending with July 31st of this year no less than 99,367 were males over eighteen years of age, and of this latter number 25,305 had entered in the first four months of the present fiscal year. It is clear, therefore, beyond peradventure that either substantial numbers of immigrants who have recently arrived in Canada are in the ranks of the unemployed, or conversely, they have displaced Canadians who are now unemployed."[90]

The closing of the immigration gates was well received across the country, especially in Saskatchewan and Alberta where the provincial governments had refused to accept Russian Mennonite refugees in November 1930. Not even the claim that these refugees stood to be banished to the prison camps in Siberia could move the Conservative government of J.T.M. Anderson.[91] The next year Alberta refused entry to the members of the Wolf Creek Hutterite Colony of South Dakota who had bought 4,908 acres of land in this southern part of the province at a cost of $302,450.[92]

It was a sign of the times that the Canadian Manufacturers' Association also removed itself from the immigration booster lobby. At the 1929 annual convention L.W. Simms, association president, questioned the necessity of importing unskilled workers in view "of the marvellous mechanical progress in automatic machinery and in serialization of processes." His successor, R.J. Hutchings of Winnipeg, called the next year for a complete halt to immigration from Central Europe: "Large numbers of unemployed and illiterate people are liabilities and not assets. Employment, at fair remuneration, should be the keynote of our immigration policy. It is not economic to import farmers to compete with those now on the land ... nor is it wise to congest cities with people unless industry is encouraged to expand and provide them with employment."[93] Hutchings might have added that in Winnipeg and other centres Anglo-Canadian businessmen were becoming increasingly disturbed by the threat that large numbers of unemployed Central European workers posed to social order.

IV

An association between European immigration and unemployment was now being made in many parts of the country. At the Western Unemployment Conferences held in Winnipeg in January 1930, the Dominion immigration authorities were censured not only for gutting the labour market, but also for allowing "the immigration societies to gather up all the available jobs for the people they brought in." A few days after the conference the Manitoba Legislature unanimously passed a resolution branding unemployment a national problem; it was "the flow of immigrants into Western Canada, many of whom had been admitted as agricultural labourers, and who have undertaken farm work for a short time only" that was the root of the problem.[94] In Ontario, Premier Ferguson went one step further announcing that his government did not intend to extend relief payments to unemployed immigrant workers. No attention, he informed one correspondent, had been paid "to our views to the matter."[95]

On March 1, 1930 the Dominion Cabinet was formally confronted with evidence that unemployment and immigration were linked by representatives from municipalities from Ontario, Manitoba, Saskatchewan, Alberta, and British Columbia. The representatives from Winnipeg and Vancouver, cities that bore the brunt of the relief of destitute immigrant workers, were to the fore in this confrontation. In the case of Winnipeg, relief costs had increased from $31,394 in 1927-28 to $1,683,836 in 1930-31.[96] In keeping with its general policy of parsimony towards the mounting economic crisis the King government steadfastly refused to admit that it had a long-term obligation towards the maintenance of immigrant workers. On the contrary, the minister of labour, Peter Heenan, tried to place the burden of responsibility on the private sector: "If businessmen," he told the municipal delegates, had to have "a surplus of men around, let them have a minimum wage or a retaining wage for their men when they don't need them. ... If they are obliged to do that they will arrange their business accordingly."[97]

The transportation companies were, in fact, already acting, but their motivation was not so much the welfare of the immigrant worker as the fear that they might have to pay for their return to Europe. During the winter of 1930-31 CNR offices in North Bay and Winnipeg had found jobs for immigrant workers with fifteen large lumber companies in northern Ontario; between October and December, 626 of these men had been placed, most of them Slavs and Finns. As the Depression advanced, however, the placement of these men became more and more difficult not only because of the scarcity of jobs, but because of their destitution. Robert England, the Western colonization manager of the CNR, gave this account of the situation to W.J. Black: "This year the wages being paid are rather lower compared to other years and no doubt this has had a great effect on the financial position of immigrants generally. At freeze-up time a lot of immigrants find it impossible to outfit themselves in winter clothing and have sufficient to carry on to winter work in Ontario."[98]

In the context of the Depression the efforts of the transportation companies and private employment agencies on behalf of immigrant workers only intensified anti-alien sentiments in Anglo-Canadian workers. In May 1931 the employment of foreigners on a reforestation project near North Bay drew an angry response from residents of the area. Canadian workers, it was alleged, had "to stand around and starve while foreigners get the first privilege."[99] The fact that large concerns like INCO and the CPR worked through private agencies rather than the Employment Service of Canada only exacerbated the situation.[100] Private employment agencies also favoured immigrant workers because they were more malleable and willing to pay "kickbacks." As a group of Russian workers recounted their experience in securing employment through the Sudbury Labour Agency of Manor & Carmichael: "We had talked to this man at the Employment Office and he said then that he would fix us up with a job later. When we went and knocked at his door, he told us to come in; we went in and sat down; we could not talk much English, so we did not speak much. He held out his hand and we both give him a ten dollar bill. ... We figured it was better to pay for a job than to be around a soup kitchen."[101]

With the municipal and provincial governments now lined up against them immigrant workers had no choice but to fall in line with the "padrone" system. In September 1934 the City of Winnipeg announced that it intended to discontinue relief payments to 500 families and 1,600 single men who had entered the country after January 1, 1929; the vast majority of these people were Central Europeans.[102] In Sarnia, Central European immigrants were not only denied financial assistance, but were fired from local public works in large numbers because of the hostility of the Anglo-Canadian community. The Sarnia *Observer* frequently ran editorials calling for the deportation of unemployed foreigners, especially those who were involved in radical immigrant organizations like the Ukrainian Workers' Council.[103]

W.B. Hurd's Census Monograph, *Racial Origins and Nativity of the Canadian People* (Ottawa, 1942) offers further insight into the desperate plight of Central and Eastern European immigrants in this period. Using data from the 1931 Census, Hurd shows that the annual level of unemployment of Central Europeans was far above the national average. Thus while in 1931 Ukrainians, Poles, and Russians were unemployed for 20.12, 19.68, and 17.16 weeks per year respectively, the average for those of British nativity was only 9.09 weeks and from "preferred" European countries like Norway and Sweden for only 13.80 weeks. His analysis also showed that amongst Central Europeans "the highest level of unemployment existed among those immigrants who had arrived during the boom years 1926-29." Again, whereas in 1921 51 per cent of the Central European population in Canada had been naturalized, the equivalent figure for 1931 was only 39 per cent. What was even more shocking was the apparent propensity of these unemployed and alien people to become involved in crime and civil unrest. Hurd's pessimistic conlusion was that these problems could not be solved by economic means alone because they were partly racial in nature: "every South, Eastern and Central European race ... exceeded the average by over 60 p.c. [which] tends to support the view that the propensity to crime is in some measure at least a product of racial background."[104]

What Hurd neglected to mention was that vagrancy was the most common crime for which Central Europeans were being charged. During the years 1929-32 thousands of immigrant workers rode the rails desperately seeking employment, and finding nothing but rejection and discrimination. A Polish immigrant's account of how arrest and deportation might be welcome typified their desperation: "I have travelled 1200 miles for work. I never knew I would come to this life. I wish I could get back. They can't even find work for there [sic] own Canadians I have spoke to Indians Poland French and they were down and out and good fellows. I cant [sic] go on like this. I will have to do something to get deported. Will you see what you can do now I think I will close now if you want to find out where I am put the police on me I cant put know address because I wont know where I shall be."[105]

By 1931 many immigrant workers believed that they would be better off in Europe, and the movement of people back across the Atlantic became a notable feature of Canadian life. It was also significant that several European countries, most notably Germany and Poland, considered schemes to repatriate their destitute nationals in Canada. A letter from the Berlin chief of police to a Canadian official caught the spirit of the times: "What are you doing to these young men. ... We sent you clean, vigorous young fellows, the cream of our manhood. They wished to start life in a new, virile country like Canada. Now, when that country cannot give them employment, they are being deported to us branded with the stigma of a conviction under your laws. We are happy to welcome them home, where they find it easier to subsist among their friends, but help them to come home with unblemished records."[106]

CHAPTER FIVE

Ethnic Radicalism and the "Red Scare" of 1931-1932

The collapse of the Winnipeg Strike, the defeat of the OBU in the coal fields of District 18 and the unsuccessful strikes in Northern Ontario and British Columbia in the fall of 1919 threw the radical labour movement in Canada on the defensive. Yet the Dominion government, which had been so much to the fore in containing the strikes of 1919, remained apprehensive. During the 1920s the radical foreign worker was still thought of by many in authority as threatening both the free enterprise system and the Anglo-Canadian way of life. In consequence, Dominion security authorities, working in close co-operation with their provincial counterparts, refined the methods by which the major radical organizations were kept under surveillance. Initially, most of the attention was devoted to the newly formed syndicalist OBU and the revived IWW. By the mid-1920s, however, the Communist Party of Canada (CPC) was seen as the greatest threat, both because of its avowed revolutionary purpose and its superior organizational structure.[1]

In its recruitment campaigns the CPC made a special effort to attract the support of ethnic workers. Given the history of immigrants in the country's radical organizations, and their important place in the extractive industries, this emphasis was not surprising. Slavs, Finns, and other Europeans were all present in the ranks of the OBU and the IWW, while the Anglo-Saxon membership of the CPC rarely exceeded 10 per cent. The large-scale immigration of the 1920s confirmed the ethnic bias of radical labour in Canada. The new immigrants faced the old facts of social and economic exploitation. Moreover, many of them had been forced to leave European homeland because of their involvement in left-wing activity.

116

In the competition among the three main radical organizations in the country the CPC was most successful in recruiting foreign workers.[2] There were several reasons for its success. Whereas the OBU and the IWW were determinedly North American, the CPC had a strong European orientation. It was also easier for foreign radicals to obtain leadership positions than in either the OBU or IWW; members of the Ukrainian Labour Farm Temple Association (ULFTA) and the Finnish organization of Canada (FOC) were especially prominent in the party offices. These ethnic organizations provided the party with both men and money. The party was also popular with immigrant workers because of its emphasis on industrial organization and its interest in the unemployed. Finally, the party's advocacy and at times use of violence strongly appealed to many European immigrant workers. Mass demonstrations and picket-line confrontations were in many instances closer to their European experience than were the subtleties of collective bargaining and parliamentary democracy.[3]

Immigrant workers found a haven in the CPC, and their energy and frustration quickly made it a force to be reckoned with in Canadian life. Yet the party's success among these workers was not without cost. The ethnic rivalries and tension which had bedevilled socialist and labour organizations in Canada in the past also disrupted the CPC.[4] The internal strains caused by ethnic loyalties were especially acute after 1925 when the Communist International (Comintern) called for the Bolshevization of all national Communist movements; in Canada this meant a reduction in the influence and independence of ULFTA and the FOC. Between 1928 and 1931 the CPC was seriously disrupted by the issue of Bolshevization, and a number of leading members of ULFTA and the FOC were either expelled from the party or were severely censured.[5]

The problems of the party in these years were magnified by the intensification of the campaign against it by Dominion and provincial authorities. This renewed effort to contain the forces of radicalism in the country culminated in August 1931 with the arrest of the major Communist leaders on charges of sedition, and the subsequent outlawing of the CPC. Simultaneously, many foreign-born Communists were deported from the country, some under Section 41 of the Immigration Act, others under the more convenient vagrancy charge. These drastic actions had widespread public support among Anglo-Canadians, demonstrating once again the free hand which governments enjoyed when they acted in defence of "the Canadian Way of Life."[6]

I

The security measures adopted by the Dominion government after the Red Scare of 1919 were specifically designed with the immigrant population in mind. Suspected agitators and radical organizations were kept under close surveillance. In connection with this the exchange of information with security officials in Britain and the United States was made more systematic. All three countries kept and circulated inventories of imigrants rejected for political reasons, of radicals deported and of known Bolsheviks.[7] The Immigration Branch, which before 1914 had been mainly concerned to let people in, was now primarily concerned with the problem of keeping undesirables out. During the 1920s its liaison with the RCMP and provincial police forces became central to its operation. More and more after 1919 applications for naturalization had to be approved by the RCMP; for those rejected the prospect of deportation was an ever-present reality.[8]

Within the country it was the membership of radical organizations, most notably the OBU, who were given the closest attention. Many security officials assumed that the OBU was a Canadian version of the IWW and that it was directly linked to Soviet Russia.[9] The attempts by the OBU in 1920 to establish branches in Ontario and Quebec evoked the greatest alarm. At the January semi-annual conference of the OBU, Joe Knight, one of the special organizers, told the delegates that the organization had to make headway among Eastern Canadian workers if it was "to conquer." Police reports indicate that most of the OBU success in the East was among unskilled urban and rural workers, and there was some fear that the organization might launch a major campaign to recruit French Canadian loggers into the Lumber Workers Industrial Union.[10]

By 1920, the LWIU with its 20,000 members was the "largest and fastest growing" part of the OBU; it was especially strong in British Columbia and in lumber communities of northern Ontario such as Port Arthur, Sudbury, and Sault Ste. Marie. But the LWIU did not live up to its early promise; indeed, by the end of the year 1920 the marks of its impending disintegration were already apparent. A bitter disagreement between the LWIU leadership and that of the OBU was one source of trouble. The OBU executive insisted that the LWIU be organized in geographical units, while the leaders of the latter union wished to maintain an industry-wide organization, and to relate to the OBU as an affiliate.[11] Some of the Anglo-Saxon leaders of the OBU, most notably R.B. Russell, Victor Midgley, Joe Knight, T.S. Cassidy and T.R. Roberts, also failed to acknowledge the strength of ethnic feeling among Finnish lumber workers who dominated the LWIU membership in Ontario. One example of this insensitivity was the requirement that meetings of the LWIU in Port Arthur be conducted in English, and then translated into Finnish, despite the homogeneous character of the local.[12]

The LWIU in British Columbia was not divided ethnically, but faced a bitter opponent in the British Columbia Loggers Association, which was bent on its destruction. During the years 1920-23 this association conducted a highly successful "open shop" campaign, importing workers from Eastern Canada through its central employment agency, and maintaining an elaborate blacklist. The members of the Association were bound not to employ "knowingly any member of the IWW, or any man known to have seditious, radical or disloyal leanings."[13]

In addition to its problems with lumberworkers, the OBU was severely challenged by the reappearance of the IWW. Abandoning its pre-1914 approach, the latter had as its determined policy not only "to go among the unorganized workers and organize them but to go into territories where the O.B.U. had already organized the workers and wean them over from the O.B.U.."[14] This campaign was directed in particular at Finnish loggers and miners, whose loyalty to the OBU was already in doubt and who had syndicalist traditions.

Simultaneously, the OBU was being weakened among its Ukrainian supporters, particularly in the coal fields of District 18, by the Communist Party of Canada (CPC). By 1922 it was apparent that many leaders of the ULFTA and the FOC, Matthew Popovich, John Navis, John Boychuk, A.T. Hill, Arvo Vaara, and John Ahlqvist among them, were firmly committed to the CPC, and out to destroy the OBU. This transition was indicative of the fact that the CPC had quickly established itself as the premier organization on the Canadian left drawing to its ranks both foreign-born and Anglo-Saxon labour activists.[15] Of the latter, Jack Kavanagh, Joe Knight, Hugh Bartholomew, William Bennett and A.S. Wells, all known OBU organizers, had been present at the founding of the CPC and the Worker's Party of Canada (WPC) in 1921. The logic of the situation was that the OBU associate itself with the CPC, but negotiations to this end proved unsuccessful, largely because R.B. Russell and other members of the OBU executive refused to countenance the dismantling of their organizations; nor would they submit to the discipline of the Comintern. But their resistance had little effect on the growth of Communist influence.[16]

II

Between its formation in July 1921 and its proscription in August 1931, the CPC passed through several stages of development. Initially it was a secret organization, highly apprehensive of repression by the state. By 1922, however, it had come out into the open, and was actively engaged in trade union activity, and was a supporter of the Canadian Labour Party. In 1924 the party began using the Communist label, and dramatically revised its organization. The most important part of the new structure was the Central Executive Committee (CEC); out of the CEC came a small group of permanent officials known as the Political Commission, or Politbureau. The Finnish Organization of Canada and the Ukrainian Labour Farm Temple Association were given special status within the party and their leaders included in the Politbureau.[17]

During the first decade of its existence the Finnish Organization of Canada provided over half of the CPC's membership. Many Finnish Canadians had fought on the Communist side in the Finnish Civil War of 1918, and had a heightened sense of class consciousness. For its part the Finnish Organization of Canada required all its members "automatically to take out a card in the [Communist] Party or be blacklisted or expelled." At the Toronto Convention of the Workers Party of Canada (WPC) in 1922 the Finnish Organization of Canada was recognized as the Finnish Federation of the WPC; in effect, without losing their independence branches throughout the country also became branches of the WPC. Above all, Finnish Communists retained their financial independence; party dues were collected by the Finnish Organization of Canada and then remitted to the Politbureau. On occasion, the Finns supplemented their dues, most notably in 1922 with a donation of $2,000 to launch the English-language Communist newspaper *The Worker*. The growth of the Finnish Organization of Canada in the 1920s far exceeded that of the CPC membership as a whole; by 1930 the organization had seventy-four branches and membership of over 6,000. It also published a weekly newspaper *Vapaus* ("Worker"), and maintained a variety of cultural and social programmes.[18]

If the FOC was stronger numerically than the ULFTA it lacked the latter's diversity. Though primarily a Ukrainian organization ULFTA also had support among Poles, Russians, and other Slavic groups. Founded in Winnipeg in 1918 after the Canadian government had declared the Ukrainian Social Democratic Party an "illegal Bolshevik Organization," ULFTA soon expanded to other parts of the Dominion. By 1929 it had about 185 branches with approximately 5,438 members, published the *Ukrainian Labour News*, and maintained a Workers' Benevolent Society.[19] In 1930 the executive of the ULFTA gave this account of its activities to the Politbureau:

> ULFTA gave Ukrainian workers and farmers in Canada the Marxist-Leninist teachings, class consciousness, proletarian art ... proletarian choirs and orchestras ... against religious and nationalist children schools it organised and established workers' children schools and took workers' children in the cities under its influence; against religious and nationalist institutions which prepare lawyers, doctors, and teachers for the Ukrainian blackguards, monarchists, Petrurities and fascists, ULFTA organized Higher Educational Courses for workers and farmers to arm them with the knowledge of Marxism and Leninist teachings for the struggle against the enemies of the working class.[20]

Quite clearly the ability of ULFTA to provide essential social services to the Ukrainian community was an important factor to its success. The educational and cultural activities it sponsored, particularly those which evoked the Old World experience, were very popular. That Matthew Popovich could sing traditional Ukrainian songs at party-sponsored concerts greatly enhanced his prestige as a party organizer. The organization's Benevolent Society and immigrant reception centres in Winnipeg, Toronto, Fort William, Saskatoon, and Edmonton confirmed its appeal to both recent and established immigrants.[21]

The ULFTA was led into the CPC by Matthew Popovich, John Navis, Daniel Loby, and John Boychuk. Since complete identification with the CPC in 1921 might have justified large-scale seizure of ULFTA property by Dominion security authorities, the organization favoured an affiliated status with the CPC rather than total absorption.[22] Nor were these fears of repression entirely misplaced. Between 1921 and 1923 both the Meighen and King governments received a number of petitions calling for the repression of the "seditious and treasonous utterances" of the - *Ukrainian Labour News*. In one of these the president of the Great War Veterans Association called upon the Dominion authorities to prosecute the editor of this paper and all those "who pander to the lowest passions of undesirable citizenship."[23]

The educational and cultural activities of ULFTA also came under fire. Here the opposition emphasized the need to defend "loyal and Canadianized Ukrainians from their Bolshevik foes."[24] In the spring of 1923 a group of Fort William Ukrainians, closely associated with the Uniate church, sued the local ULFTA branch. Their complaint was that the Fort William Prosvita Society, established in 1910, had been illegally transformed" into a Revolutionary, Communistic and Bolshevik Society in affiliation with the Third International of Moscow." The original society, it was claimed, had through its hall and various programmes "sought to spread culture among the Ukrainian people," membership having been open to all Ukrainians "irrespective of their religious connections or the state to which any of the members used to belong."[25] Significantly, their case was handled by Dowler & Dowler, one of the leading law firms in Fort William, who seemed to have approached the matter for its ideological implications as well as for its legal ramifications. In a letter to the Commissioner of the RCMP, W.A. Dowler pointed out the importance of decisive government action "to retain the loyalty of those Ruthenians who have become Canadian citizens ... and uphold them against the revolutionary bunch." His appeal was well received. The RCMP was already alarmed by the success of the ULFTA, and there was even talk of charging the association under Section 98 of the Criminal Code.[26]

The FOC was similarly harassed. In August 1923 the RCMP investigated a number of reports that "Red" Finns had terrorized their "White" opponents in certain communities of northern Ontario. According to one report the Reds had set up investigation committees "to test newcomers ... as to their political beliefs." Defending the rights of Canadian Finns who were "loyal to the institutions of this country" soon became an important RCMP and Ontario Provincial Police function.[27]

Communist-controlled trade unions also now came under severe police scrutiny. In these areas activity was concentrated in the coal fields of Nova Scotia and Alberta and the lumber camps of northern Ontario. The Communist infiltration of District 26 of the UWMW was largely the work of J.B. McLachlan, the dynamic secretary-treasurer of the union. A founding member of the CPC, McLachlan worked closely with Communist organizer Tom Bell in publishing the radical newspaper *Maritime Labour Herald*; he also assisted Jack Macdonald and Malcolm Bruce, two other Communist organizers of Scottish background, in their recruitment efforts in Cape Breton.[28] In 1923 McLachlan was convicted on charges of seditious libel and conspiracy. In the same year his local's charter was suspended by the headquarters of the UMWA; this together with local OBU competition and the depressed state of the coal market contained the growth of the CPC in Nova Scotia.[29]

Alberta coal mines, however, with their strong tradition of labour radicalism and "foreign" influence offered a much better fighting ground to the CPC in the 1920s. Unstable coal prices, a high percentage of recent immigrants among the local labour force and union weaknesses all combined in the 1920s to produce abominable working and living conditions in the region.[30] The main vehicle for Communist activity in the coal fields of Alberta was the Mine Workers Union of Canada (MWUC). Founded in 1925 the MWUC set out to organize "all the coal and metal workers of the Dominion of Canada;" the union's initial assault was on Alberta and eastern British Columbia. The union had as its targets both mine owners and its working-class IWW and OBU rivals. Most of the jleaders of the MWUC were Anglo-Saxons: Lewis Macdonald ("Kid Burns"), Jan Lakeman, and James Sloan were among the most prominent. Ukrainian leaders of the union included John Stokuluk and D. Bungla.[31] In 1925 Lewis Macdonald was the dominant force in the organization not only because of his reputation as a professional boxer, but because of the organizational skills he and his friends brought from the coal fields of Nova Scotia. On one occasion the commissioner of the Alberta police informed the attorney general of the province, W. Brownlee, that the worst element in the province were from Cape Breton "men who were implicated in the strike at Sidney ... followers of McLaughlin [sic] ... members of the 3rd International ... absolute Reds."[32] Yet if the Cape Bretoners led, the ranks of those who followed consisted mainly of foreign-born miners. This account of the confrontation between the Alberta police and the MWUC at Drumheller reveals the violence which the growth of this daring new union entailed:

I had a number of constables on duty and as soon as stone throwing started, I warned the crowd to cease and when they did not I ordered my men to draw their revolvers. We then forced the crowd to back off the tracks to the street. These men [strike-breakers] proceeded towards the mine, but halfway up they were met by a crowd of women who again stoned them. ... Some men, led by Lewis McDonald, on seeing the constables busy with the women ... rushed down the hill and raided the powder house ... McDonald has since been charged with assault causing grievous bodily harm. ... I went towards the mine premises for the purpose of rescuing the men who were being stoned, and had a number of stones thrown at myself, as well as considerable abuse from the women. In this instance, as well as previous occasions, it has been found that the women are much more difficult to handle.[33]

The involvement of foreign workers in such encounters soon prompted the commissioner of the provincial police to ask the RCMP and the Immigration Branch to "check up on unnaturalized foreigners in the Drumheller Valley," and deport any "found to be Communists."[34] This position was strongly endorsed by the mine managers of the region, who seized upon the illegitimate status of the CPC and IWW to discard all collective bargaining procedures. In 1925, R.M. Young, president of the Western Coal Operators Association, was advised by the manager of the Thiel Detective Agency that the temporary success of the IWW in the Alberta mines might not be a bad thing since they were "an easier organization to break up and disperse than the UMWA because of the more stable qualities of the latter."[35]

The lumber companies in both British Columbia and northern Ontario were equally anxious to discredit all union organization, and to prevent "undesirables" from reaching their bush camps. To a considerable extent blacklists, company guards and co-operative provincial and local police kept the CPC and other radical organizations at bay. But it was impossible to prevent the odd *animateur* from slipping through. Lumber workers were highly mobile, and occupational pluralism was often a way of life.[36]

CPC organizers enlarged upon the work which prominent members of the FOC, most notably A.T. Hill, Alf Hautamaki, and E. Holm, had performed for the OBU. Indeed, when the Communists formed their own organization in 1923, they continued to use the name Lumber Workers Industrial Union (LWIU).[37] The Communist union encountered bitter resistance from both the IWW and the lumber companies and its progress was slow until 1926. In that year the LWIU and its IWW opponents joined forces in a strike which shut down the mammoth logging industry of the Thunder Bay District for over eight weeks. Strike-breakers were imported and police harassment was commonplace; but despite their lack of a strike fund the 2,000 loggers who had walked out outlasted the lumber companies and gained higher wages and better working conditions.[38] Community support for the strike was a major factor in this working-class victory. The Finnish

Union Co-operative in Port Arthur fed over 600 workers a day, while in rural areas farmers, especially those of Finnish background, provided potatoes, milk, and poultry to the strikers free of charge. Union organizers were also quite successful in persuading strike-breakers, many of whom were recent immigrants, to abandon work in the lumber camps.[39]

Although *The Worker* publicly described the strike as "a splendid illustration ... of the united front of two union organizations," its union leadership privately regarded the strike as "a real organizational experience" which would enable the LWIU "to gain great prestige and authority among Lumberworkers." Yet the way ahead proved hard. By 1929 depressed economic conditions had largely negated the gains obtained during the Thunder Bay strike. Moreover, further attempts at strike action encountered violent company resistance.[40] In October 1929, for example, two LWIU organizers, Viljo Rosval and John Voutilaimen, disappeared during the bloody Shabaqua Strike. Both *The Worker* and *Vapaus* charged corporate assassination when, in March 1930, their bodies were found "face down in six inches of water." No police investigation was conducted, however, and the CPC was given two martyrs; the funeral of "the fallen heroes" in Port Arthur was attended by more than 4,000 workers.[41]

The same spring the party created a new organization the Lumber and Agricultural Workers Industrial Union (LAWIU), with its headquarters in Port Arthur. Agricultural workers and poor farmers had, of course, long been regarded by both the Comintern and the CPC executive as members of the proletariat. They too were locked into a destructive wage and price system which was manipulated by powerful financial and agricultural interests. Worse still, many had been indoctrinated with the ethic of Canadian capitalism, while others exhibited reactionary "peasant values." The agricultural proletariat held promise for the party but it was not without its false assumptions.[42] A 1930 Comintern Report made specific reference to this problem:

> The kulak goal looms large in the calculations of many. Further, to many of them their position as agricultural laborers working for $35. a month is an immense improvement on the conditions they left behind them in Europe, and they feel no urge to struggle for more especially as such a struggle might cause the loss of their job, and thus prove to be, in their estimation a step backward from their goal of becoming farmers. Even those who have revolutionary tendencies are hampered

by the lack of knowledge of the language and customs of the new country they find themselves in, and many are afraid to take part in any movement that might lead to their deportation.[43]

In its organizational effort among farmers the CPC made no distinction between immigrants and native-born. In 1925 the Progressive Farmers' Educational League (PFEL) was organized in Western Canada by Tom McEwen, J.M. Clarke, Walter Wiggins, and Carl Axelson. Its headquarters was in Saskatoon but there were many branches throughout the Prairies, and it proved particularly attractive to farmers of Ukrainian and Finnish background. In October 1930 the PFEL was transformed into the Farmers' Unity League (FUL).[44] During the next year the FUL conducted a major recruiting programme, particularly through its newspaper *The Furrow*; in addition, both the ULFTA and the FOC were instructed "to use their organizers to set up Party units in agricultural districts, and mobilize Finnish and Ukrainian farmers ... for the left wing."[45]

The party also concerned itself with the fate of the migrant agricultural worker. The unsuccessful British harvest excursion of 1928 gave the Communists both recruits and publicity. At a series of public meetings, and in the pages of *The Worker* and the *Ukrainian Labour News*, CPC organizers described how these immigrants had been duped by the promise of high wages and good working conditions; they had arrived in the country only to be exploited by "the Canuck John Farmer" and his railroad and steamship allies.[46] The episode enabled the leadership of the CPC to demonstrate to their Ukrainian and Finnish membership that capitalist exploitation transcended ethnic background, that British workers could be treated as brutally as those from Eastern Europe.[47]

The hope of the Communists was that the British harvesters and other migratory workers would extend the occupational, geographical, and ethnic character of their union. The party discarded the term "migratory" because of the syndicalism which had been amply manifested in the migratory organization of the IWW. On the ethnic front the LAWIU sought to build upon the existing Finnish base of support by attracting French Canadians and Slavs.[48] The party had long regarded French Canadian lumber workers as potential recruits, though it recognized that the Roman Catholic Church powerfully influenced "the ignorant ... French workers." At one stage it was thought that if the union moved its headquarters to Montreal it would be in a position "to organize the french [*sic*] loggers."[49] Such a move would also reduce "the dangerously Finnish character" of the LAWIU; it would lose "its narrow national character, and become a real union of the Canadian workers."[50] Although the switch was never made the Politbureau became increasingly frustrated by the ethnic problems of this union.[51]

Ukrainians and Finns had been the great strength of the CPC but they had, on occasion, been quite contemptuous of other ethnic groups, especially Jews and Blacks. In 1931 Tom McEwen complained bitterly about the way in which Slavic prejudice had disrupted the party's organizational efforts among oppressed Black workers in the Windsor area.[52] Similarly, Ukrainian Communists were accused of having a very bad attitude towards women: "They say a woman talks too much and can't be trusted and enuf [*sic*] if their husbands are in the party. In Lethbridge ... they even suspended one from the meetings. ... It is very important to carry on this in the UKE [*sic*] press. They have the old peasant attitudes on this question."[53] For the Politbureau, which was primarily English-speaking, maintaining good relations with the ULFTA and the FOC was a never-ending problem. One aspect of the problem was seen as the lack of "dependable English-speaking men" at both the local and national level. When Tom McEwen was shifted from Winnipeg to party headquarters in Toronto, the English-speaking rank and file in the Prairie city were outraged: "in our district we need somebody whom they [the Ukrainians] will at least respect – it is hard to have influence over them, unless it is one of their own." Nor were local English-speaking members prepared to accept the appointment of Matthew Popovich or Jacob Penner as the new district organizer; this, they warned, would change the Winnipeg Communist Party into "a pure isolated Ukrainian group."[54] In Port Arthur and Sudbury similar tensions existed between Finnish and English-speaking members. In April 1931 McEwen informed the district organizer in Fort William that it was necessary to fight continuously against this "not speaking English crap" when dealing with the FOC.[55]

Interference from Moscow further complicated the internal problems of the CPC. On major policy decisions the Canadian party was bound by the dictates of the Comintern. During the 1920s two decrees of the International Organizations seriously disrupted the CPC. For a long time the Comintern had been concerned about the number of foreign workers in the North American Communist movement, and their organization into semi-autonomous language federations. The retention of national loyalties jeopardized the development of a broad class consciousness; in North America the progress of Communism meant a common working-class language. That language could only be English. In 1925 the American and Canadian parties were informed that they should base their organization on occupation rather than language; on the factory floor immigrant workers should be made "to fraternize with other Communists, and hopefully, even with fellow workers who were not Communists and did not belong to any ethnic group."[56]

The second major internal development to alter dramatically the course of Canadian Communism came in 1928. In that year the Comintern, now dominated by Joseph Stalin, forecast an imminent disaster for capitalism which required immediate and complete working-class mobilization. In keeping with this spirit the CPC in January 1930 disbanded the TUEL and threw itself into the organization of industrial unions in every sector of the economy. Its chosen instrument was the Workers' Unity League (WUL). Within a year, under the umbrella of the WUL, eleven unions with a membership of 12,000 had been established. Needless to say these unions became involved in the most bitter and prolonged strikes.[57]

Canadian Communism survived the shifts in Comintern policy, but in the short run the dictums of class war and Bolshevization were deeply divisive. In 1929 Maurice Spector and Jack Macdonald, both prominent members of the Politbureau, strenuously objected to both aspects of the new party line; for this disobedience they were expelled from the Politbureau and their places taken by Tim Buck and his followers. Simultaneously John Ahlqvist and Avro Vaara, leading members of the FOC, were disciplined for challenging Buck's international viewpoint. Later, Matthew Popovich and John Navis, and several Jewish Communists, were similarly disciplined.[58]

The Party's assimilationist policy stirred up opposition in the FOC and the ULFTA. The Finnish were the first to take up arms against a "threat to the peasant ethnic traditions that they had maintained for nearly a generation in their workers' clubs and halls." In doing so they were well aware of the tremendous counterattack which their American brethren had launched in 1925-26. In the United States the Bolshevization campaign was branded by Finns as a conspiracy on the part of Jews to take over the American Communist Party, and to destroy "the Finnish workers' social life."[59] Canadian Finns did not prove quite as aggressive, but they denied the validity of the Comintern's directive as formulated at the 1929 CPC Convention: "The chief objectives of the language organizations must be to become real mass organizations, which are to draw the foreign born workers into the general stream of the Canadian Labour Movement (unions, mass organizations such as the Womens Labour League, CLDL, etc.)"[60]

The forms of FOC resistance varied. On the one hand, Ahlqvist, Vaara, and other leading Finnish communists strongly supported Jack Macdonald in his power struggle with Tim Buck. Moreover, when Buck won they challenged the legitimacy of a number of his directives. In December 1929 the secretary of the FOC informed Buck that his organization would maintain its connection with *Työmies* ("Liberty"), the American Finnish newspaper, and would not blacklist American Finns expelled far from their country's Communist Party.[61] The actions of the existing Politbureau were viewed as creating "hard feelings" and posed "the danger of a split." More importantly, the FOC rejected an order that Arvro Vaara, the outspoken editor of *Vapaus* be moved from Sudbury to Party headquarters in Toronto, presumably to bring him and his followers into line.[62]

This act of defiance quickly led to the suspension of Ahlqvist, Vaara, and J. Wirta. In attempting to contain this "serious and significant breach of party discipline" Tim Buck and his allies appealed through *The Worker* for the support of Canadian Finns "against the outright opportunitist [*sic*] elements within their ranks. Though the "rebels" had considerable community support, A.T. Hill and some other Finns in the Port Arthur and Sault Ste. Marie areas supported Buck against them.[63] This division strengthened Buck's case with the Comintern, and contributed to his eventual triumph. In March 1930 the Comintern confirmed its Bolshevization policy in even stronger language than before: "All narrow nationalism, sectarianism and the like must be fought by our Party fractions within these organizations. The present system of obligatory membership in the CP for those workers who join the Finnish society for social reasons must be abandonded. Only those who are convinced communists can be recruited into the Party. The Finnish Society must become a broad mass organization and be utilized by the Party fraction as a recruiting ground for the Party."[64]

The next month a Special Commission of the International body, appointed to investigate the trouble between Buck and "the right wing members" of the FOC, submitted its report. The commission found that the dissident Finnish members had "grieviously erred," and now had but two choices: to submit or else leave the party.[65] The accused chose the former course and in its April edition *Vapaus* carried Arvo Vaara's recantation: "I realize that my weightiest mistake has been, that I refused the task to which the Political Committee of the Party instructed me. It was a bad error. The struggles of the working class before us ... cannot be won if ... the instructions of the working class general staff Comintern and the leadership of its Parties are not strictly carried out." For its part the Politbureau allowed Vaara to continue as "nominal ... editor" of *Vapaus* though the day to day operation of the paper would be the responsibility of the Toronto headquarters.[66]

The legacy of these traumatic events was a suspicious and inwardly hostile Finnish leadership. Later, the "loyal" A.T. Hill was charged with attempting to use his position to return to Finland a wealthy man. The Politbureau was also in future years to doubt the commitment of the FOC to the policy of industrial unionism; in northern Ontario the progress of the LAWIU remained painfully slow.[67]

The Ukrainian Labour Farm Temple Association faced similar charges of "federalism and sectarianism." In February 1930, for example, the Politbureau complained that some members of the ULFTA executive were divided in their loyalty and were "striving to demoralize the party ranks and discredit the leading party committee and functionaries." Buck and his supporters soon moved on to specific charges and in the next two months a number of Ukrainian activists found themselves suspended from Party activity.[68] Led by Popovich and Navis the ULFTA fought back claiming that the charges of "sectarianism and right wing opportunism" were not being properly investigated, and were, for the most part, "unjustified." The Comintern treated the ULFTA appeal as it had treated the FOC: it demanded submission. While admitting that Communist leaders in Canada had on occasion failed to suppress anti-Ukrainian sentiments within the party, the Comintern's directive was blunt: "The ECCI calls ... upon the Ukrainian comrades to work in the closest harmony with and under the direction of the Party leadership."[69] Until the ULFTA eliminated "narrowness and national exclusiveness" its important task of guiding Ukrainian workers and farmers into the "revolutionary trade union movement" would be seriously hampered. What the ULFTA needed was a programme of Canadianization. English classes should be offered to Ukrainian members, and the *Ukrainian Labor News* should discard its narrow focus and "tie up the struggles of the Ukrainian workers with the general proletarian struggle in Canada ... and the struggle of the international proletariat." The ULFTA was ordered not to let the protection of property become "a barrier ... to militant class programmes." All bourgeois cultural activities and pastimes should also be "gotten rid of" and "The many non-revolutionary plays which are extremely empty and often directly harmful and indeed are sometimes outright bourgeois trash, which are employed for 'want of something better' must be replaced by a real revolutionary programme of plays and proletarian films ... local courses and classes should be strengthened ... including courses in English. It is also necessary to increase physical culture and to develop as rapidly as possible the workers' sport movement among the Ukrainian workers."[70]

In January 1931 the Politbureau announced that Matthew Popovich and John Navis, who had previously rejected "the Polcom statement on the working class mass organizations," would soon be confessing their guilt. Their subsequent recantation appeared both in *The Worker* and the *Ukrainian Labor News*.[71]

The CPC leadership did, however, use the carrot as well as the stick in attempting to bring the ULFTA into the mainstream of party life. In July 1931, for example, Buck overruled the Fort William District Bureau when it refused to pay the expenses of M. Kostaniuk, a delegate to the annual ULFTA convention in Winnipeg. In doing so he acknowledged the importance of the Ukrainian organization to the Party: "It must always be remembered that the Ukrainian masses constitute the third largest language group in Canada. Not only that, but they are the most highly organized, and in several respects it is in the Ukrainian movement (Red and White) that political developments find their clearest and most classical expression in Canada."[72]

In June, 1931 *The Worker* commenting on the twelfth annual convention of the ULFTA stated that Ukrainian Party members had discarded "the old sectarian theories that only Ukrainians should organize Ukrainians and that only English should organize English." During the summer and fall of 1931 *The Worker* glowingly reported the entry of other ethnic groups into the party, and the improvement of relations among Finns, Ukrainians, and Anglo-Saxons.[73] In Winnipeg a separate Polish local was launched by Dan Holmes (Chomicki), a prominent member of the District Bureau. Mike Cacic was likewise successful among

Serbs, Slovaks, and Croatians; in July 1931 he was named "national organizer of the South Slav Bureau of the Party."[74]

If the Communists were to succeed with building industrial unions in a hostile environment then ethnic harmony within the party was essential. Steel, the needle trades and meat packing were all "missionary" areas for the CPC, in which they faced the most bitter corporate opposition. Suspected WUL organizers were often summarily dismissed, and wholesale blacklisting was widespread. Mike Melrichuk, a Winnipeg meat-packer, described the problem of a typical organizer to Tom McEwen, director of the WUL, in June 1931: "I have been working in Swift Canadian Packing plants in Winnipeg for 7 years. Since time ago they faired [sic] me for treing to organised workers ther into Food Workers Industrial Union of W.U.L., of C. . Befor I wose successful in bring the workers ther together a stool peogon got amongst us and on report of the stool I wose faired."[75] Nor was the situation facing the Communists much better in the mining and lumbering industries, where they had long been active. In Sudbury, Finnish members of the MWUC were so afraid of INCO retaliation that they prevented their union from sending a petition of protest about safety standards to the Ontario Department of Mines.[76]

Yet despite every form of government and corporate harassment the WUL gained ground. By the summer of 1931 Tom McEwen could give this promising account of the party's union movement:

> Our organization is the Canadian Section of the Red International of Labor Unions. Our present membership ... stands around ten or twelve thousand and we are growing every day. ... We have fairly well established in Nova Scotia but have still a lot to do before we can chase the rotten BESCO tool of the UMW out of there. ... we have a strong movement among the miners of Alberta, and only a few weeks ago two thousand more decided to affiliate with us. In B.C. we are gradually making headway, but the blacklist against fighting trade unionists is so strong that our progress is necessarily very slow."[77]

In addition to the work among industrial workers, McEwen was able to report that, since January 1, 1931, 20,000 cards had been issued for the National Unemployed Workers Association (NWUA), and that this body now had an active membership of 16,000. Demonstrations by unemployed across the country substantiated this bold assertion of Communist strength. The presence of many Anglo-Saxon workers in the ranks of the organized unemployed was another mark of the party's growing strength. Even in Quebec, especially among the French Canadian unemployed, there now seemed reason for hope.[78] The new elan manifested itself in violent confrontations with the police. During the Winnipeg visit of Gideon Robertson, Dominion minister of labour, to Winnipeg in June 1931, violence flared between the demonstrators and the local police. Ben Winter, a leading member of the Manitoba Bureau, provided McEwen with this description of the encounter: "Altho the police came ready and prepared under the instructions to smash the demonstration, I might say that the workers put up one of the best fights that Winnipeg has ever witnessed. From their own report, 14 police were injured, including an Inspector and a few sergeants. Last Sunday nite the regular Sunday meeting of the Communist Party was held at the Market Sqare. The workers were jubilant, and felt more confident in themselves after Friday's results."[79]

III

Such confrontations were symptomatic of the years 1929-31. The Communists were on the rise and their business and political opponents were more determined that they should be suppressed. The climax came in August 1931 when ten of the leaders of the Politbureau were charged with seditious conspiracy and the party declared an illegal organization. Simultaneously, efforts were made to drive foreign-born Communists out of the country, hundreds being deported under Section 41 and the vagrancy provisions of the Immigration Act. The main instrument of Communist retaliation was the Canadian Labour Defence League (CLDL). This organization provided funds for the bail, fines, and legal fees, and sought to mobilize public opinion for the victims of "capitalist oppression." That its success was only marginal was evident in the steady stream of "foreign" Communists heading backward across the Atlantic, many to fascist countries.[80]

Toronto and Winnipeg as well as the industrial communities of northern Ontario and British Columbia were the major arenas in which the struggle between Canadian communism and the forces of "law and order" was fought. In Toronto, as elsewhere, anti-communism and anti-alien sentiment was closely identified. In January 1929 Brigadier-General Denis C. Draper, Chief Constable of Toronto, announced that in future "all proceedings and addresses at all public meetings [were] to be in the English language"; he also stipulated that "no disorderly or seditious reflections on the form of government or the King, or any constituted authority [would] be allowed." These measures were soon implemented. Many public halls and "places of public amusement" which had allowed communist meetings to be conducted "in a foreign language" now had their licences suspended. When the Communists resorted to impromptu street corner meetings the police were there with their clubs and horses. This tough response received widespread support not only from traditional patriotic organizations like the Orange Lodge and the Canadian Legion, but also from the city's newspapers.[81] A January 1929 editorial of the *Mail & Empire* caught the mood of the times: "The majority of those who have a *gripe* about police interference ... are not Canadian by birth or persons who have lived all their lives under British institutions. They need reminding that the laws of Canada are binding upon them. No sovietism or other form of anarchism they have been indoctrinated in in alien countries or by alien teaching will find a footing here. ..."[82]

In Winnipeg the business community had more reason than most to fear Communist subversion. Winnipeg businessmen could well remember when their city had been virtually controlled by "alien bolsheviks." Moreover, during the 1920s the predominantly immigrant North End had provided a powerful base for CPC activities. The election of William Kolisnyk as alderman in Ward Three in December 1926 only served to confirm the worst fears of the Anglo-Saxon leaders,[83] and the *Winnipeg Free Press* captured this mood when it described Kolisnyk, after his election, as "the local officer of the Bolshevik army which marches under the red banner."[84]

In 1929, Major-Colonel Ralph Webb, Winnipeg's mayor moved to eradicate "any sort of a Comunistic menace." Webb's initiative was typical of the times: he attempted to prevent the CPC from holding meetings, and he pressured first the King and later the Bennett governments to deport Communist agitators "back to Russia, the country of their dreams." In February 1931 Webb warned R.B. Bennett that unless decisive action was taken by Dominion authorities Winnipeg's Anglo-Saxon community might resort to force to defend its property and to prevent "Moscow interference with the citizens and the development of our country."[85] Webb argued that his call for action had widespread support in the city, Ukrainians, and other central Europeans not excepted. Subsequently, Bennett was contacted by the National Press, a Winnipeg-based Ukrainian organization, which requested financial assistance; in its efforts "to combat communism." By describing the real condition in Russia the Slavic newspapers of the National

Press could effectively counter the *Ukrainian Labour News* and other CPC publications.[86]

During the spring and summer of 1931 pressure for Dominion intervention against the Communists grew. In April 1931 the Sudbury Council adopted the following resolution: "That the City Council of Sudbury go on record, asking the Dominion government to deport all undesirables and Communists, and a copy of this resolution be forwarded to the Government at Ottawa, also to all Municipalities in the Dominion asking them to endorse Sudbury's action." Between April 15 and June 26 over eighty municipalities wrote to Prime Minister Bennett indicating their support of the Sudbury proposal.[87]

Provincial governments soon joined this crusade. In June 1931 Premier S.F. Tolmie informed the Dominion government that the labour trouble in British Columbia was almost out of control; the province had been pushed to the brink by "foreign agitators" – "some of whom were adopting English and Scotch names [thus] giving the public a false impression." Deportation, Tolmie argued, had two advantages: it would remove "foreign agitators without waiting for conviction by court or jury," and it would encourage the loyal Anglo-Saxon population. It is difficult, he wrote, "to say how long we can hold back the law abiding population from themselves dealing with this element and [the] public results would be terrible."[88] The Taschereau government in Quebec issued a similar appeal though its tendency was to blame Communist activities on *Jewish radicals*.[89] But it was the support of the Ontario government which put the anti-Communist campaign over the top. In August 1929, while the Toronto police were on the offensive against the CPC, Premier G. Howard Ferguson urged Mackenzie King to amend the existing immigration regulations in two important respects. His first suggestion was that the naturalization period be extended to ten years; during this time "undesirables" "who are dangerous and who disseminate sedition might be deported from the country." He also called for the deportation of Communist agitators rather than their criminal prosecution; here, he argued, that it was "very difficult to secure a conviction for sedition ... and a jail term merely makes martyrs of these individuals and stimulates them to greater action."[90]

American policy towards the Communists also influenced Canadian attitudes. In August 1930, H.M. Wrong, a member of the Canadian Legation in Washington, informed the secretary of state for external affairs, O.D. Skelton, that in the United States "there had been a considerable increase in the number of prosecutions of 'reds'." As a result, the American government had established a Special Committee of Enquiry into Communist influence, especially among the immigrant working class. Wrong's own response to this development was light-hearted; the more responsible newspapers had "treated the investigation with indifference or as a subject for levity which served to enliven their columns during the season when there is a scarcity of news."[91] By January 1931, however, Wrong's report had acquired a more serious tone. The American investigators had shown that the Communist Party had an active membership of about 12,000 in the country backed up with "500,000 to 600,000 Communist sympathizers." The recommendation of the American investigations was that the Communist Party be outlawed, and that immigrant members of it, "whether naturalized or not be deported from the country.[92]

By the summer of 1931 there were indications that the Bennett government was moving in the same direction. In March 1931 the deputy minister of immigration asked the commissioner of the RCMP to keep him informed when "budding revolutionaries" were applying for passports. "We will probably find," he wrote, "that some of them are Canadian born but we will undertake to make things very interesting for them in establishing their status under the Immigration Act if they leave Canada and seek to return."[93] Yet another aspect of the Canadian policy of restriction was the introduction into the Senate of an Alien Identification Bill: under this measure "all aliens in Canada would be required to register somewhere, at the nearest post office or wherever the Government regulation provides." This measure, it was argued, would make it possible for the RCMP "to know what people arrive from Moscow or any other foreign place." The bill did not pass because it "stigmatized [all] newcomers to Canada." But this did not mean that the Dominion government was backing down.[94] During 1931 the number of "foreigners" deported under Sections 40 and 41 of The Immigration Act increased significantly; the former section of the Act was used most extensively because, as A.L. Jolliffe, superintendent of immigration, informed his officers, "in these types of procedures "very little background information would be required."[95]

The Communist response to the mounting arrests and deportation was manifold. The party became more secretive about its activities, and began screening its recruits very carefully. Tom McEwen warned, however, that a siege mentality could prevent the party's expansion: "If we ... develop a mania that every worker who comes in our ranks and shows great eagerness to work must be a stool pigeon, we will fail to develop leadership from among the masses, we will be scared of our own shadow." The party also developed a more efficient courier system while some members of the Politbureau dropped their official titles.[96]

In the case of imprisoned members the party sought redress through the Canadian Labour Defence League. This common front organization had been formed in 1925 to prevent "unwarranted persecution and imprisonment of workers who take an active part in the struggles of the working class against master class oppression." Between 1925 and 1931 the CLDL provided strike assistance and legal aid on a large scale. In 1928 it gave $1,550 to the strikers at the National Steel Company plant in Hamilton, Ontario; the next year it donated $2,800 to Arvo Vaara's defence in Sudbury against a charge of seditious libel. In 1930 it helped fund the investigation into the disappearance of LWIU organizers J. Voutalainer and V. Rosevall. By 1931 the organization had 123 branches: thirty-seven were dominated by Ukrainians and twenty-seven by Finns.[97] At its July 1931 Conference the CLDL created a special branch called "The Defence of the Foreign Born," out of concern for the numerous Canadians who had been "slated for deportation ... [to] death or prison in European fascist countries." According to A.E. Smith, the secretary of the CLDL, the new branch would seek to extend the work of the parent organization to include "Italian, Greek, Latvian and Czechoslovakian" organizations. The ultimate goal was to create a network of local councils which would report all cases of "class war prisoners" to the Toronto headquarters of the CLDL.[98]

The Communist Party put up a brave front, but the truth of the matter was that the Politbureau was pessimistic about its chances of preventing further arrests and deportations. In July 1931 the Politbureau was informed that arrested Communist organizers were having "the maximum penalty ... dished out every time." Moreover, the demand for defence funds far exceeded the resources of the CLDL; bail was often unobtainable for arrested members and fines went unpaid with resultant prison terms. Communists deported from the country in this period included J. Pantaja, Tony Botrokoff, and Joe Farbey all of whom had been arrested for their involvement in local strikes and demonstrations.[99] In July 1931 H. Sula, district organizer for Alberta, informed the Politbureau that his naturalization record was being investigated; he predicted that Dominion authorities were now tracking down the leading members of the party "to find out ... how they have been behaving; and if there is some formal reasons for possible deportations and revoking their [naturalization] papers." On July 11, 1931 the *Ukrainian Labour News* charged that the Bennett government had already prepared a list of prominent Communists "to be deported"; repression, however, would not work "for Communism in Canada both among Anglo-Saxon and foreign workers was a product of Canadian circumstances."[100]

Dominion authorities were now poised to complete the clean-out of the Communist Party. On August 11, 1931, eight days after Parliament had adjourned, the RCMP, Ontario Provincial Police and the Toronto Municipal Police descended upon the offices of the CPC, the WUL, and *The Worker*. Simultaneously, the homes of the Toronto-based members of the Politbureau were raided. By the end of the day the following faced charges of seditious conspiracy: Tim Buck, Tom McEwen, A.T. Hill, John Boychuk, Sam Carr, Mike Caci, Malcolm Bruce, and Mike Golinsky. On September 2, the name of Matthew Popovich was added to this list. At their trial in November these men were charged with under Section 98 of the Criminal Code of being members of an "unlawful association", and of being involved in seditious conspiracy.[101] Their trials lasted ten days during which time the Crown produced a variety of evidence obtained from party headquarters. The prosecution also benefited from two RCMP undercover agents Detective Zaneth, who had played such an important role in the 1919 Winnipeg Strike trials, and Sergeant Jack Leopold, who until his expulsion in 1928 had served as a high-ranking CPC official in Saskatchewan. On November 14 Buck McEwen, Hill, Boychuk, Popovich, Carr, and Bruce were sentenced to five years' imprisonment while Cacic was given a two-year term. Deportation was recommended for those that were not native-born once they had served their prison terms.[102]

In the same month as the "Toronto Eight" were convicted the commissioner of the RCMP sent a list of thirty-five foreign born Communists to the superintendent of immigration and colonization; this list included the names of many Ukrainian and Finnish Communists based outside Toronto. The most notable of these were John Navis, Danial Lobay, John Stokaluk, Dan Holmes, John Ahlqvist, Alfred Hautamaki, Martin Pohjansalo and Arvo Vaara. For many of the men mentioned on the list the deportation sheds in Halifax were soon an unpleasant reality. In May 1932, for example, Arvo Vaara and Martin Pohjansalo were seized and deported to Finland; a similar fate awaiting Dan

Holmes, who was returned to Poland, a country he had not seen since 1913.[103]

In time, however, many Canadians became concerned over the tendency of police forces across the country to disregard the civil rights of the foreign-born. Among the immigrants themselves there was widespread alarm that the techniques of arrest and deportation were being used as a "corporate lash" to maintain labour docility. These fears were played upon by the CLDL whose publications graphically described the plight of "class war prisoners." The CLDL's civil rights campaign gained ground on September 29, 1931, when the RCMP clashed with striking miners in Estevan, Saskatchewan; according to *The Worker* three of the miners were killed outright and many were seriously injured in this "brutal and unwarranted attack."[104] The Communists' attempts to discredit the RCMP were further advanced when members of the force entered, without warrant, the Saint Mary Parish Hall in Regina, in search of party organizers; the Mounties were subsequently censured by the Archbishops' Council of the city for the "gross insult to common decency and to the Roman Catholic Church."[105]

Events such as these facilitated the growth of the CLDL. This body increased its branches from 70 to 350, and its membership from 7,000 to over 20,000 between the spring of 1930 and the summer of 1933. This expansion was accompanied by the affilation of some locals of the Trades and Labor Congress and the All Canadian Congress of Labour. Two events nurtured this developing common front: the attempt made on Tim Buck's life in Kingston Penitentiary, in October 1932, and the sensational trial and acquittal of the accused, A.E. Smith, in March 1934.[106]

Gradually the punitive measures which had been enforced against the Communists were relaxed. In 1934 Buck and the other Communist leaders were released from jail. In the same year Mitchell Hepburn, the newly elected Liberal premier of Ontario, "put an end to the anti-Communist measures associated with his Tory predecessors." Though it was still a proscribed organization, the party ran a number of candidates in the October 1935 Dominion election. None was successful and it was not until Fred Rose's victory in the Cartier by-election in 1942 that the party obtained a voice in the House of Commons. The 1935 result, however, was not without benefit to the party. The new King government quickly repealed both Section 98 of the Criminal Code and Section 41 of the Immigration Act.[107]

Party membership was also on the rise; from a figure of 4,000 in 1931 it advanced in 1939 to 16,000. The CPC took further en-

couragement from its industrial union activity. In 1934 the Politbureau had claimed that 75 per cent of the 317,547 days lost the
previous year were attributable to Communist-led unions. And if
the Comintern's 1934 order to disband the WUL had temporarily
lessened Communist influence in the Canadian labour movement, the coming of the CIO in the late thirties more than
compensated for the loss. By the outbreak of war in 1939 the
Communists were well established in such major unions as the
United Electrical Workers, the International Union of Mine, Mill
and Smelter Workers, and the International Woodworkers of
America.[108]

The impact of the party on Canadian labour relations was un-
doubted, but at heart it remained an immigrant movement.
True, the party had made headway among Anglo-Saxon and
French Canadian workers, especially the unemployed; but in
general these were only temporary converts. Canadianization of
the party was more evident at the top than the bottom. In 1937
only a quarter of the members of the Central Committee were of
Eastern European origin, and the FOC and the ULFTA had lost
much of their previous influence. The rank and file of the Party
also looked somewhat different. There was a relative decline in
Finnish and Ukrainian participation but it had been offset by the
accession of other European ethnic groups.[109]

IV

Essentially the Communist Party was a social movement on the
fringe of Canadian society. Because of its immigrant base, and its
commitment to the Comintern it was never able to establish
itself among a significant group of English- or French-speaking
workers. Yet the legacy of the CPC is not without importance.
During the 1920s the party was the only working-class organization which, in a sustained way, sought out the thousands of exploited foreign workers. For these men, hampered as they were
by poverty and linguistic differences, the Communist Party was
the only avenue of protest. While most CPC strikes failed, and
few CPC candidates were elected, the party still provided immigrant workers with an opportunity to channel their grievances
into organized protest. Nor was their protest ineffective. That authority had to turn to the repression of the years 1929-34 is itself
evidence of significant CPC influence.

The party also provided a bridge between the Old World and
Canadian society. Within its ranks enterprising European "comrades" were given an opportunity to become involved in trade

union and political activity. For the rank and file the CPC offered a variety of services through its special branches and through the many locals of the ULFTA and the FOC. Here Ukrainian and Finnish members could feel at home while gradually integrating themselves into the larger Canadian community. The Comintern's Bolshevization decree of 1929 made the party less effective in this role, and resentment among Ukrainians and Finns considerably weakened it. The leaders of the CPC recognized the short-term dangers inherent in this policy, but accepted Canadianization of the immigrant as essential in the long run to the development of a working-class movement in the country. Ironically, the CPC was no more tolerant of cultural pluralism than its Anglo-Canadian bourgeois enemy.[110]

Conclusion

The arrival of thousands of European immigrants between 1896 and 1931 profoundly affected Canadian society. The development in this period of the frontier regions of Northern Ontario and the Prairies owed much to these hardworking people. In harvesting wheat, laying track, cutting timber and extracting coal, immigrant workers were at the forefront. Yet despite their willingness to accept the most arduous jobs and to live frugally few of them seemed to have improved their material condition very quickly. Low wages and irregular seasonal employment were their lot. For the most part, they existed near the border between subsistence and destitution. Sickness and injury could wipe out the accumulation of years of back-breaking toil, leaving a man helpless in a strange land.

Canadian society did not indulge those immigrants who failed its willowing tests. During periods of economic recession deportations were frequent. In practice the German notion that "an expendable labour force takes its problems away with it when it is re-exported" had many Canadian adherents. Nor did governments in Canada do much to facilitate the integration of the immigrant communities into the larger life of the Dominion.[1] The task of Canadianizing the immigrant was left essentially to private agencies – Frontier College, the YMCA and the Protestant churches. The voluntary agencies had to make it on their own, as Dominion and provinces squabbled in true Canadian fashion over whose jurisdiction encompassed the responsibility for immigrant education. Moreover, in attempting to inculcate Anglo-Canadian and Protestant values the voluntary agencies, however well intentioned, often aggravated the immigrant's sense of his own cultural identification – a pride that was perhaps his most important asset in dealing with the vicissitudes of life in a land that at once promised and threatened.[2] The Canadian Trades and Labor Congress, with its exclusive craft orientation, was no more successful in reading these workers.[3]

Shunned or patronized by traditional native institutions, alienated immigrant workers turned to groups who sought to transform Canadian life through revolution: the Industrial Workers of the World, the One Big Union, and the Communist Party of Canada. But even within these fringe organizations their deeply felt particularities could pose problems. Class and ethnicity proved as hard to reconcile in Canada as elsewhere. Thus, when the Communist Party of Canada attempted to reduce the influence of its foreign-language federations in the name of working-class solidarity it met with stiff resistance. To many Ukrainian and Finnish workers in Canada, cultural assimilation was too high a price to pay even for the proletarian revolution.[4]

Notes

Introduction
1. Donald Avery, "Continental European Immigrant Workers in Canada, 1896-1919: From 'Stalwart Peasants' to Radical Proletariat," *Canadian Review of Sociology and Anthropology*, 12, 1 (1975), pp. 53-63.
2. Harold Troper, *Only Farmers Need Apply* (Toronto, 1972); Robin Winks, *The Blacks in Canada* (Toronto, 1971); J.S. Woodsworth, *Canada and the Orient* (Toronto, 1941); C.J. Woodsworth, *Strangers within Our Gates* (Toronto, 1909).
3. Rowland Berthoff, *British Immigrants in Industrial America, 1790-1950* (Cambridge, 1953); Helen Cowan, *British Emigration to British North America: The First Hundred Years* (Toronto, 1961); Lloyd Reynolds, *The British Immigrant: His Social and Economic Adjustment in Canada* (Toronto, 1935).
4. *Canadian Magazine*, 25 (1905), pp. 497-99.
5. Reynolds, *British Immigrant*, pp. 178-201; Edmund Bradwin, *The Bunkhouse Man* (Toronto, 1972).
6. Robert England, *The Central European Immigrant in Canada* (Toronto, 1929); *Report of the Royal Commission on Bilingualism and Biculturalism*, Book IV (Ottawa, 1968).
7. *Ukrainian Rural Settlements, Report of the Bureau of Social Research* (Winnipeg, January 25, 1917); Gerald Rosenblum, *Immigrant Workers: Their Impact on American Labour Radicalism* (New York, 1973); Vladimin Kaye, *Early Ukrainian Settlement in Canada, 1896 to 1900* (Toronto, 1964).
8. Charlotte Erickson, *American Industry and the European Immigrant, 1860-1885* (Cambridge, 1957); George Haythorne and Leonard Marsh, *Land and Labor: A Social Survey of Agriculture and the Farm Labour Market in Central Canada* (Toronto, 1941).

9. Peter Stearnes, "The Unskilled and Industrialization: A Transformation of Consciousness," Paper Presented at the Eighth Annual Conference on Social-Political History: Urban and Community Structures in Europe and America, October 10-11, 1975, Brockport, New York.

10. O.J. Firestone, *Canada's Economic Development, 1867-1953* (London, 1958); Avery, "Continental European Immigrant Workers."

11. Charlotte Erickson, *Emigration from Europe, 1815-1914* (London, 1976); Philip Taylor, *The Distant Magnet: European Emigration to the U.S.A.* (New York, 1971); Francis Hyde, *Cunard and the North Atlantic, 1840-1973* (London, 1975)

12. Luciano Iorizzo, "The Padrone and Immigrant Distribution," in S.M. Tomasi and M.H. Engel, *The Italian Experience in the United States* (Staten Island, N.Y., 1970); G. Prpic, *The Croatian Immigrants in America* (New York, 1971); Humbert Nelli, "The Padrone System: An Exchange of Letters," *Labor History*, 17, 3 (1976) pp. 44 ff.

13. G. Prpic, *Croatian Immigrants*, pp. 20-41; R.J. Vecoli, "Contadini in Chicago: A Critique of the Uprooted," *Journal of American History*, 51 (December 1964); Tamara Hareven, "The Laborers of Manchester, New Hampshire, 1912-1922," *Labor History*, 16, 2 (1975), pp. 249-65.

14. Bradwin, *Bunkhouse Man*; Martin Robin, *Radical Politics in Canadian Labour, 1880-1930* (Kingston, 1968).

15. W.R. Böhning, *The Migration of Workers in the United Kingdom and the European Community* (London, 1972), pp. 2-3. Stephen Castles and Godula Kosack, *Immigrant Workers and Class Structure in Western Europe* (Toronto, 1973).

16. Böhning, *Migration of Workers*, pp. 62-63.

17. *Ibid.*, pp. 62-72.

18. Norman Macdonald, *Canadian Immigration and Colonization, 1841-1903* (Toronto, 1968); Troper, *Only Farmers*; Maldwyn Jones, *American Immigration* (Chicago, 1960).

19. *Abstracts of Reports of the Immigration Commission*, vol. I (Washington, 1911), p. 24.

20. Böhning, *Migration of Workers*, pp. 35-37.

21. Macdonald, *Canadian Immigration*; Immigration Branch Records, PAC (hereinafter cited as IB with file no.) file 594511, W.D. Scott to Gerald Brown, April 7, 1921; Ivan Head, "The Stranger in our Midst: A Sketch of the Legal Status of the Alien in Canada," *The Canadian Yearbook of International Law, 1964* (Vancouver, 1964), pp. 123-24.

22. W. Burton Hurd, "Racial Origins and Nativity of the Canadian People," *Seventh Census of Canada, 1931*, vol. XIII, Monographs (Ottawa, 1942), pp. 537-818; Leonard Marsh, "The Problem of Seasonal Unemployment," unpublished typescript, Research Project No. 22, 1933, McGill Social Research Series.

23. Peter Stearnes, "The Unskilled and Industrialization"; Herbert Gutman, "Work, Culture and Society in Industrializing America, 1815-1919," *American Historical Review*, June 1973; Tamara Hareven, "Laborers of Manchester," pp. 249-50.

24. John Macdonald and Leatrice Macdonald, "Chain Migration, Ethnic Neighborhood Formation and Social Networks," *Milbank Memorial Fund Quarterly*, 52 (January 1964), pp. 82-97; Diana Brandino, "The Italians in Hamilton," unpublished MA thesis, University of Western Ontario, January, 1977; Ivan Avakumovic, *The Communist Party of Canada* (Toronto, 1975), pp. 20-45.

25. Avery, "European Immigrant Workers"; Michiel Horn (ed.), *The Dirty Thirties: Canadians in the Great Depression* (Toronto, 1972), pp. 159, 213, 261-304.

26. In this work the term "ethnic" is usually associated with the "biological affiliation and ancestry" which corresponded to the major categories in the Canadian Census of the period 1901-31. The term "alien" has somewhat less legitimacy; nevertheless it was used in a number of statutes and orders-in-council. "Foreigner" was the least official, but was used extensively in the debates of legislative bodies, in government correspondence and in English-Canadian newspapers. See the *Royal Commission on Bilingualism and Biculturalism, Book IV*, pp. 6-11. Also Marilyn Jean Barber, "The Assimilation of Immigrants in the Canadian Prairie Provinces, 1896-1918: Canadian Policies" (unpublished Ph.D. thesis, University of London, 1975); Robert England, *Central European Immigrant*; John Porter, "Dilemmas and Contradictions of a Multi-Ethnic Society," Paper Presented to Section II, Royal Society of Canada, St. John's Newfoundland, June 8, 1972.

27. Warren Kalbach and Wayne McVey, *The Demographic Bases of Canadian Society* (Toronto, 1971); *Royal Commission of Bilingualism and Biculturalism, Book IV*; Brinley Thomas, *Migration and Economic Growth: A Study of Great Britain and the Atlantic Community* (Cambridge, 1973), p. 44.

28. Brinley Thomas, *Migration and Economic Growth*; Floyd Alvin Farrar, "Migration and Economic Opportunity in Canada, 1921-1951," unpublished Ph.D. thesis, University of Pennsylvania, 1962; R.A. Easterlin, *Population, Labour Force and Long Swings in Economic Growth: The American Experience* (New York, 1968); W.B. Hurd and J.C. Cameron, "Population Movements in Canada, 1921-1931; Some Further Considerations," *Canadian Journal of Economic and Political Science*, 1, 2 (May 1935); Nathan Keyfitz, "Growth of Canadian Population," *Population Studies*, 4 (June 1950), pp. 54-55.

29. Marcus Lee Hansen, *The Atlantic Migration, 1607-1860, A History of the Continuing Settlement of the United States* (Cambridge, 1940); Hansen, *The Immigrant in American History* (Cambridge, 1940); Oscar Handlin, *The Uprooted: The Epic Story of the Great Migrations that Made the American People* (Boston, 1951); Vladimir Kaye, *Early Ukrainian Settlement*; Reino Kero, "The Return of Emigrants from America to Finland," Paper Presented at the Conference on the Finnish Experience in the Western Great Lakes Region: April 26, 1974; Donald Fleming and Bernard Bailyn (eds.), *Dislocation and Emigration: The Social Background of American Immigration* (Cambridge, 1973).

30. Susan Mann Trofimenkoff and Alison Prentice (eds.) *The Neglected Majority: Essays in Canadian Women's History* (Toronto, 1977); Jacques Rouillard, *Les Travailleurs du Coton au Quebec, 1900-1915* (Toronto, 1974); Monica Boyd, "Occupations of Female Immigrants and North American Immigration Statistics," *International Migration Review*, 10, 1 (Spring 1976); Claire La Vigna, "Women in the Labour Movement, 1860-1914: A Comparison of the Italian and Canadian Record," Paper presented at the Conference on the Italian Immigrant Women in North America, Toronto, October 28 and 29, 1977.

31. Bradwin, *Bunkhouse Man*; Alfred Fitzpatrick, *The University in Overalls* (Toronto, 1920): Brandino, "Italians in Hamilton."

Chapter One

1. O.J. Firestone, *Canada's Economic Development, 1867-1953* (London, 1958), p. 65; *Fifth Census of Canada*, 1911 (Ottawa, 1913), pp. 2, 42-44; Robert England, *The Central European Immigrant in Canada* (Toronto, 1929); George Haythorne and Leonard Narsh, *Land and Labour: A Social Survey of Agriculture and the Farm Labour Market in Central Canada* (Toronto, 1941), pp. 213-30.

2. IB, 571672, W.F. McCreary to J.A. Smart, June 21, 1897.

3. H.C. Pentland, "The Development of a Capitalistic Labour Market in Canada," *Canadian Journal of Economics and Political Science* (November 1959), p. 450.

4. *Ukrainian Rural Settlements, Report of the Bureau of Social Research* (Winnipeg, January 25, 1917); J.W. Dafoe, *Clifford Sifton in Relation to His Times* (Toronto, 1931), pp. 318-19; Canada, House of Commons, *Debates*, 1905, p. 7686; *ibid.*, 1914, p. 1611. There are also extensive references to this trend in IB, 29490 and IB, 195281.

5. Avery, "Canadian Immigration Policy," pp. 16-25; Dafoe, *Sifton*, pp. 95-100.

6. *Sessional Papers* (SP), 1902, No. 13, p. 7; *ibid.*, 1896, no. 13, p. 7; Dafoe, *Sifton*, p. 319.

7. Emerson Hough, *The Sowing* (Winnipeg, 1909), pp. 27, 62; *Sessional Papers*, 1910, no. 25, p. 110.

8. Haythorne and Marsh, *Land and Labour*, pp. 181-92. The Census of 1911 showed that there were 142,384 farm labourers in Canada; of these, 58,132 or 41% were immigrants. *Census*, 1911, vol. VI, pp. 30-31.

9. IB, 741096, W.S. Herron to W.D. Scott, November 6, 1907.

10. Norman Macdonald, *Canadian Immigration and Colonization, 1841-1903* (Toronto, 1968), pp. 95-100, 200-9; IB, 321912, John Dyke to T.M. Daly, minister of the interior, April 28, 1893.

11. IB, 48176, W.F. McCreary to secretary, Department of the Interior, December 8, 1897.

12. IB, 113228, No. 4, James A. Smart to Clifford Sifton, July 13, 1900; *ibid.*, J.A. Smart to the North Atlantic Trading Company, July 17, 1900. Between 1899 and 1906 this mysterious syndicate of European agents had a virtual monopoly on the recruitment of agriculturalists for Canada in Central Europe and the Scandinavian countries. Despite an official inquiry of its operation by the House of Commons Select Committee on Agriculture and Colonization in 1906 neither James A. Smart, former deputy minister of the interior nor W.T.R. Preston, former superintendent of emigration in London, England, would divulge the names of the directors of the North Atlantic Trading Company. "Evidence," Select Committee on Agriculture and Colonization, 1906, pp. 231-2 (PAC); W.T.R. Preston, *My Generation of Politics and Politicians* (Toronto, 1927), pp. 125-222. IB, 113228, No. 11, F.C. Blair to Dr. Edwards, October 24, 1921.

13. IB, 17480, No. 1, L.M. Fortier, acting superintendent of immigration branch to W.W. Cory, acting deputy minister of the interior, September 21, 1907; IB, 946587, No. 1, Report of Immigration Account to W.C. Black, deputy minister of immigration and colonization, March 31, 1922; *Proceedings of the Trade and Labour Congress*, 1908, p. 48.

14. IB, 389803, J.A. Smart to W.D. Scott, May 31, 1905; *ibid.*,

Scott to Frank Oliver, July 14, 1905; *ibid.*, Smart to Oliver, January 10, 1907.

15. IB, 595173, No. 4, W.D. Scott to W.W. Cory, January 16, 1912.

16. Lloyd Reynolds, *The British Immigrant* (Toronto, 1935), pp. 46, 289, 306; "Report of the W.T.R. Preston," *Sessional Papers*, 1900, No. 13, p. 13; *Laurier Papers*, 72945, Reverend Charles Gordon to Laurier, May 7, 1903; IB, 595173, J. Obed Smith to Scott, February 12, 1907.

17. George Haythorne, "Harvest Labor in Western Canada: An Episode in Economic Planning," *Quarterly Journal of Economics*, 1932-33, pp. 533-44; IB, 29490, No. 3, J. Obed Smith to Scott, July 8, 1909; Sir Thomas Shaughnessy Papers (PAC, Microfilm), to Alfred Jones, August 3, 1906.

18. Ottawa *Free Press*, July 17, 1911; IB, 29490, Smith to Pedley, October 15, 1901; *Debates*, 1904, p. 7302.

19. IB, 29490, No. 1, Smith to Scott, August 1, 1901; *Ukrainian Rural Settlements*, pp. 4-6. William de Geldwr, *A Dutch Homesteader on the Prairies* (Toronto, 1973), pp. 12-13, translated by Herman Ganzevoort.

20. Philip Tayler, *The Distant Magnet: European Emigration to the U.S.A.* (New York, 1971), p. 80; Francis Hyde, *Cunard and the North Atlantic, 1840-1973: A History of Shipping and Financial Management* (London, 1975), pp. 140-92.

21. H.A. Innis, *A History of the Canadian Pacific Railway* (Toronto, 1971), pp. 139, 170, 224, 264; Shaughnessy Papers, Shaughnessy to Archer Baker, August 5, 1908; *ibid.*, Shaughnessy to Robert Rogers, December 2, 1911. With the absorption of the Allan line into the newly created Canadian Pacific Ocean Steamship service in 1915, an additional eighteen ships were added to the Atlantic service. The Pacific fleet, which dated back to 1889, was also expanded during this period. The CPR also benefited from lucrative mail subsidies from both the Canadian and Imperial governments. Innis, *Canadian Pacific*, pp. 139, 170, 224; Thomas Appleton, *Ravenscrag: The Allan Royal Mail Line* (Toronto, 1974), pp. 120-30.

22. Hough, *The Sowing*, p. 92. *Labour Gazette*, February 1912, pp. 720-21; *ibid.*, May 1913, p. 116.

23. Shaughnessy Papers, Archer Baker to Shaughnessy, August 5, 1908; Innis, *Canadian Pacific*, pp. 263-64.

24. James Hedges, *Building the Canadian West* (New York, 1939), pp. 129-30; Harold Innis, *Settlement and the Mining Frontier* (Toronto, 1936), pp. 370-75; IB, 39145, McCreary to Smart, May 17, 1900.

25. IB, 39145, Smart to McCreary, June 5, 1900; *ibid.*, Blake Robertson to Oliver, October 10, 1907.

26. A.R.M. Lower, *Settlement and the Forest Frontier* (Toronto, 1936), pp. 22, 134; Sifton Papers, 82801, H.A. McKibbon, sec., Port Arthur Board of Trade to Sifton, November 5, 1901; Martha Allen, "A Survey of Finnish Cultural Economic Development in the Sudbury District" (unpublished MA thesis, University of Western Ontario, 1954), pp. 4-20; *Project Bay Street* (Lakehead, 1974); Arvi Heinonen, *Finnish Friends in Canada* (Toronto, 1930), pp. 35-60.

27. Paul Phillips, *No Power Greater* (Vancouver, 1967), pp. 45, 77; Haythorne and Marsh, *Land and Labor*, pp. 200-25, Innis, *Mining Frontier*, pp. 173, 221.

28. *Sessional Papers*, 1899, vol. 33, no. 70, "Report of Mr. R.C. Clute on the Commission to Inquire into the Death of McDonald and Fraser on the Crow's Nest Pass Railway," p. 16.

29. IB, 39501, Smart to Shaughnessy, October 26, 1897; *ibid.*, Shaughnessy to James A. Stewart, October 27, 1897. F.A. Talbot, *The Making of a Great Canadian Railway* (London, 1912), pp. 133-59, 238-76.

30. IB, 39145, Smart to D. McNicoll, 2nd vice president, CPR, May 12, 1903; *Ukrainian Rural Settlements*, pp. 4-35.

31. IB, 39145, Smith to Pedley, July 1, 1901; Mackenzie King to Thomas Shaughnessy, July 3, 1901, cited by John Wilson, *The Calcium Light* (St. Louis, 1902), p. 46; Sir Clifford Sifton Papers (PAC), 83178, McCreary to Sifton, July 3, 1901.

32. *Report, Royal Commission to Inquire into the Immigration of Italian Labourers to Montreal, and Alleged Fraudulent Practices of Employment Agencies* (Ottawa, 1904), pp. 25, 95, 144.

33. Laurier Papers (PAC), 160620, Charles Hays to Laurier, October 4, 1909, IB, 594511, No. 3, J.O. Reddie to W.D. Scott, April 1, 1910; *Labour Gazette*, 12 (June 1912), p. 721.

34. IB, 594511, Survey of Labour Needs of Railroad Contractors, Memorandum, W.D. Scott, April 5, 1909; IB, 39145, J. Bruce Walker, Winnipeg commissioner, to Scott, May 19, 1908; *Labour Gazette*, 1906-7, p. 261; IB, 594511, No. 3, Survey of Railroad Contractors, in 1910 revealed that of 27 major companies the average wage varied from $1.50 per diem in New Brunswick to $2.50 in British Columbia.

35. James Mavor Papers, University of Toronto Archives, James Mavor to George Cox, April 2, 1907; IB, 809068, W.W.B. McInnes to Scott, April 5, 1909; Scott to M.J. Reid, Sept. 18, 1910; *Christian Guardian*, April 2, 1913.

36. IB, 594511, Survey of Labour Needs of Railroad Contractors Memorandum, W.D. Scott, April 5, 1909; IB, 39145, J. Bruce Walker, Winnipeg commissioner, to Scott, May 19, 1908.

37. IB, 594511, No. 3, J.M. Langley, chief of police to mayor of Victoria, August 28, 1911; *ibid.*, J. Bruce Walker to Scott, March 12, 1912; Extensive correspondence by immigration officials on this problem of restriction is located in IB, 594511, Nos. 2-6. What also troubled Canadian Immigration officials was the difficulty of returning to the United States immigrants who had not been naturalized there and who were "undesirable." IB, 594511, No. 3, F.H. Larned, acting commissioner-general, Immigration and Naturalization, U.S. Government, June 16, 1909.

38. Laurier Papers, 182131 Duncan Ross to Laurier, February 27, 1911; IB, 594511, W.W. Cory to Scott, July 16, 1910; Mackenzie King Diary (PAC), January 10, 1911; Mackenzie King Papers, 1910, Memorandum B. Robertson, July 1910; IB, 594511, No. 4, J.O. Ben Smith (PAC) circular letter, July 1910.

39. IB, 594511, No. 5, Donald Mann to W.D. Scott, August 6, 1912; *ibid.*, Timothy Foley to Robert Rogers, March 27, 1912.

40. IB, 594511, No. 4, W.D. Scott to Dr. W.J. Roche, January 18, 1913; *Christian Guardian*, April 2, 1913; IB, 594511, No. 6, W.D. Scott to R.H. Chadwick, Secretary, Trades and Labour Council, Moose Jaw, May 22, 1915.

41. Innis, *Canadian Pacific*, pp. 146, 164; Martin Robin, *The Company Province*, pp. 111, 125-30.

42. SP, 1910, No. 25, pp. 41, 42, cited in Innis, *The Mining Frontier*, p. 307.

43. Shaughnessy Papers, Shaughnessy to William Whyte, August 3, 1900; *Report of the Alberta Coal Commission, 1925* (Edmonton, 1926), pp. 183-190.

44. Shaughnessy Papers, Shaughnessy to Thomas Skinner, January 20, 1906; *ibid.*, Shaughnessy to William Whyte, November 26, 1908; Innis, *Mining Frontier*, pp. 293-314; Phillips, *No Power Greater*, pp. 55-57.

45. Professor Arthur Coleman, "Address," February 29, 1912, *Empire Club of Canada*: Addresses ... During the Session of 1911-12 (Toronto, 1913), p. 163; *Canadian Mining Journal*, June 15, 1907, p. 195.

46. *Census of Canada*, 1911, vol. V, pp. vi, xviii, xx, 7, 74, 88, 155; "Report of Superintendent of New Ontario," Acts and Proceedings of the General Assembly of the Presbyterian Church in Canada," 1914, p. 20.

47. *Alberta Coal Commission, 1925*, p. 181.

48. *The Labour Gazette*, September, 1904, p. 262; *Report of the Ontario Commission on Unemployment* (Toronto, 1916), p. 121. Most of these agencies were located in large transportation centres – Toronto (24), Montreal (18), Winnipeg (17), Edmonton (14), Vancouver (13), and Sudbury (11). Major companies such as the Central Employment Agency and the Star Employment Agency had branches in several cities as did the employment arms of the Canadian Pacific Railway, the Grand Northern and Grand Trunk Pacific. (IB, 801518, Inventory of Employment Agencies licensed under PC 1028 and PC 1064 in the year 1913.)

49. IB, 801518, Henry Stanford to W.D. Scott, January 25, 1908.

50. *Royal Commission ... of Italian Labourers*, 1904, p. 155; IB, 775789, cited in letter of J.G. Young, immigration agent, Sydney, to Scott, November 10, 1913; IB, 819863, W.D. Scott to Robert Rogers, December 5, 1911.

51. *Statutes of Canada*, 1897, 60-61. V., c.11,1; James J. Atherton, "The Department of Labour and Industrial Relations, 1900-1911" (MA thesis, Carleton University, 1972), pp. 240-60.

52. Sifton Papers, 103827, W.L. Hagler to minister of labour, January 18, 1902; Clute, Royal Commission on Mining Conditions.

53. Laurier Papers, 85632, E. Kirby to T.L. Blackstone, January 31, 1901; Andrew R. McCormack, "The Origins and Extent of Western Canadian Labour Radicalism: 1860-1919" (unpublished Ph.D. thesis, University of Western Ontario, 1973), pp. 103-18; King diary, 1901, p. 276.

54. Shaughnessy Papers, PAC Shaughnessy to William Whyte, December 10, 1908.

55. *Answers* (London, England), April 23, 1910; IB, 594511, No. 4.

56. *Royal Commission ... of Italian Labourers*; Montreal *Star*, June 1, 1904; *Debates*, 1904, pp. 7898.

57. IB, 686314, Dr. Freyesleben to Oliver, June 28, 1907.

58. *Ibid.*, testimony of Franciszek Wlodzniski of Sokal, Galicia; *ibid.*, copy of agreement issued by Davis & Nagel Company to Carl Ditnar, May 4, 1907. IB, 686314, "Report of Immigration Inspector Henry Stanford to W.D. Scott," November 14, 1907.

59. *Ibid.*, testimony of Max Rabin, enclosed in letter sent by Dr. Freyesleben to Oliver, June 28, 1907, *ibid.*, Edward Bayley, to Colonel A.P. Sherwood, commissioner of the Dominion Police, August 13, 1907; *ibid.*, W.W. Cory to J.J. Foy, Ontario Attorney General, September 27, 1907.

60. Diary of Mr. Angus Bell (Lakehead University) of the contracting firm of Bell & McMillan, sub-contractors on the Foley, Welsh & Stewart portion of the National Transcontinental in 1913 between Cochrane and Harriganaw River, Quebec.

61. Statistics tabulated from SP, 1913, No. 36, "Report of the Deputy Minister of Labour," p. 72; Edmund Bradwin, *The Bunkhouse Man* (Toronto, 1972), pp. 153, 200, 212.

62. The Department of Labour had the responsibility of enforcing the Fair Wages Regulation of 1900 which imposed minimum standards on employers who were receiving federal subsidies. As a private company, the CPR was not covered by these regulations and on at least one occasion Thomas Shaughnessy expressed surprise at the "exorbitant money" the company doctors were charging the workers. Edmund Bradwin, *The Bunkhouse Man*, pp. 81, 144-53; SP, 1907, "Report of the Deputy Minister of Labour," pp. 64-67; *Labour Gazette*, July 1912, pp. 40-42; Shaughnessy Papers, Shaughnessy to William Whyte, May 15, 1907.

63. SP, 11912, No. 36, pp. 88-100; IB, 686314, "Report of Henry Stanford to W.D. Scott," November 14, 1907; *Eastern Labour News*, May 24, 1913; Bradwin, *Bunkhouse Man*, p. 234.

64. *Alberta Coal Commission, 1925*, pp. 183, 220-30; W.H.P. Jarvis, *Trials and Tales in Cobalt* (Toronto, 1908), p. 110; Innis, *Mining Frontier*, pp. 320-28.

65. Vernon Jensen, *Lumber and Labour* (New York, 1945), pp. 92-145; Myrtle Bergren, *Tough Timber: The Loggers of B.C. - Their Story* (Toronto, 1966), pp. 24-30, 67-80; *British Columbia Federationist*, June 7, 1918.

66. Statistics tabulated from *Sessional Papers*, 1907-8, No. 25, pt. 2, "Report of the Superintendent of Immigration"; *ibid.*, 1915, No. 25, pt. 2, "Report of the Superintendent of Immigration."

67. W. Burton Hurd, *Racial Origins and Nativity of the Canadian People* (Census Monograph No. 4 (Ottawa, 1937), p. 586; Frontier College Collection (PAC), Twelfth Annual Report.

Chapter Two

1. Oscar Handlin, *The Uprooted* (Boston, 1951), pp. 90-105; John Higham, *Strangers in the Land* (New York, 1966), pp. 50-165.

2. Vera Lysenko, *Men in Sheepskin Coats* (Toronto, 1957), p. 101.

3. Walter Galenson (ed.), *Comparative Labour Movements* (Englewood Cliffs, N.J., 1952); Seymour Lipset and Reinhard Bendix, *Social Mobility in Industrial Society* (Berkeley, 1959); John

Laslett, *Labor and the Left: A Study of Socialists and Radical Influences in the American Labor Movement, 1881-1924* (New York, 1970); Gad Horowitz, *Canadian Labour in Politics* (Toronto, 1968); Martin Robin, *Radical Politics and Canadian Labour 1880-1930* (Kingston, 1968).

4. Gerald Rosenblum, *Immigrant Workers: Their Impact on American Labour Radicalism* (New York, 1973), pp. 60-82, 124-39, 146-67, 175.

5. John Porter, *The Vertical Mosaic* (Toronto, 1966), p. 60.

6. See the Annual Reports of the Immigration Branch, *Sessional Papers* (SP), 1890-1905; John W. Dafoe, *Clifford Sifton in Relation to His Time* (Toronto, 1931), pp. 132-44, 318-23; Norman Macdonald, *Canada: Immigration and Colonization* (Toronto, 1968), pp. 240-80.

7. Toronto, *Empire*, October 2, 1890.

8. Toronto *Mail and Empire*, April 10, 1899. The author has examined some 22 daily newspapers which commented negatively on the influx of Ukrainian immigrants between March and May 1899. See IB, 60868, No. 1.

9. *The Independent* (Vancouver), July 23, 1904.

10. C.A. Magrath, *Canada's Growth and Some Problems Affecting It* (Ottawa, 1910), pp. 53, 71-74; Henry Vivian, "City Planning," Address to the Ottawa Canadian Club, October 22, 1910, *Addresses Delivered before The Canadian Club of Ottawa, 1910* (Ottawa, 1911), pp. 100-8; Dr. Charles Hodgetts, "Unsanitary Housing", *Addresses to the Second Annual Meeting of the Commission on Conservation*, Quebec City, January 17, 1911 (Ottawa, 1911), pp. 32-42; J.S. Woodsworth, *My Neighbour* (Toronto, 1911), pp. 28-156.

11. Annual Report of the Commissioner of the RNWMP, A. Bowen Perry, *Sessional Papers*, 1904-14. This viewpoint was confirmed by the municipal police chiefs, especially at the 1913 annual convention. *Chief Constables Association, Ninth Annual Convention*, Halifax, June 25-27, 1913, IB, 813739, No. 11.

12. Ralph Connor, *The Foreigner* (Toronto, 1909), p. 34.

13. J.S. Woodsworth, *Strangers within Our Gates* (Toronto, 1909), pp. 136, 195, 226; *The Christian Guardian*, September 8, 1909; *ibid.*, July 16, 1913, Handlin, *Uprooted*, p. 94.

14. Joseph Barton, *Peasants and Strangers: Italians, Rumanians and Slovaks in an American City, 1890-1950* (Cambridge, Mass., 1975), pp. 9-77; John Briggs, Italians in Italy and America: A Study of Change and Continuity in Three American Cities 1890-1930 (Ph.D. Thesis, University of Minnesota, 1972), pp.

5-49. Peter Stearnes and Daniel Walkowitz (eds.), *Workers in the Industrial Revolution* (New Brunswick, N.J., 1974), pp. 25-34, 72-82. Thomas Childers, "The Austrian Emigration: 1900-1914," in *Dislocation and Emigration: The Social Background of American Immigration*, Donald Fleming and Bernard Bailyn (eds.), Perspectives in American History, vol. VII (Cambridge, Mass., 1973), pp. 275-375.

15. Childers, *Austrian Emigration*, p. 325; Barton, "Immigration," pp. 16-35.

16. Childers, *Austrian Emigration*, p. 321; Vladimir Kaye, *Early Ukrainian Settlement in Canada* (Toronto, 1964), pp. 5-27, 34, 47-50, 126-33.

17. John S. Macdonald and Leatrice D. Macdonald, "Chain Migration, Ethnic Neighborhood Formation and Social Networks," *Milbank Memorial Fund Quarterly*, 52 (January 1964), pp. 82-97; Charles Tilly and C. Harold Brown, "On Uprooting Kinship, and the Auspices of Migration," *International Journal of Comparative Sociology*, (1967), pp. 138-64.

18. *Ukrainian Rural Settlements, Report of the Bureau of Social Research* (Winnipeg, January 25, 1917), pp. 4-6, 59; Reino Kero, "The Return of Emigrants from America to Finland," Presentation at the Conference on The Finnish Experience in the Western Great Lakes Region: New Perspectives, April 26, 1974.

19. *Report, Royal Commission to Inquire into the Immigration of Italian Labourers to Montreal, and Alleged Fraudulent Practices of Employment Agencies* (Ottawa, 1904), pp. 25, 95, 144. See IB, 686314.

20. Childers, *Austrian Emigration*, p. 362; U.S. Immigration Commission, *Report of the Immigration Commission*, vols. IV, XXXVII (Washington, 1911); Charlotte Erickson, *American Industry and the European Immigrant: 1860-1885* (Cambridge, Mass., 1957), pp. 77-82; Kero, "Return of Emigrants," pp. 16-19.

21. Donald Avery, "Dominion Control over the Recruitment and Placement of Immigrant Industrial Workers in Canada, 1890-1918," unpublished paper presented at the Conference on Canadian Society in the Late Nineteenth Century, January 18, 1975.

22. The Report on the Housing Survey of Certain Selected Areas of Winnipeg, made March and April 1921 (City of Winnipeg Health Department, PAM).

23. Woodsworth, *My Neighbor* (Toronto, 1972), pp. 43-155; George Prpic, *The Croatian Immigrants to America* (New York, 1971), pp. 153-54.

24. A.V. Spada, *Italians in Canada* (Montreal, 1969), pp. 35-128; Project Bay Street (Port Arthur): Sponsored by the Finlandia Club and the Secretary of State, September 1974.

25. M.H. Marunchak, *The Ukrainian Canadians: A History* (Winnipeg, 1970), pp. 99-114; Lysenko, *Sheepskin Coats*, pp. 98-112.

26. Rudolph Vecoli, "Prelates and Peasants: Italian Immigrants and the Catholic Church," *Journal of Social History*, Spring 1969, pp. 217-68.

27. Maurice Neufeld, *Italy: School for Awakening Countries* (New York, 1961), pp. 195-316.

28. Letterbook of the Cristorofo Colombo Society of Trail, British Columbia Constitution (microfilm), PAC.

29. Maranchuk, *Ukrainian Canadians*, pp. 154-73; Bay Street Project; Hyman Berman, "Education for Work and Labor Solidarity: The Immigrant Miners and Radicalism on the Mesabi Range," unpublished manuscript, Immigration Archives, University of Minnesota, pp. 4-20.

30. E.P. Thompson, *The Making of the English Working Class* (New York, 1967); Neil Smelser, *Social Change in the Industrial Revolution; An Application of Theory to the British Cotton Industry* (Chicago, 1959).

31. Clark Kerr and A. Siegel, "The Inter-Industry Propensity to Strike: An International Comparison," in A. Kornhauser *et al.* (eds.), *Industrial Conflict* (New York, 1954), pp. 191-98; Eric Hobsbawm, *Primitive Rebels: Studies in Archaic Forms of Social Protest Movements in the 19th and 20th Century* (Toronto, 1959).

32. Lawrence Schofer, "Patterns of Worker Protest: Upper Silesia, 1865-1914," in Peter Stearnes and Daniel Walkowitz, *Workers in the Industrial Revolution: Recent Studies of Labor in the United States and Europe* (New Brunswick, N.J., 1974), pp. 32; Edward Shorter and Charles Tilly, *Strikes in France, 1830-1968* (London, 1974), p. 16.

33. Shorter and Tilly, *Strikes*, p. 13; John Laslett, *Labor and the Left*, pp. 192-230.

34. Neufeld, *Italy*, pp. 195-257; Sidney Tarrow, *Peasant Communism in Southern Italy* (London, 1967), pp. 12-73, 101-4.

35. Arthur May, *The Hapsburg Monarchy, 1867-1914* (Cambridge, Mass., 1960), pp. 223-25; Arthur Whiteside, *Austrian National Socialism before 1918* (The Hague, 1962), pp. 42, 78-88; Richard Pipes, *Social Democracy and the St. Petersburg Labor movement, 1885-1897* (Cambridge, Mass., 1963), pp. 1-16; 95-105.

36. Berman, "Immigrant Miners," pp. 15-45; J. Donald Wilson

"Matti Kurikka: Finnish-Canadian Intellectual," *BC Studies*, No. 20 (Winter 1973-74), pp. 50-66. Martha Isobel Allen, "A Survey of Finnish Cultural, Economic and Political Development in the Sudbury District of Ontario" (unpublished MA thesis, University of Western Ontario, 1954), pp. 7-35.

37. Pipes, *Social Democracy*, p. 1.

38. Berman, "Immigrant Miners, pp. 21-55; David Brody, *Labor in Crisis: The Steel Strike of 1919* (New York, 1965), pp. 40-43.

39. IB, 801181, Constable Carvan to Colonel Sherwood, Commissioner of the Dominion Police, July 9, 1908.

40. Royal Canadian Mounted Police Records (hereafter RCMP Records) PAC, 321, Sergt. W.J. Redmond to Inspector Davidson.

41. *Ibid.*, vol. 1605, Sergt. Piper to Supt. Primrose, September 24 and 28, 1907.

42. CPR, Sir Thomas Shaughnessy Papers, Letterbook 75, Shaughnessy to Jerome Internocia, Acting Consul General for Italy, July 28, 1901.

43. *Royal Commission ... Italian Labourers* (1904), pp. 58-60.

44. Captain C. Wetherall, Stipendiary Magistrate to H.H. Killaly, Assistant Engineer, Board of Works, March 26, 1844 cited in Ruth Bleasdale, Irish Labourers on the Cornwall, Welland and Williamsburg Canals in the 1840's" (MA thesis, University of Western Ontario, 1975), p. 59.

45. Ely Culbertson, *Strange Lives of One Man: An Autobiography* (Chicago, 1940), p. 273.

46. Eggleston (Edmonton, 1955), p. 66.

47. C. Kerr and A. Siegel, "The Inter-Industry Propensity to Strike: An International Comparison", in A. Kornhauser *et al.* (eds.), *Industrial Conflict* (New York, 1954), pp. 191-93.

48. Lysenko, *Sheepskin Coats*, p. 53.

49. Peter Friedlander, *The Emergence of an U.A.W. Local, 1936-1939: A Study of Class and Culture* (Pittsburg, 1975); Jean Morrison, "Community and Conflict: A Study of the Working Class and Its Relationships at the Canadian Lakehead, 1903-1913" (MA thesis, Lakehead University, 1974), pp. 9-69.

50. *Report of a Preliminary and General Social Survey of Fort William* (1913), pp. 5-24; Directed by the Department of Temperance and Moral Reform of the Methodist Church and the Board of Social Service and Evangelism of the Presbyterian Church, pp. 5-24.

51. Morrison "Working Class," pp. 70-76.

52. Port Arthur *Daily News*, October 1, 1906.

53. Morrison, "Working Class," pp. 76-85; Department of National Defence Papers, PAC, 363-17, Report Colonel S.B. Steele, DOC, Military District #10, to Secretary of the Militia Council, August 12, 1909.

54. Melvyn Dubofsky, *We Shall Be All: A History of the Industrial Workers of the World* (Chicago, 1969), pp. 4-35; A.R. McCormack, "The Industrial Workers of the World in Western Canada: 1905-1914," Canadian Historical Association, *Historical Papers*, 1975, pp. 167-91.

55. McCormack, "Industrial Workers"; Wayne State, IWW Records, Vol. 24-17, Louis Moreau to Fred Thompson, March 8, 1967. Peter Stearnes, *Revolutionary Syndicalism and French Labor: A Cause without Rebels* (New Brunswick, N.J., 1971), pp. 25, 105.

56. SP, 1912, no. 36, Department of labour, pp. 88-100; Donald Avery, "Canadian Immigration Policy and the 'Foreign Navvy', 1896-1914," *Historical Papers*, Canadian Historical Association, 1972, pp. 147-50.

57. *British Columbia Federationist* (Vancouver) April 5, 1912; *ibid.*, June 8, 1912.

58. Moreau to Thompson.

59. Montreal *Witness*, April 2, 1912; IB, 594511, No. 5, Donald Mann to Robert Rogers, August 26, 1912; *ibid.*, Memorandum, Office of the Minister of the Interior to W.W. Cory, Deputy Minister, April 2, 1912; *The Labour Gazette*, August, 1912, p. 191.

60. Calgary *Herald*, April 4, 1912; Edmonton *Journal*, April 5, 1912; Vancouver *Sun*, April 8, 1912.

61. McCormack, "Industrial Workers."

62. Department of Labour, *Strikes and Lockouts*, vols. 558-61, J.D. McNiven to Gerald Brown, Assistant Deputy Minister of Labour, August 20, 1912; Vincent St. John to Minister of Labour, August 6, 1912.

63. McCormack, "Industrial Workers"; Paul Phillips, *No Power Greater* (Vancouver, 1967), pp. 52-58.

64. Vernon Jensen, *Heritage of Conflict* (New York, 1968), pp. 245-49; Charles McMillan, Trade Unions in District 18, 1900, (MA thesis, University of Alberta, 1969), pp. 103-20; Western Federation of Miners' Collection, (WFM), University of British Columbia, vols. 151-58, *passim*.

65. McMillan, *Trade Unions*, pp. 86-88; Phillips, *No Power Greater*, p. 57.

66. Proceedings of the Annual Convention of District 18 of the UMW of A. (Glenbow Archives) 1910, pp. 60-72; *ibid.*, 1911, pp.

17-42; *ibid.*, 1912, pp. 9-16, 28-46, 62-74.

67. R.C. Clute, "Commission on Mining Conditions in British Columbia: Evidence," typescript, 1899, *passim.*

68. "Proceedings ... Convention of 1912", p. 55.

69. *Ibid.*, p. 84.

70. *Ibid.*, p. 51.

71. *Ibid.*, pp. 60, 310, 320; WFM Collection, vol. 160, A. Shillard, Secretary Treasurer to Membership, February 23, 1911; *Dominion Law Reports*, vol. 8, 1913 (Toronto, 1913), p. 264. The case was argued before the Privy Council by Joseph Martin of Vancouver and L.P. Eckstein of Fernie.

72. M.I.A. Bulmer "Sociological Models of the Mining Community," *Sociological Review*, 1975, pp. 64-81.

73. "Proceedings ... Convention of 1912", pp. 9-20, 65-80.

74. Victor Greene, *The Slavic Community on Strike: Immigrant Labor in Pennsylvania Anthracite* (Notre Dame, 1968), pp. 50-121, 207-16; "Proceedings ... Convention of 1911," pp. 8-17.

75. RCMP Records, file 790, translation of letter, enclosed letter Inspector E.J. Camies to Supt. J.O. Wilson, "K Division," April 7, 1906.

76. *Ibid.*, Supt. Wilson to Comm. Perry, May 2, 1906.

77. "Proceedings ... Convention of 1912," pp. 27, 38, 67-69; Joseph Kirschbaum, *Slovaks in Canada* (Toronto, 1967), pp. 68-75.

78. WFM Collection, vol. 160, James Roberts, Secretary to the Membership, February 19, 1912.

79. The IWW also attempted made to organize workers in the rapidly expanding lumber industry, especially in British Columbia and northern Ontario. The problems were, however, more formidable. Camps were smaller and less stable, and owners adept at the blacklisting of Wobbly organizers. Myrtle Bergen, *Tough Timber* (Toronto, 1966), pp. 24-35; Vernon Jensen, *Lumber and Labor* (New York, 1945); A.T. Hill, "The Historical Basis and Development of the Lumber Workers' Organization and Struggles in Ontario" (typescript in possession of the author).

80. Marunchak, *Ukrainian Canadians*, pp. 108-116; *Chervony Prapor* November 15, 1907.

81. Ralph Carter Elwood, *Russian Social Democracy in the Underground: A Study of the RSDRP in the Ukraine, 1907-1914* (Netherlands, 1974), pp. 3, 159, 266; David Lane, *The Roots of Russian Communism: A Social and Historical Study of Russian Social Democracy, 1897-1907* (New York, 1968), pp. 5, 63, 85-134; Yuzyk, *Ukrainians*, pp. 18-20, 96-98.

82. *Chervony Prapor*, November 8, 1907; Lysenko, *Sheepskin Coats*, pp. 110-20; *Robochny Narod*, January 22, 1914.
83. Yuzyk, *Ukrainians*, pp. 96-98; Marunchuk, *Canadian Ukrainians*, pp. 99-160.
84. *Robochny Narod*, January 22, 1914.
85. *Ibid.*, May 6, 1914; *ibid.*, January 8, 1914; *ibid.*, December 12, 1913.
86. *Ibid.*, June 9, 1915; *ibid.*, December 14, 1916. Nadia O.M. Kazymyra, "The Defiant Pavlo Krat and the Early Socialist Movement in Canada," forthcoming in *Canadian Ethnic Studies*. Pavlo Krat was an early example of the Ukrainian Socialist exile.
87. Yuzyk, *Ukrainians*, pp. 96-99; Elwood, *Social Democracy*, pp. 150-62.
88. Ernie Chisick, "Development of Winnipeg's Socialist Movement, 1900-1914" (MA thesis, University of Manitoba, 1972), pp. 87-95; *Manitoba Free Press*, November 25, 1910.
89. *Robochny Narod*, May 6, 1914.
90. Michael Karni (ed.), *For the Common Good* (Superior, Wisconsin, 1977), pp. 10-21, 28-64, 167-94.
A small group of activists in Port Arthur and Sudbury such as A.T. Hill, John Ahlqvist and Arvo Vaara, all of whom had been active in Finnish left wing politics elsewhere, were responsible for the establishment of Finnish Socialist locals between 1908-1911. Bay Street Project; Morrison, "Community and Conflict," pp. 80-110; A.T. Hill, "Historic Basis and Development of the Lumber Workers Organization and Struggles in Ontario," mimeo, in possession of the author.
91. In their own ways Jewish and Italian workers were also drawn into various forms of collective protest and political action in Canada. For example, in 1906 a local of the Jewish Socialist Party was established in Winnipeg. Although Italian workers did not establish a socialist organization as such in Canada they were subscribers to American radical newspapers such as the socialist *La Parola dei Socialisti* (Chicago), the syndicalist *Il Proletario*, and the anarchist *La Questione sociale* (Paterson, New Jersey). Edwin Fenton, *Immigrants and Labor, A Case Study: Italians and American Labor, 1870-1920* (New York, 1975), pp. 120-200; IB, 761900, A.D. Stewart to W.D. Scott, March 4, 1908.
Moses Rischin, "The Jewish Labor Movement in America", *Labor History*, 4, 3 (1963), pp. 227-47; Melvyn Dubofsky, "Organized Labor and the Immigrant in New York City, 1900-1918," *Labor History*, 4, 2, (1961), pp. 182-201; Chisick, Socialist Movement, pp. 54-57.

92. Melvyn Dubofsky, "The Origins of Western Working Class Radicalism, 1890-1905", in Stearnes and Walkowitz, *Workers in the Industrial Revolution*, pp. 390-92; Gerald Rosenblum, *Immigrant Workers*, pp. 60-82, 146-75.

93. Michael Piva, "The Decline of the Trade Union Movement in Toronto, 1900-1915," Paper Presented at the Canadian Historical Association Conference, 1975; Peter Stearnes, "National Character and European Labour History," in Stearnes and Walkowitz (eds.), *Workers in the Industrial Revolution*, p. 15.

94. Tamara Hareven, "The Laborers of Manchester, New Hampshire, 1912-22: The Role of Family and Ethnicity in Adjustment to Industrial Life," *Labor History*, vol. 16, 2 (1975), pp. 249-65.

95. Bulmer, "Sociological Models," pp. 64-72; Jorgen Dahlie, "Socialist and Farmer: Ole Hjelt and the Norwegian Radical Voice in Canada, 1908-1928," forthcoming in *Canadian Ethnic Studies*.

96. During the 1910 Session of the House of Commons the member for West Huron, E.L. Lewis, introduced a private members bill calling for the restriction of immigration from the area of Europe south of 44° north latitude and east of 20° east longitude in order to prevent Canada from becoming "a nation of organ grinders and banana sellers," *Debates*, 1909-10, p. 3134; *ibid.*, 1914, p. 140.

97. IB, 800111, J.H. Ashdown to Frank Oliver, April 9, 1908.

Chapter Three

1. A.R. McCormack, "The Origins and Extent of Western Canadian Labour Radicalism: 1860-1919" (unpublished Ph.D. thesis, University of Western Ontario, 1973); *Labour Gazette*, pp. 820-21, pp. 286-332.

2. Public Archives of British Columbia, Richard McBride Papers, PABC, Box 166, P. Wathner, provincial secretary, to McBride, September 10, 1914; *ibid.*, Report of December 18, 1914; *ibid.*, City reveiver, Sandon B.C., to provincial secretary, December 15, 1914.

3. *Robotchny Narod* (RN) March 14, 1914; On November 12, 1913 the *Guardian* reported that over three thousand Bulgarian navvies had returned to Europe during the fall of that year.

4. *Fifth Census of Canada*, 1911 (Ottawa, 1913), vol. II, p. 367; *Canadian Annual Review* (CAR), 1915, p. 353.

5. *Revised Statutes of Canada*, 1927, Chapter 206, vol. IV, pp. 1-3; *Canadian Gazette*, August 15, 1914. Sir Robert Borden

Papers, (BP), PAC, 56666, C.H. Cahan to C.J. Coherty, Sept. 14, 1918.

6. Major General W.D. Otter, *Internment Operations*, 1914-20 (Ottawa, September 30, 1920), pp. 2, 6, 12; CAR, 1916, p. 433.

7. CAR, 1916, p. 433; Joseph Boudreau, "The Enemy Alien Problem in Canada, 1914-1921" (unpublished Ph.D. thesis, University of California, 1964), pp. 50-103.

8. *The Canadian Ruthenian*, August 1, 1914.

9. *Ibid.*, August 8, 1914; Department of Militia and Defence Headquarters (hereafter DND), file C-965 #2, Report, Agent J.D. Sisler, August 9, 1914. There were numerous other reports in this file.

10. Some of the strongest support for internment camps came from prominent citizens in heterogeneous communities. In Winnipeg, for example, J.A.M. Aikins, a prominent Conservative, warned that the city's enemy aliens might take advantage of the war "for the destruction of property, public and private". BP, 106322, Aikins to Borden, November 12, 1914.

11. *Canadian Mining Journal*, August 15, 1914.

12. IB, 775789, T.D. Willans, travelling immigration inspector to W.D. Scott, June 9, 1915; D.H. McDougall, general manager, Dominion Iron and Steel Corporation, May 29, 1915.

13. *The Northern Miner* (Cobalt) October 9, 1915; Car, 1915, p. 355; DND, file 965, No. 9, Major E.J. May to Colonel E.A. Cruickshank, district officer in command of military district #13, June 28, 1915.

14. W.D. Otter, Internment Operations, pp. 6-12; Arthur Meighen Papers (PAC), 106995, Meighen to Borden, September 4, 1914. The European dependents of these alien workers obviously had to live on even less because after August 1914 it was unlawful to send remittances of money out of the country. Chief Press Censor, 196, Livesay to Chambers, December 4, 1915.

15. British Columbia Provincial Police (BCPP), file 1355-7, John Simpson to Chief Constable of Greenwood to Colin Campbell, supt. of the BCPP, Jan. 26, 1916.

16. IB, 29490, No. 4, W. Banford, Dominion immigration officer to W.D. Scott, May 13, 1915; McBride Papers, McBride to Premier Sifton (Alta.), June 30, 1915. About 20,000 Canadian troops had also been used in gathering the harvest during 1915.

17. IB, 29490, No. 6, W.D. Scott "Circular Letter to Canadian Immigration Agents in the United States," August 2, 1916.

18. Sir Joseph Flavelle Papers (PAC), 74, Scott to Flavelle, director of imperial munitions, August 11, 1916; IB, 29490, No. 6, J.

Frater Taylor, president of Algoma Steel to Flavelle, August 17, 1917. The number of American Immigrants entering the country was 41,779 in 1916 and 65,739 in 1917.

19. *British Columbia Federationist*, January 18, 1918; *Vancouver Sun*, February 7, 1918.

20. IB, 75789, A. Macdonald, Employment Agent, Dominion Coal Company to Scott, July 25, 1916.

21. CAR, 1918, p. 330; *ibid.*, 1916, pp. 325-28; *Statutes of Canada*, 9-10 Geo. V, xciii. The reaction of the Trades and Labor Congress to the treatment of enemy alien workers varied. On one hand they endorsed the "patriotic" dismissals in 1915, and supported the scheme to relocate enemy aliens on homesteads on the uncultivated lands of New Ontario. In June 1916, however, the congress executive, concerned over the possibility that the Dominion government intended to use large numbers of enemy aliens in the mines of Northern Ontario, strongly protested the practice of utilizing forced labour. *Proceedings of the Thirty-first Annual Session of the Trades and Labor Congress of Canada* (1915), pp. 16-17; *ibid.*, 1916, p. 43.

22. Otter, *Internment Operations*, pp. 9-14; Secretary of State papers (PAC), Internment Operation Section, file 5330, No. 7, Major Dales, Commandant Kapuskasing to Otter, November 14, 1918; Desmond Morton "Sir William Otter and Internment Operations in Canada During The First World War", (March 1974), pp. 32-58.

23. BP, 43110, Mark Workman to Borden, December 19, 1918; *ibid.*, 43097, Borden to A.E. Blount, July 1, 1918.

24. CAR, 1915, p. 354; Internment Operation Papers, Otter to F.L. Wanklyn, CPR, June 12, 1916.

25. A.R. McCormack, *Labour Radicalism*, pp. 362-76; Martin Robin, *Radical Politics and Canadian Labour, 1880-1930* (Kingston, 1968), pp. 138-39.

26. *Robotchny Narod*, August 19, 1914; *ibid.*, April 21, 1915; *ibid.*, December 12, 1916.

27. On June 23, 1915, the *Robotchny Narod* reported that 14 members of the Ukrainian Social Democratic Party had been arrested at Fernie and another 28 at Michel.

28. *Ibid.*, June 16, 1915.

29. *Ibid.*, July 10, 1916; *ibid.*, November 7, 1917; *ibid.*, July 11, 1917.

30. *Ibid.*, June 23, 1915; Paul Krat was one of the leading organizers of the party until 1917 when he was expelled for "deviant behaviour."

31. *Ibid.*, March 25, 1917. The Ukrainian Social Democrats strongly endorsed the Bolshevik cause; in November 1917, for example, the "First All Ukrainian Workers Convention" in Winnipeg sent official greetings to the Soviets. It was significant, however, that one important aspect of the USDP support was the belief that the Bolsheviks would ensure self determination for the Ukraine. RN, November 7, 1917.

32. *Ibid.*, July 25, 1917; *ibid.*, August 1, 1917.

33. Chief Press Censor, PAC, 144-A-2, Chambers to W.H. Maxwell, translation officer, Postmaster General, New York, August 10, 1917; Livesay to Chambers March 7, 27, 1916.

34. Censor, Chambers to Fred Livesay, Western press censor, February 7, 1916; McCormack, *Labour Radicalism*, pp. 432-62. In April 1917, Leon Trotsky, one of the heroes of the October Revolution, had been temporarily interned in Nova Scotia while on his way back to Russia. He was, however, released after the Kerensky government exerted pressure on the British authorities. Rodney, *International*, p. 17; DND, C-2051, Major-General Fiset, deputy minister of defence to deputy minister of marine, December 18, 1917; *ibid.*, Walter Long, British Colonial Secretary to Governor-General, Duke of Connaught, May 23, 1918.

35. Melvyn Dubofsky, *We Shall Be All: A History of the Industrial Workers of the World* (Chicago, 1969), pp. 314-15; IB, 917093, No. 1, W.D. Scott to T.G. Winter, Minnesota Commission of Public Safety, July 16, 1917; *ibid.*, Bruce Walker, Winnipeg commissioner to Scott, August 2, 1917.

36. DND, file 2102, Major General Fiset to W.D. Scott, August 26, 1918; Borden papers, 56617, Colonel Sherwood, commissioner of the Dominion Police to minister of justice, March 19, 1918.

37. Department of Justice, 1918, file 934, registrar of alien enemies, Kamloops to Sherwood, June 19, 1918; BP 56629, R. Allen, special agent, Hollinger Consolidated Mines to Sherwood, April 8, 1918.

38. BP, 123189, W.F. Langworth to J.J. Garrick, March 14, 1917. IB, 917722, Fred Hardy, secretary IWW Recruiting Union to Bruno Kaario, May 27, 1918.

39. Thomas Crerar Papers (Douglas Library, Queen's University), A. Murray to Crerar, October 5, 1917; BP, 126353, A.E. Boyle Secretary, Winnipeg Board of Trade to Borden, October 5, 1917.

40. Canadian Pacific Railway Records (hereafter CPR Records), Glenbow Institute, file 518, T.W. Crothers to P.L. Naismith, to

Sir Augustus Nanton, November 3, 1916; BP, 120385, Report, Inspector Tuckin to officer commanding D Division, October 4, 1917; *ibid.*, 120421, Arthur Meighen to Borden, February 9, 1918.

41. BP, 120361, W.A. Wood, President of the Vallance Coal Company, Alta., to Borden, May 16, 1917; *Building Bulletin*, (Winnipeg), August 15, 1918.

42. DND, C-2665, Major-General Ketchen, officer commanding Military District 10, to secretary of the Militia Council, July 7, 1917; Justice papers, 1919, file 2059, registrar of alien enemies, Winnipeg, to Colonel Sherwood, August 17, 1918.

43. BP, 56656, C.H. Cahan to Borden July 20, 1918; *ibid.*, 56668, Cahan to Borden, September 14, 1918.

44. CPC, 144-A-2, Chambers to secretary of state, September 20, 1918.

45. BP, 56668, Cahan to Borden, September 14, 1918. The fourteen illegal organizations also included the IWW, the Group of Social Democrats of Anarchists, the Chinese Nationalist League, and the Social Democratic Party; although the later organization was removed from the list in November 1918. BP, 56698, Cahan to Borden, October 21, 1918.

46. William Rodney, *Soldiers of the International: A History of the Communist Party of Canada, 1919-1929* (Toronto, 1968), pp. 7-19; CPC, 147-A, Colonel Chamber to H. Wolafsky (Eagle Publishing Co.), March 3, 1919.

47. *Statutes of Canada* (1919), 9-10 Geo. V, pp. 1xxi-1xxiii; Borden Papers, 48169, C.H. Cahan to Borden, October 29, 1918.

48. Censor, 144-A-1, Chambers to Major-General Ketchen, October 3, 1918; *Western Labor News*, (Wpg.) October 5, 1918. There was a considerable regional difference in the severity of the sentences imposed on aliens found guilty under PC 2381 and PC 2384. In industrial communities such as Port Arthur, Sault Ste. Marie, and Winnipeg the radical aliens received heavy fines ($2,000-$5,000) and/or long prison sentences (three to five years). BP, 60974, Memorandum, solicitor general to minister of justice, May 23, 1919.

49. *Western Labor News*, December 28, 1918; Mounted Police Records (Headquarters files) on the Winnipeg Strike, Vol. 7, R.B. Russell to Joseph Knight, December 10, 1918.

50. OBU Collection (Manitoba Archives), W. Yates to A.S. Wells, December 11, 1917; Midgely to D. Thompson, December 27, 1918.

51. James Eayrs, *In Defence of Canada: From the Great War to the*

Great Depression (Toronto, 1967), p. 30.

52. *Winnipeg Telegram*, January 28, 1919.

53. Internment Operations, file 6712, Major-General Otter to acting minister of justice, Dec. 19, 1918; Justice Records, 1919, vol. 227, Report, chief commissioner Dominion Police for director of public safety, November 27, 1918.

54. BP, 83163, Sir Thomas White to Borden, February 3, 1919. On February 28, 1919 the German government lodged an official complaint with British authorities over "the reported plan of the Canadian government to deport all Germans from Canada." IB, 912971, Swiss ambassador, London, England to Lord Curzon, February 28, 1919.

55. DND, C-2817 (2), comptroller, RNWMP to Lieutenant Colonel Davis, April 7, 1919; *ibid.*, comptroller to Davis, May 14, 1919.

56. *Vancouver Sun*, March 26, 1919; Mathers Royal Commission on Industrial Relations, "Evidence," Sudbury hearings, May 27, 1919, testimony of J.L. Fortin, p. 1923, Department of Labour Library.

56. *Montreal Gazette*, June 14, 1919.

58. In April 1918 an amendment to the Dominion Land Act denied homestead patents to non-naturalized residents; the subsequent amendments to the Naturalization Act in June 1919 also made it extremely difficult for enemy aliens to become naturalized. Justice Papers, 1919, file 2266, Albert Dawdron, acting commissioner of the Dominion Police, to the minister of justice, July 28, 1919. *Statutes of Canada*, 1918, 9-10 Geo. V, c. 19, s. 7; *Debates*, 1919, pp. 4118-33.

59. Censor, 196-1, E. Tarak to Chambers, January 11, 1918 (translation).

60. IB, 963419, W.D. Scott to James A. Calder, minister of immigration and colonization, December 11, 1919; *Toronto Telegram*, April 1, 1920; Meighen Papers, 000256, J.A. Stevenson to Meighen, February 24, 1919; *Canadian Ruthenian*, February 5, 1919.

61. Mathers Royal Commission, "Evidence," Victoria hearings, testimony of J.O. Cameron, president of the Victoria Board of Trade; *ibid.*, Calgary hearings, testimony of W. Henderson; *ibid.*, testimony of Mortimer Morrow, manager of Canmore Coal Mines.

62. Censor, 292, Cahan to Sir Thomas White, January 7, 1919; *ibid.*, W.E. Playfair, memorandum to Chambers, February 11, 1919.

63. DND, C-2051, Major-General Gwatkin to Cahan, January 4, 1919.

64. A.T. Hill Memoirs (in possession of the author); OBU Collection, J.W. Ahlqvist circular letter, March [?], 1919.

65. *Ukrainian Labor News*, July 12, 1919; DND, C-2665, Agent's Report to Commissioner Perry NWMP, May 22, 1919. *The Ukrainian Labor News* began publication in March 1919, with Matthew Popovich as editor.

66. Meighen Papers, 00519, Report, supt. E. Division (B.C.) to Commissioner Perry, May 7, 1919.

67. BP, 62036, comptroller, RNWMP to George Yates, secretary to Borden, June 19, 1919; DND, C-2051, Lieutenant Colonel A.F. Hamilton, director of cable censorship, to Chambers, February 13, 1919.

68. "Proceedings of District 18 of the United Mine Workers of America Conference, February 1919" (Glenbow Institute), typescript.

69. Robin, *Radical Politics*, pp. 170-80.

70. *District Ledger* (Fernie), April 26, 1919; OBU Collection, Midgley to H. Blac, May 13, 1919; *ibid.*, list of contributors, Cumberstone Local of UMWA; Anne Waywitka, "Drumheller Strike of 1919," *Alberta Historical Review* (Winter 1973), pp. 1-6.

71. *Ukrainian Labor News*, May 10, 1919.

72. OBU Collection, Carl Berg (Edmonton) to Midgley, April 24, 1919; *ibid.*, Midgley to Berg, April 28, 1919.

73. DND, file 3042, General Godson-Godson to General Gwatkin, May 10, 1919; Justice Records, 1919, file 113, A.A. Mc, comptroller, to deputy minister of justice, January 14, 1919.

74. Royal Canadian Mounted Police Records, Criminal Investigation Branch (PAC), R.J. Mansfield, secretary, Alien Investigation Branch, to Commissioner Perry, February 26, 1919; *ibid.*, E.L. Newcombe, deputy minister of justice, to A.L. Cawdron, acting commissioner of the Dominion Police, March 15, 1919.

75. DND, C-2665, Major General Leckie, officer commanding British Columbia, to Major General Ashton, April 26, 1919; *ibid.*, C-2817, Major A.E. Jukes to Lieutenant Colonel Davis, May 9, 1919.

76. *Ibid.*, C-2817, A.E. Jukes to Davis, May 3, 1919.

77. Alan Artibise, *Winnipeg: A Social History of Urban Growth, 1874-1914* (Montreal, 1975), pp. 223-45; *Manitoba Free Press*, November 3, 1918.

78. RN, August 1, 1917; *ibid.*, February 20, 1918.

79. DND, C-2665, Secret Agent No. 47, Report (Wpg.), to Supt. Starnes, RNWMP, March 24, 1919.

80. RCMP Records, Blumenburg Deportation Inquiry, July 15, 1919, testimony of Albert Reames, Secret Agent, RNWMP, p. 37; *Winnipeg Telegram*, January 29, 1919.

81. OBU Collection, R.B. Russell to Victor Midgley, January 29, 1919.

82. *Manitoba Free Press*, May 7, 1919; *Western Labor News*, April 4, 1919. The Alien Investigation Board was legitimized by the passage of Order-in-Council PC 56 in January 1919 which transferred authority to investigate enemy aliens and to enforce PC 2381 and PC 2384 from the Dominion Department of Justice to the provincial attorney general. Between February and May the board processed approximately 3,000 cases; of these 500 were denied certificates. RCMP Records, Comptroller to Commissioner Perry, March 20, 1919; *Manitoba Free Press*, May 7, 1919.

83. Meighen Papers, 000279, D.A. Ross to Meighen, April 9, 1919.

84. D.C. Masters, *The Winnipeg General Strike* (Toronto, 1959), pp. 40-50; David Bercuson, *Confrontation at Winnipeg* (Montreal, 1974), pp. 103-95.

85. Murray Donnelly, *Dafoe of the Free Press* (Toronto, 1968), p. 104; RCMP Records, 1919, vol. I, Major-General Ketchen to secretary of the Militia Council, May 21, 1919; *The Citizen* (Wpg.), June 5-20, 1919.

86. *Manitoba Free Press*, May 22, 1919.

87. Bercuson, *Confrontation at Winnipeg*, pp. 125-68; *Western Labor News*, Special Strike Edition No. 19, June 7, 1919.

88. RCMP Collection, 1919, vol. II, Special Agent W.H. McLaughlin to Supt. Stearnes, June 14, 1919. Similar trends were evident in Edmonton and Calgary. Borden Papers, OC, File 564, No. 2, Report, RNWMP supt., District 7 (Alberta).

89. BP, 61936 Gideon Robertson to F.A. Acland, deputy minister of labour, June 14, 1919.

90. P.M. Christophers, president of District 18 actually suggested "a general strike throughout the West" if the Dominion government sent troops into Winnipeg. OBU Collection, Christophers to Midgley, May 19, 1919.

91. BP, 61913, Robertson to Borden, June 14, 1919.

92. Diary of Sir Robert Borden, June 13-17; RCMP, CIB, vol. 70, J.A. Calder, to Commissioner Perry, June 16, 1919; IB, 961162, Calder to Perry, June 17, 1919.

93. Masters, *Winnipeg Strike*, pp. 100-5.

94. Tom Moore to E. Robinson, June 24, 1919 cited by *Manitoba Free Press*, November 21, 1919; Borden Diary, June 20,

1919; *The Canadian Railroader*, June 29, 1919; BP 61936, Robertson to Acland, June 14, 1919.

95. *Manitoba Free Press*, June 18, 1919; BP 62012, Andrews to Meighen, June 18, 1919.

96. *Ukrainian Labor News*, July 16, 1919; Norman Penner (ed.), *Winnipeg: 1919: The Strikers' Own History of the Winnipeg General Strike* (Toronto, 1973), pp. 175-81.

97. *Manitoba Free Press*, July 2, 1919; *Ukrainian Labor News*, July 14, 1910.

98. RCMP Collection I, Supt. Starnes to Comm. Perry, May 27, 1919; Almazoff hearings, August 16; Blumenberg hearings, August 15; Charitinoff hearing, August 15; Schoppelrie hearing, July 18.

99. RCMP, Criminal Investigation Branch CIB, vol. 70. Perry to Supt., Lethbridge District, July 5, 1919; *Manitoba Free Press*, September 21, 1919.

100. IB, 912971, No. 3, T.J. Murray, Telegram to J.A. Calder, October 30, 1919; Justice Records, 1919, file 1960, deputy minister of justice, to Murray and Noble, November 5, 1919.

101. DND, C-2817, Major Jukes to Lieutenant Davis, September 6, 1919; British Columbia Loggers Association Minute Book, August 8, 1919 (UBC Archives); *ibid.*, December 12, 1919.

102. Western Coal Operators' Association (Glenbow Institute), W.R. Wilson, president of the Crow's Nest Coal Company to W. McNeill, president of the Western Coal Operators Association; *ibid.*, Samuel Ballantyne, chairman of the UMWA International Commission to McNeill, September 2, 1919; OBU, George Dingwall, Rossland, B.C., to Midgley, May 20, 1919.

103. WCOA Collection, F. Scaltritti to Coal Commissioner W.H. Armstrong, September 13, 1919; *ibid.*, D.H. Quigley, manager, North American Collieries, to McNeill, October 4, 1919.

104. *Ukrainian Labor News*, October 29, 1919.

105. In October 1918 the United States Congress had passed an amendment to the "Act to Exclude and Expel from the United States Aliens Who Are Members of the Anarchist and Similar Classes"; Emma Goldman, Alexander Berkman and 247 other "Reds" were deported to Russia under this measure in December 1919. John Higham, *Strangers in the Land* (New York, 1966), p. 308-24; IB, 961162, No. 1, F.C. Blair, secretary of immigration and colonization, memorandum to J.A. Calder November 4, 1919; *ibid.*, John Clark, American Consul-General, Montreal, to F.C. Blair, June 19, 1920.

106. *Ibid.*, A.J. Cawdron to supt. of immigration, June 24, 1919;

ibid., assistant director, CIB, RCMP, to F.C. Blair, August 4, 1920.

107. Rodney, *Soldiers of the International*, pp. 29-31; interview with John Boychuk (Glendon College, York University). IB, 563236, commissioner of Border Chamber of Commerce, to Scott, August 14, 1919.

108. DND, C-2817 Major General Gwatkin to S.D. Meuburn, minister of militia, August 5, 1919; *ibid.*, J.A. Calder to Sir George Foster.

109. IB, 563236, No. 7, deputy attorney general of Ontario to F.C. Blair, November 6, 1919.

110. Higham, *Strangers in the Land*, pp. 308-24; *Debates*, 1919, pp. 1916, 1969, 228-90.

111. *Industrial Canada*, July 1919, pp. 120-22.

112. Ivan Avakumovic, *The Communist Party in Canada: A History* (Toronto, 1975), pp. 1-53.

113. Governor General's Office (PAC), vol. CIII, "Report of Operative, Intelligence Branch of the United States War Office," cited in C.F. Hamilton, CIB, RCMP to A.F. Sladen, private secretary to governor-general, August 31, 1921.

Chapter Four

1. *Debates*, 1919, pp. 771, 1867-73, 2280-90; CAR, 1919, pp. 503-21.

2. Figures compiled from the *Royal Commission on Bilingualism and Biculturalism*, Book Four (Ottawa, 1968), pp. 238-46; Robert England, *Colonization of Western Canada* (London, 1936), pp. 313-14; *Select Standing Committee on Agriculture and Colonization: Minutes of Proceedings and Evidence and Report*, 1928, Appendix No. 8 (Ottawa, 1928). Hereafter, *Select Committee*, 1928.

3. W. Burton Hurd, "Racial Origins and Nativity of the Canadian People," *Seventh Census of Canada*, 1931, vol. xiii, Monographs (Ottawa, 1942), pp. 537-818; Floyd Alvin Farrar, "Migration and Economic Opportunity in Canada, 1921-1951" (unpublished Ph.D. thesis, University of Pennsylvania, 1962), pp. 20-53; Leonard Marsh, "The Problem of Seasonal Unemployment," unpublished typescript, Research Project No. 22 McGill Social Research Series. Of the 215,978 immigrants from Central and Southern Europe who arrived in Canada between 1925 and 1931 the largest numbers were Ukrainians (57,657) Poles (30,649), Hungarians (28,624), Jews (22,107), Slovak (19,167), and Italians (11,608); England *Western Canada*, pp 312-13.

4. "An Act to amend an Act of the present session entitled An Act to amend The Immigration Act 1919," *Statutes of Canada*

1919, 9-10 Geo. v, Chap. 26, s. 41.

5. *Ibid.*; IB, 72552, No. 6, F.C. Blair, secretary, Immigration and Colonization (IC), deputy minister, IC, August 11, 1921.

6. "PC 1203, 1919", *Statutes of Canada*, 1919, 9-10 Geo. v, vols. I-II, p. x; George Woodcock and Ivan Avakumovic, *The Doukhobors* (Toronto, 1968) pp. 240-56.

7. Wellington Bridgman, *Breaking Prairie Sod* (Toronto, 1920), p. 256. During the 1920s European immigrants were officially categorized as "preferred" and "non-preferred" immigrants. Not surprisingly, the application of the non-preferred label aroused deep resentment on the part of many European governments. IB, 28885, No. 6, F.C. Blair to J.A. McGill, general agent, CPR, November 21, 1923.

8. *Maclean's Magazine*, August, 1919, pp. 46-49.

9. IB, 651, No. 3, Blair to McFadden & McMillan Lumber Company, Fort William, August 27, 1919.

10. *Ibid.*, 28885, No. 5, Blair to president of Algoma Steel Corporation (Sault Ste. Marie), September 20, 1920.

11. *Sessional Papers* (hereafter SP), 1920, vol. LVI, no. 18, "Annual Report of the Superintendent of Emigration for Canada in London, England, Lt. Colonel J. Obed Smith," pp. 30-32; IB, 2183, No. 2, J. Obed Smith to F.C. Blair, February 28, 1921.

12. IB, 651, No. 3, P.C. Walker, agent for Shepard & Morse Lumber Company to Blair, October 14, 1919.

13. IB, 775789, R.M. Wolvin, President Dominion Steel Corporation to W.R. Little, September 24, 1920.

14. *Canadian Mining Journal* (CMJ), February 25, 1920.

15. Ontario Department of Labour, 1920, "Report of Labour Conditions in Gold and Silver Mining Districts in Northern Ontario, October, 1920"; deputy minister of labour to W.R. Rollo, minister of labour, October 15, 1920; CMJ, October 15, 1920.

16. IB, 594511, C.P. Riddell, general secretary, Railway Association, to Sir George Foster, acting prime minister, February 23, 1920.

17. *Ibid.*, Blair to Riddell, April 9, 1920; *ibid.*, Blair to minister of immigration and colonization, April 22, 1920.

18. *Vancouver Sun*, July 10, 1920; Vancouver *World*, August 17, 1920.

19. Department of Labour, *Annual Report* 1927-28; *Labour Gazette*, December 1920, pp. 1630-34.

20. SP, 1922, vol. XVIII, "Report of the Supt. of Emigration for 1921," pp. 24-25; England, *Western Canada*, pp. 75-90.

21. "PC 183, January 31, 1923," cited in *Select Committee*, 1928, pp. 818-20.

22. *Statutes of Canada*, 1923, 13-14 Geo. V, Chap. 28, Section 5., "Chinese Immigration Act, 1923"; CAR, 1923, pp. 45-46; Toronto *Globe*, August 7, 1923; IB, 9309, *passim*; Patricia Roy, "The Oriental 'Menace' in British Columbia," in *Studies in Canadian Social History* (Toronto, 1974), edited by Michiel Horn and Ronald Sabourin, pp. 287-97.

23. *Annual Departmental Reports* (hereafter ADR), 1924-25, vol. III (Ottawa, 1926).

24. ADR, 1925-26 (Ottawa, 1927), *Report of the Deputy Minister of Labour*, p. 6; *ibid*, *Reports of the Department of Immigration and Colonization*, 1921-29, *passim*.

25. SP, 1914, PC 1028; IB, 785450, M.B. Scarth to W.D. Scott, December 9, 1913. In Ontario there had been 56 convictions for violation of the law between May and December 1914. *Report of the Ontario Commission on Unemployment* (Toronto, 1916), pp. 121-22.

26. CAR, 1918, p. 490.

27. *Debates*, 1918, pp. 841, 1034-38; *Annual Reports of the Department of Labour, Employment Service Branch*, 1921-31, *passim*.

28. Ontario Department of Labour (PAO), Office of the Deputy Minister, L.G. Clarke to J.A. Mille, Toronto, October 21, 1919; Lawrence Fric, "The Role of Commercial Employment Agencies in the Canadian Labour Market" (unpublished Ph.D. thesis, University of Toronto, 1973), pp. 42-68. In 1924 the Trades and Labour Congress called upon the Dominion government "to place amongst the prohibited classes labour hired to replace strikers, or those hired without the sanction of the Employment Service", *Proceedings of the TLC, 1924, p. 42.*

29. *Debates*, 1919, pp. 1870-90; CAR, 1920, pp. 242-45; Reynolds, *British Immigrant*, pp. 50-116; W.G. Smith, *A Study in Canadian Immigration* (Toronto, 1920), pp. 150-85.

30. *The Dafoe-Sifton Correspondence, 1919-27* (Altona, Manitoba, 1966), pp. 41-42, edited by Ramsay Cook. C. Sifton to J.W. Dafoe, November 18, 1920; IB, 28128, No. 4, Blair to W.C. Kennedy, December 7, 1920. England, *Colonization*, pp. 90-98.

31. *Grain Growers' Guide*, December 23, 1925; Hurd, "Racial Origins", pp. 708-15. Reynolds, *British Immigrants*, 95-98.

32. IB, 2446, No. 8, Egan to Robert Forke, August 2, 1927; *United States Daily*, May 13, 1927. The emigration of Canadian citizens to the U.S.A. averaged about 100,000 a year throughout the 1920s. Howard Palmer, "Nativism and Ethnic Tolerance in Alberta, 1920-1972" (unpublished Ph.D. thesis, York University, 1972) pp. 10-30.

33. Flavelle Papers (Queen's University), Flavelle to Frederick Hyde, Managing Director, Midland Bank, London, England, December 4, 1924. *Industrial Canada* (Toronto), April 26, 1924; *ibid.*, January 7, 1927.

34. *Grain Growers' Guide*, May 4, 1921; England, *Colonization*, pp. 79-87.

35. *Guide*, January 21, 1925; *ibid.*, October 1928. The British and Canadian governments subsidized the transportation costs of British harvesters who came to Canada in the fall of 1923. George Haythorne, "Harvest Labor in Western Canada: An Episode in Economic Planning", *Quarterly Journal of Economics*, 47 (1932), pp. 533-44.

36. John Herd Thompson, *The Harvests of War: The Prairie West 1914-1918* (Toronto, 1978).

37. CNR Colonization Records (hereafter CNR-Col.) PAC, vol. 8486, file 33852, C.W. Peterson to Colonel Dennis, March 23, 1926; CAR, 1922, no. 269.

38. *Canadian Mining Journal*, October 5, 1923.

39. England, *Colonization*, pp. 78-86; ADR, 1924-25, pp. 20-33; King Papers, 71356, W.A. Buchanan to King, December 14, 1923.

40. King Papers, 94824, Beatty and Thornton to King, February 14, 1925.

41. IB, 216882, No. 1, W.J. Egan to Edward Beatty, July 29, 1925; King Papers, 94852, Beatty to King, August 18, 1925; *ibid.*, 94859, Beatty to King, August 18, 1928.

42. *Ibid.*, King to Beatty, August 27, 1925.

43. IB, 94861, 216882, No. 1, F.C. Blair, memorandum, September 10, 1925; James Hedges, *Building the Canadian West* (New York, 1939), pp. 360-90.

44. IB, 216882, No. 1, Blair to Egan, September 10, 1925; IB, 926, No. 2, W.D. Black, director of colonization, CNR, to Blair, March 1, 1926.

45. Calgary *Herald*, April 27, 1925; John Irmie, editor of Edmonton *Journal* to C.A. Macgrath, June 9, 1925 cited in Palmer, "Nativism and Ethnic Tolerance," p. 82. Pro-business service clubs such as the Kiwanis International hailed the agreement as a major step in lifting Canada out of the economic recession. Howard Ferguson Papers (PAO), 1925, Immigration File, E.A. Cunningham, chairman of Kiwanis to Ferguson, October 29, 1925.

46. *Canadian Congress Journal*, June 1922, p. 287.

47. United Church, Board of Home Missions (UCA), file 1, Dr.

C.E. Manning to Egan, November 26, 1925; *Guide*, January 21, 1925; *ibid.*, September 30, 1925.

48. IB, 216882, No. 1, W.J. Egan to J. Bruce Walker, Winnipeg commissioner, October 21, 1925; Egan to J. Robb, minister of immigration, August 26, 1925.

49. Palmer, "Nativism and Ethnic Tolerance," p. 89; Hedges, *Canadian West*, pp. 360-65.

50. Hedges, *Canadian West*, pp. 366-90; CNR-Col., vol. 5629, file 5121-1, W.J. Black to F.J. Freer, CNR, supt. of land settlement, Winnipeg, July 13, 1927; IB, 216882, No. 6, Blair to Egan, October 5, 1927. There was a preponderance of single and unaccompanied males who came out to Canada from continental Europe. In 1926, for example, out of a total of 38,028 immigrants 28,979 or 76% were males; in 1927 the figure was 78%. This trend was especially pronounced among immigrants from Czechoslovakia (92%), Jugo-Slavia (90%), Austria (85%), Lithuania (80%), Poland (78%), Hungary (76%), and Roumania (74%). *Select Committee*, pp. 762-63.

51. D.H. Miller-Barston, *Beatty of the C.P.R.: A Biography* (Toronto, 1951), pp. 50-55; IB, 216882, No. 5, W.J. Black to Blair, May 30, 1927; Hedges, *Canadian West*, pp. 257, 35-55, 361-386; CNR-Col., vol. 842, Johnson to Black, December 2, 1927; *ibid.*, vol. 5629, file 5121-1, F.B. Tomanek, Catholic Czechoslovakian Immigration Society to Black, November 5, 1928.

52. Canadian Pacific Railway Colonization Records (hereafter /CPR-Col.), Glenbow Institute, Calgary, file 740, J. Colley, assistant supt. of colonization, to C.A. Van Scoy, January 9, 1929; *ibid.*, file 682, Colley to Van Scoy, October 7, 1927.

53. *Ibid.*, 1039, Colley to J. Schwartz (labour agent), March 21, 1931; IB, 216882, No. 5, Walter Woods, district supt., Land Settlement Branch, to Major John Barnett, superintendent, May 18, 1927.

54. IB, 216882, No. 6, memorandum F.C. Blair, June 7, 1927.

55. CPR-Col., 1039, Colley to M. Bosworth, November 7, 1930; Miller-Barston, *Beatty of the CPR, pp. 53-65*.

56. IB, 216882, No. 7, Supt. J.G. Rattray, Land Settlement Branch to W.J. Egan January 10, 1928; *ibid.*, No. 10, W.S. Woods to Rattray, January 30, 1929.

57. *Alberta Labor News*, March 27, 1926.

58. Dept. of Labour (Alberta), 1927 files (PAA), Report Provincial Dept. of Labour for Premier Brownlee, March 11, 1927.

59. "P.C. 534, April 8, 1926), cited in *Select Committee on Colonization*, 1928, p. 820, ADR (1926-27), p. 59.

60. IB, 594511, Black to Egan, June 4, 1926.

61. *Ibid.*, Egan to Black, September 7, 1926.

62. IB, 216882, No. 6, Blair to Egan, June 15, 1927.

63. *Ibid.*, No. 3, J.H. McVety, general supt. of Labour Bureau, to A.D. Skinner, division commissioner, December 25, 1926; *ibid.*, No. 5, W.R. Clubb, Manitoba minister of labour, to MacKenzie King, May 25, 1927.

64. *Ibid.*, No. 6, Blair to Egan, June 15, 1927; *ibid.*, Blair to Charles Stewart (Minister of Immigration), May 27, 1927; *Select Committee on Immigration*, 1928, pp. 409-21.

65. CNR, vol. 8386, file 33852, Colonel J.S. Dennis, to Black, February 23, 1926.

66. *Ibid.*, C.W. Peterson to Dennis, March 23, 1926; *ibid.*, Dennis to George Walker CPR Solicitor, Calgary, March 9, 1926.

67. IB, 216882, No. 6, Blair to Robert Forke, minister of immigration, August 1, 1928; *ibid.*, Edward Beatty to Charles Stewart, June 30, 1928; Haythorne, "Harvest Labor in Western Canada," pp. 533-44.

68. IB, 907095, T.W. Bell, chairman, Grand Lodge of British America, Immigration Department, Toronto, to Lodge #1895, Coleman, Alberta, September 12, 1928; Montreal *Star*, August 8, 1928; *Guide*, October 1, 1928.

69. *Proceedings, T.L.C.*, 1928, Resolution of the Ontario Provincial Council of Carpenters (#61). The T.L.C. had also severely criticized the 1923 movement of British Harvesters. King Papers, 76789, Tom Moore to King, Sept. 10, 1923.

70. ADR, 1928, pp. 49-50; IB, 216882, No. 9, W.S. Woods, Supt. of Land Settlement to Col. Rattray, June 5, 1928.

71. IB, 348818, Leask, Saskatchewan, to Blair, June 11, 1928; Toronto *Telegram*, September 13, 1928.

72. CAR, 1928-29, pp. 162-63; MEP, July 18, 1928; *Canadian Congress Journal*, March 1928. Board of Home Missions (UCA), file 7-8, F. Albert Moore, Secretary, United Church of Canada to J.H. Edmison, October 11, 1926; *ibid.*, Moore to Dr. C.E. Manning, April 22, 1927.

73. *Guide*, June 1, 1928.

74. IB, No. 348818, Resolution of the Prince Albert NAC, May 21, 1928. Bennett Papers, 241067, Resolution, Assembly #2, Native Sons of Canada, November, 1930. The *Orange Sentinel* (Toronto) also maintained a fierce anti-alien position as well as charging that Canadian immigration policy was determined by the Roman Catholic hierarchy. *Sentinel*, may 12, 1927; *ibid.*, February 28, 1929.

75. The defeat of the Gardiner government during the 1929 provincial election, largely on religious and immigration issues, did much to force the King government to reassess its immigration policy. Patrick Kyba, "The Saskatchewan General Election of 1929" (unpublished MA thesis, University of Saskatchewan, 1964), p. 23.

76. Saskatoon *Star*, June 5, 1928.

77. Saskatoon *Beacon*, December 28, 1928; *Orange Sentinel*, May 12, 1927; Regina *Star*, January 2, 1929.

78. *Proceedings, T.L.C.*, 1928, pp. 164-68.

79. *Ibid.*

80. *Guide*, May 1, 1928; Resolution, Lethbridge UFA Local, cited in Palmer, "Nativism and Ethnic Tolerance," p. 97

81. Toronto *Globe*, February 9, 1928.

82. *Debates*, 1928, pp. 3924.

83. IB, 216882, No. 8, F. Franke, Austrian consul general, to Forke, August 15, 1928; *ibid.*, No. 10, A.V. Seferovitch, consul general Serbes, Croates and Slovenes, to Forke, June 6, 1929; Albert de Haydin, Hungarian consul general, cited in Calgary *Herald*, August 12, 1927.

84. *Select Committee on Immigration* (1928), pp. 347-48. Sir Henry Thornton was somewhat more cautious, and he admitted that it was not always possible "to make a good Canadian out of the first foreigner" who arrived in Canada; *ibid.*, p. 328.

85. *Ibid.*, pp. 367-407.

86. *Ibid.*, pp. 670-80; Regina *Leader*, November 24, 1927; Ottawa *Citizen*, February 13, 1928.

87. *Select Committee on Immigration* (1928), pp. x-xi.

88. IB, 216882, No. 8, A.L. Jolliffee to Egan, August 14, 1928; Dept. of labour, file 617 (24-2), Egan to H.H. Ward, Deputy Minister of Labour, January 15, 1930.

89. CAR, 1928-29, pp. 158-59; Dept. of Labour, file 617 (24-2); IB, 216882, No. 11, Egan to Stewart, February 19, 1930.

90. CAR, 1929-30, pp. 86, 94-102; IB, 216882, No. 12, W.A. Gordon to Thornton and Beatty, October 31, 1920; Bennett Papers, 241109, W.A. Gordon, letter to the provincial premiers, February 14, 1931.

91. CAR, 1930-31, p. 257; Frank Epp, *Mennonite Exodus: The Rescue and Resettlement of the Russian Mennonites Since the Communist Revolution* (Altona, 1962), pp. 240-300.

92. MFP, January 31, 1930; Bennett Papers, 241142, G.G. Serkav, to Bennett, July 21, 1931.

93. "Annual Review by L.W. Simms, President of the Canadian Manufacturer's Association, *Canadian Manufacturer's Annual*

Meeting, Halifax, June 4-6, 1929, p. 9; *ibid.*, June 2, 1930, Toronto, "Annual Review by President R.J. Hutchings," p. 9.

94. Winnipeg *Tribune*, January 30, 1930; "Votes and Proceedings of the Legislative Assembly of Manitoba, February 3, 1930," Dept. of Labour (file 617) (24-2).

95. Ferguson Papers (PAO), 1930, Ferguson to A.J. Moore, January 6, 1930.

96. Dominion Dept. of Labour, File 617 (24-2) "Minutes of an Interview of Representatives of Certain Municipalities in Ontario, Manitoba, Saskatchewan, Alberta and British Columbia and of the Provincial governments of Manitoba, Saskatchewan, Alberta and British Columbia with the Cabinet, Feb. 26, 1930, Ottawa, March 1, 1930." Bracken Papers (PAM), 1933, City of Winnipeg Unemployment Relief Dept.

97. Montreal *Gazette*, February 4, 1930.

98. CNR-Col. 8386, file 3600-20, manager of Eastern District to Black, December 17, 1929; *ibid.*, Robert England, Winnipeg manager of Colonization, to Black, September 2, 1930; *ibid.*, October 7, 1930.

99. Ontario Department of Labour, 1931, James Gallagher, N. Bay to Minister of Labour, May 12, 1931.

100. *Ibid.*, W.C. Dobbs, supt. of employment agencies, to H.C. Hudson, deputy minister of labour, March 24, 1931.

101. *Ibid.*, Affidavit, John Kostiuk and William Pendryk, Sudbury, March, 1932, enclosed in letter Hudson to Dr. J.D. Monteith, minister, Department of Public Works and Labour, March 9, 1932.

102. Bracken Papers, 1933, "City of Winnipeg Unemployment Relief Report."

103. Henry Blank, "Industrial Relations in Sarnia, Ontario, with Specific Reference to the Holmes Foundry Strike of March, 1937" (unpublished MA thesis, University of Western Ontario, 1975), pp. 115-18; Sarnia *Observer*, May 7, 1932; *ibid.*, February 27, 1933.

104. W.B. Hurd, "Racial Origins," pp. 586, 698, 699, 719.

105. IB, 216882, No. 9, Wasyl Czaban (Mundare, Alberta), enclosed in letter from Woods to Blair, December 13, 1939; Henry Radecki and Benedykt, *A Member of a Distinguished Family: The Polish Group in Canada* (Toronto, 1976), pp. 192-93.

106. Tolmie Papers, UBC, vol. 8, file 8-32, Stephen Raymer, J.P., memorandum to Tolmie, April 7, 1932.

Chapter Five
1. Martin Robin, *Radical Politics and Canadian Labour, 1880-*

1930 (Kingston, 1968); Stuart Jamieson, *Times of Trouble: Labour Unrest and Industrial Conflict in Canada, 1900-66* (Ottawa, 1968), pp. 1-276; David Mitchell, *1919: Red Mirage* (New York, 1970); William Rodney, *Soldiers of the International: A History of the Communist Party of Canada, 1919-1929* (Toronto, 1968); Ivan Avakumovic, *The Communist Party in Canada* (Toronto, 1975); Norman Penner "The Socialist Idea in Canadian Political Thought" (unpublished Ph.D. thesis, University of Toronto, 1975), pp. 136-400.

2. Tom McEwen, *The Forge Glows Red: From Blacksmith to Revolutionary* (Toronto, 1974), pp. 85-137; Tim Buck, *Thirty Years, 1922-1952: The Story of the Communist Movement in Canada* (Toronto, 1952), pp. 1-106; Irving Abella, *Nationalism, Communism and Canadian Labour* (Toronto, 1973), 1-22, 66-85.

3. Paul Yuzuk, *The Ukrainians in Manitoba* (Toronto, 1953), pp. 96-112; William Marunchak, *The Ukrainian Canadians: A History* (Winnipeg, 1970), pp. 356-425; R. Jalkenen, *The Finns in North America: A Social Symposium* (Hancock, Michigan, 1969), pp. 100-223.

4. Nathan Glazer, *The Social Basis of American Communism* (New York, 1961), pp. 13-90; Rodney, *Soldiers of the International*, pp. 81-96, 118-58.

5. Avakumovic, *Communist Party*, pp. 14-71; Buck, *Thirty Years*, pp. 58-102; Penner, "Socialist Idea," pp. 187-90.

6. *Canadian Annual Review* (CAR), 1930-31, pp. 453-55; Buck, *Thirty Years*, pp. 82-139; Michiel Horn, "Keeping Canada 'Canadian'; Anti-Communism and Canadianism in Toronto, 1928-1929," *Canadian Magazine*, vol. 3, No. 1 (September 1975), pp. 35-37.

7. IB, 961162, No. 1 F.C. Blair, secretary, IC, memorandum to C.H. Ireland, secretary, minister, IC, November 24, 1919; *ibid.*, John Clark, American consul general, to Blair, June 19, 1920.

8. IB, 961162, No. 1, A.J. Cawdron, acting chief commissioner RCMP, to Supt. IB, June 24, 1919; *ibid.*, assistant director, CIB unit, RCMP, to Blair, August 4, 1920; *Sessional Papers*, 1923, No. 28 "Annual Report to the Commissioner, RCMP," pp. 12-13.

9. Arthur Meighen Papers (PAC), 018443, Murray Clark to Sir George Foster, July 20, 1920; IB, 917093, A.J. Cawdron to Blair, September 15, 1921.

10. One Big Union Collection (OBU), UBC Archives, Report of the First Annual Convention of the OBU, January, 1920; Department of National Defence Records (DND), PAC, file 44721, Report Agent, April 9, 1920; *ibid.*, Report, May 3, 1920.

11. Paul Phillips, *No Power Greater* (Vancouver, 1967), pp. 82-88; OBU, circular letter, Victor Midgley, February 2, 1921.

12. OBU, Report of the First Annual Convention, January 1920; R.B. Russell, To T.D. Roberts, Organizer, January 29, 1924; Lumber Workers Industrial Union Records, (LWIU) Port Arthur Branch, Lakehead University, Minute Books, October 1919 to September 1920.

13. B.C. Loggers' Association Minute Book (UBC Archives), Book 203, pp. 21-34, "minutes of meeting, December 5, 1919"; Mountain Lumber Manufacturers' Association, Minute Book, /UBC Archives; OBU, Tom Wall, Prince George District Organizer to Carl Berg, Regional Organizer, Edmonton, September 30, 1919; *British Columbia Federationist*, April 13, 1922.

14. OBU, Minutes of the General Executive Meeting, April 29, 1924; *ibid.*, Russell to Roberts, August 29, 1925.

15. *Ibid.*, Russell to Roberts June 19, 1924; *ibid.*, Roberts to R.H. Dunn, June 15, 1926; Tim Buck, *Thirty Years*, pp. 25-32; "Interview between R.B. Russell and Lionel Orlikow," transcript, PAM.

16. Rodney, *Soldiers*, pp. 28-52; Avakumovic, *Communist Party*, pp. 16-28.

17. Avakumovic, *Communist Party*, 31-39. In the years 1921-25 the ULFTA and the FOC were referred to as Language Bureaus; between 1926 and 1929 they were called National Agitation and Propaganda Committees (Agitprop); in 1929 they were re-classified as Fraction Bureaus. Members of the Jewish Social Democratic Party were also drawn into the CPC. Rodney, *Soldiers*, pp. 78-79, 85-86, 131.

18. Buck, *Thirty Years*, pp. 26-28. The Finns were also the largest group in the American Communist Party. Glazer, *American Communism*, pp. 40-42.

19. William Marunchuk, *The Ukrainian Canadians* (Winnipeg, 1970), pp. 395-408; Department of Justice, 1926, file 293, C. Starnes to deputy minister of justice, October 27, 1926.

20. *Rex v. Buck et al.*, "Declaration by Minority of Central Executive Committee and National Agit Prop Committee of CPC Addressed to the Executive Committee of the Communist International," Exhibit #158.

21. Governor General Office (PAC), vol. 103, C.F. Hamilton to A.F. Sladen, private secretary to governor general, August 31, 1921, cited report of U.S. Security operative, "The Weekly report of revolutionary activities prepared in the Intelligence Branch of the United States War Office."

22. Rodney, *Soldiers*, pp. 83-86; *Rex v. Buck et al.*, "Declaration by Minority," Exhibit #158.

23. Dept. of Justice Files (PAC), 252, files 832-29, H. Wray, president, GWVA, to Sir Lomer Gouin, minister of justice, November 14, 1923; *ibid.*, Mary Bollert, national secretary of the Imperial Order of Daughters of the Empire, to the minister of immigration and colonization, June 27, 1921; *ibid.*, Charles Roland, President of the Employers' Association of Manitoba to Gouin, December 6, 1923.

24. *Ibid.*, 1923, file 1847, Cortlandt Starnes, commissioner /RCMP, to Gouin, July 17, 1922; E.L. Newcombe, deputy minister of justice, to James Murdock, minister of labour, May 8, 1923.

25. *Ibid.*, 1923, file 624, W.A. Dowler to C. Starnes, March 21, 1923. A writ was issued on January 29, 1923 in the Supreme Court of Ontario.

26. *Ibid.*, Memorandum for Minister of Justice, July 28, 1923; *ibid.*, Dowler to Starnes, March 25, 1923; King Papers, 69227, Starnes to King, August 21, 1922; Alberta Provincial Police Files (APP), Starnes to Brownlee, Alberta minister of justice, February 9, 1923.

27. IB, 563236, No. 1, Alseli Rauanheimo to F.C. Blair, secretary, TC, June 10, 1923; Dept. of Justice, 1924, file 1109, C. Starnes to Ernest Lapointe, June 4, 1924; *Fort William Chronicle*, April 29, 1930.

28. David Frank, "The Cape Breton Coal Industry and the Rise and Fall of the British Empire Steel Corporation" (unpublished research paper Dalhousie University, summer 1977); Rodney, *Soldiers*, p. 167.

29. Canadian Communist Party Records (CPC), Ontario, Attorney General Files, PAO, 1-A-0018, J.B. McLachlan to Buck, May 4, 1925; *ibid.*, 1-A-0239, McLachlan to Buck, April 11, 1930.

30. David Bercuson, "Labour Radicalism and the Western Industrial Frontier: 1897-1919", *Canadian Historical Review*, vol. 58, 2 (June 1977), pp. 154-74; William J. Cousins, "A History of the Crow's Nest Pass" (unpublished MA thesis, University of Alberta, 1952), pp. 130-50.

31. APP, circular letter, Coleman, September 8, 1925, "To the officers and members of all local unions in Alberta and Eastern British Columbia"; *ibid.*, Report of Agent #13, December 11, 1925; *The Worker*, June 29, 1925.

32. APP, Report, Inspector J.J. Nicholson, October 24, 1924; *ibid.*, commissioner, APP, to Attorney General J. Brownlee, September 5, 1923.

33. *Ibid.*, Report J.J. Nicholson, July 25, 1925.

34. *Ibid.*, Commissioner to Brownlee, July 25, 1925. Lewis Macdonald (Kid Burns) and 23 others were charged with a variety of offences ranging from assault to unlawful assembly. The coal companies in the Drumheller Valley for their part, rigorously applied the blacklist system against all suspected radicals. APP, Canadian Labour Defence League to Premier Brownlee, February 1, 1926.

35. *Ibid.*, Jesse Gough (Manager of Western Block Mine) to Brownlee, August 20, 1925; Western Coal Operators Association (Glenbow), file 101, C.E. Pratt to R.M. Young, March 20, 1924.

36. Phillips, *No Power Greater*, pp. 77-111; Irene Howard, *Vancouver's Svenskar: A History of the Swedish Community in Vancouver* (Vancouver, 1970), pp. 57-80.

37. CPC, 1-A-0470, Ewen to G. Lamont, Vancouver, November 27, 1930; Hill, "Lumber Workers."

38. *Industrial Solidarity* (IWW Paper), October 6, 1926; *The Worker*, October 16, 1926.

39. *OBU Bulletin*, October 4, 1926; *The Worker*, October 28, 1926.

40. *The Worker*, November 13, 1926; CPC, 1-A-0111, Report, November 1926; *ibid.*, 1-A-0375, Report of June 25, 1930.

41. *The Worker*, February 8, 1930; Hill "Lumber Workers."

42. *The Worker*, April 19, 1930; CPC, 10-C-2454, Report on the Agricultural Proletariat," 1930; I. Avakumovic, "The Communist Party of Canada and the Prairie Farmer: The Interwar Years," in *Western Perspectives I, Papers of the Western Studies Conference, 1973*, edited by David J. Bercuson (Toronto, 1974), pp. 78-87. Walter Wiggins, "Hired Man in Saskatchewan," *The Marxist Quarterly* (Winter 1964), pp. 75-84.

43. CPC, 10-C-2454, "Report on the Agricultural Proletariat, 1930."

44. Avakumovic, "Prairie Farmer," pp. 79-83; McEwen, *The Forge*, pp. 53-118.

45. *Ibid.*, CPC, 1-A-0521, "Decisions Arising from the Communist Party Agrarian Conference held in Saskatoon, October 25-26, 1930"; APP, M. Lymborn to Premier Brownlee, November 21, 1932.

46. *The Worker*, August 11, 1928; McEwen, *The Forge*, pp. 60-75.

47. *Ukrainian Labor News*, October 16, 1928.

48. CPC, 3-A-1537, A. Hautamaki to J.E. Moe, Vancouver, January 14, 1931; *ibid.*, 3-A-1585, McEwen to Port Arthur District Conference, March 24, 1931.

49. Undoubtedly the most unresponsive ethnic group to the Communist appeal were the French Canadians. Throughout the 1920s there were probably fewer than fifty French Canadian members of the party; indeed, in the Ottawa-Hull area CPC organizers could not even have their literature translated into French. CPC, 2-A-1022, McEwen to J. Litterick, June 30, 1931; Buck *Thirty Years*, pp. 29-31.

50. *Ibid.*, 2-A-1022, McEwen to J. Litterick, Organizer, Montreal, June 30, 1930; *ibid.*, 3-A-1535, A. Hautamaki to McEwen, January 14, 1931.

51. The Italians were another group which appeared relatively immune to Communist influence, especially in Montreal and Toronto. Once again the influence of the Roman Catholic Church might have been a decisive factor. CPC, 3-A-1612, Jim Barker to McEwen, April 16, 1931; Samuel L. Baily, "Italians and Organized Labor in the United States and Argentina: 1880-1919," in *The Italian Experience in the United States*, edited by S.M. Tomasi and M. Engel (New York, 1970), pp. 111-23.

52. *Ibid.*, 2-A-1233, McEwen to A. Seal (Windsor), June 27, 1931; Donald Critchlow, "Communist Unions and Racism: A Comparative Study of the Responses of United Electrical Radio and Machine Workers and the National Maritime Union to the Black Question During World War II, *Labour History*, 17, 2, (Spring 1976), 230-44.

53. CPC, 1-A-0144, M.M. (identity unknown) to McEwen, Jan. 15, 1929; *ibid.*, 1-A-0157, Beckie Buhay, Business Manager, *Worker*, to McEwen, July 17, 1929.

54. *Ibid.*, 1-A-0140, Bertha (identity unknown, although probably Ben Winter) to Buck, Aug. 20, 1929; McEwen, *The Forge*, pp. 125-66; Jacob Penner, "Recollections of the Early Socialist Movement in Winnipeg," *The Marxist Quarterly* (Summer 1962), pp. 23-31. Some Winnipeg Party members also claimed that the party had thrown away an opportunity to achieve parliamentary respectability since Winnipeg was "the only centre in the whole American Continent where the 'Communist Party' has any opportunity of having its representative elected to any legislative body." CPC, A-1-23, Holmes to Buck, August 21, 1929.

55. CPC, 3-A-1602, Ewen to Jim Barker, April 3, 1931.

56. Rodney, *Soldiers*, pp. 81-89; Glazer, *American Communism*, pp. 46-47.

57. Avakumovic, *Communist Party*, pp. 54-74; Buck, *Thirty Years*, 58-81.

58. McEwen, *The Forge*, pp. 128-30. Alex Inkeles, *Social Change* *in Soviet Russia* (Cambridge, Mass., 1968), pp. 17-27, 43-51; Roger Pethybridge, *The Social Prelude to Stalinism* (London, 1974), pp. 1-185.

59. Avro Kontainan, "The Finns and the Crisis over Bolshevization in the Workers' party, 1924-25," paper presented at the Conference on the Finnish Experience in Western Great Lakes Region, Duluth, Minnesota, April 26, 1974; Glazer, *American Communism*, pp. 41-58. A.F. Upton, *The Communist Parties of Scandinavia and Finland* (London, 1973), pp. 105-81.

60. CPC, Box Nine, Envelope 15, Letter, Political Secretariat, /ECCI, to Central Committee, CPC, Moscow, October 3, 1929.

61. CPC, 1-A-0102, secretary, FOC, to Secretariat, CPC, December 30, 1929; *The Worker*, April 12, 1930.

62. Rodney, *Soldiers*, pp. 156-58; *The Worker*, February 21, 1931.

63. *Worker*, May 18, 1929; *ibid.*, November 30, 1929; *ibid.*, April 12, 1930.

64. CPC, Box Nine, Envelope 15, "Resolution of the Political Secretariat of the ECCI on the Situation and Tasks of the Communist Party of Canada" Moscow, n.d. (1930).

65. *Ibid*; 9-C-1320, "Report, On the Question of Communist Work in the Ukrainian Workers' Organization of Canada, March [?], 1930."

66. *The Worker*, April 12, 1930; Minutes of Politbureau Meeting, August 14, *Rex v. Buck et al.*, "Hill Testimony, Minutes of Politbureau Meeting, August 14, 1930," p. 655; *ibid.*, "Directive, Joint Meeting, National Finnish Faction & Editorial Board," *Vapaus*, November 2, 1930, p. 650.

67. CPC, 2-A-1323, Hill to Party Secretariat, February 17, 1931; *ibid.*, 2-A-1484, Buck to R. Salo, April 10, 1931.

68. *Ibid.*, 1-A-0091, Joseph Grodowsky to Plenum, CEC, July 13, 1929; *ibid.*, 9-C-1305, Political Committee Meeting, following the meeting of the Party Fraction of ULFTA, February 13, 1930; *Worker*, March 15, 1930.

69. *Ibid.*, 9-C-1308, T. Kobzey, General Executive of ULFTA to all branches of ULFTA, March ?, 1930; *ibid.*, 1-A-0492, Buck to District Bureau #7, (Wpg.), April 30, 1930; *ibid.*, 9-C-1336, Statement, National Ukrainian Agitprop, March 1930.

70. *Ibid.*, Box Nine, Envelope 15, Resolution of the Political Secretariat of the ECCI on the Situation and Tasks of the Communist Party of Canada, n.d. (1930).

71. *Worker*, January 17, 1931; *Ukrainian Labor News*, February 3, 1931; CPC, 1-A-0492, Buck to District Bureau #7 (Wpg.), April 30, 1930.

72. *Ibid.*, 2-A-1514, Buck to D. Barabash, July 4, 1931.
73. *The Worker*, June 27, 1931; *ibid.*, May 30, 1931.
74. *Ibid.*, July 18, 1931; IB, 513111, Immigration Board of Inquiry, letter D. Holmes to S. Carr, March 23, 1931; "Rex v. Buck et al., Testimony," p. 184. In May, 1931 *The Worker* enthusiastically announced the formation of a Lithuanian Local.
75. CPC, 2-A-1896, M. Melrichuk to Ewen, June 6, 1931; *Western Miner*, November 19, 1931.q
76. CPC, 1-A-0427, Worker Unity League memorandum for Sudbury Conference, November 25, 1930; *ibid.*, 2-A-1515 D. Barabash to Ewen, July 3, 1931.
76. *Ibid.*, 2-A-0866, McEwen to Thomas McDermott, Queen's Bay, New Brunswick, June 17, 1931. Other Groups of workers who were organized included freight handlers, railroad navvies, workers in the needle trades, and iron and steel workers.
78. *Ibid.*, 3-A-2310, McEwen to James Sloan, July 30, 1931.
79. *Ibid.*, 3-A-1931, Ben Winter to McEwen, June 30, 1931; *The Worker*, July 4, 1931.
80. Jerry Petryshyn, "A.E. Smith and the Canadian Labor Defence League" (unpublished Ph.D. thesis, University of Western Ontario, 1977), pp. 100-83.
81. Horn, "Keeping Canada 'Canadian'," pp. 35-37; McEwen, *The Forge*, pp. 172-85.
82. *Toronto Mail & Empire*, September 6, 1929; *ibid.*, October 12, 1929; *Debates*, 1931, May 17, 1931.
83. A.B. McKillop, "The Communists as Conscience: Jacob Penner and Winnipeg Civic Politics, 1934-1935," in *Cities in the West: Papers of the Western Canada Urban History Conference* (Ottawa, 1976), pp. 181-209; J.E. Rae "The Politics of Class: Winnipeg City Council, 1919-1945," in *The West and the Nation: Essays in Honour of W.L. Morton, Edited by Carl Berger and Ramsay Cook* (Toronto, 1976), pp. 232-49.
84. WFP, December 1, 1926; W.N. Kolisnyk, "In Canada Since the Spring of 1898," *Marxist Review*, January-February 1961.
85. R.B. Bennett Papers (PAC), 94478, Webb to Bennett; *ibid.*, 94536, Webb to Bennett; April 16, 1931; *ibid.*, Webb to Bennett, May 29, 1931.
86. *Ibid.*, 94105, G. Kurdydyk to Bennett, December 20, 1931; *ibid.*, 94100, Kurdydyk to Bennett, January 15, 1931.
87. *Ibid.*, 94533, J. McKeron, City Clerk, Sudbury to Bennett, April 23, 1931; *ibid.*, 94539-94805, *passim.*
88. *Ibid.*, 94763, Premier Tolmie to Bennett, June 13, 1931. Premier W.T.R. Anderson of Saskatchewan made a similar appeal;

ibid., 94563, Anderson to Bennett, April 28, 1931.

89. *Ibid.*, 95663, Honoré Raymond, Montreal to Bennett, May 12, 1931; IB, 563263, Charles Lanctot, attorney general to W.A. Gordon, minister, IC, May 5, 1931.

90. Department of Justice, 1929, file 293, Ferguson to King, August 11, 1929; Howard Ferguson Papers (PAO), 1930, Ferguson to Tolchard, May 10, 1930. The total number of deportation from Canada rose from 1,886 persons in 1927-28 to 7,025 in 1931-32; a 27.3% increase. Ontario and Manitoba were the provinces which most dramatically increased the level of expulsions: in Ontario they increased from 646 to 2,828 (338%) and in Manitoba from 279 to 1,014 (263%). *Report of the Department of Immigration and Colonization for the Fiscal Year Ending March 31, 1936* (Ottawa, 1936), p. 77.

91. Department of External Affairs Files (PAC), file 1574, H.M. Wrong to O.D. Skelton, August 19, 1930.

92. *Ibid.*, Wrong to Skelton, January 21, 1931. In September 1931 the American Consul in Toronto asked the Ontario Attorney General "for any information arising out of the prosecution of the Communist leaders that (would) help ... to counteract Communist propaganda in the United States." Dept. of External Affairs, file 1574, Report T.S. Belcher, Assistant Commissioner RCMP, to O.D. Skelton, September 3, 1931.

93. IV, 274585, deputy minister, IC, to C. Starnes, April 13, 1929. Attempts were made in April, 1930 to prevent Tom Sula, a prominent member of the Sudbury local, from getting back into the country. Ferguson Papers, 1930, Immigration File, Charles Stewart to Ferguson, April 25, 1930.

94. *Debates of the Senate*, 1931, May 21(140), June 11(225-47); Minutes of the City Council of Winnipeg (PAM), July 14, 1931. Parliament was adjourned on July 23 before the Bill could come to a vote; of course, some nineteen days later the Communist Party was declared an illegal organization.

95. IV, 817510 Thomas Gelley, Winnipeg Commissioner to A.L. Jolliffe, supt., IC, September 5, 1931; *ibid.*, Jolliffe to Gelley, October 2, 1931. The number of immigrants deported for criminality or other civil reasons increased from 673 in 1927-28 to 1,276 in 1931-32. Unfortunately, immigration records do not specify exactly how many of these people were deported under Sections 40 and 41. The Canadian Labor Defence League, however, regularly published lists of Communists who were being deported for "political reasons." *Report of Immigration and Colonization, 1936*, p. 77; Robert Kenny Collection (University of Toronto Library)

"Statistics on Cases Handled by the C.L.D.L., 1929–Feb. 1930."

96. CPC, 3-A-2086, McEwen to F. Bray, Calgary, April 12, 1931; *ibid.*, McEwen to James Sloan, Calgary, July 7, 1931.

97. *Ibid.*, 11-C-2832, Circular Letter CLDL to Labour Unions and all other working class organizations, October 8, 1925.

98. CPC, 11-C-2843, general secretary, CPC, to Defence of Foreign Born Conference January 23, 1931; *ibid.*, Minutes and Reports, CLDL July Conference; *Worker*, December 27, 1930; *ibid.*, March 28, 1931; *ibid.*, July 18, 1931.

99. CPC, 3-A-2265 Mike Gilmour to McEwen, July 3, 1931; *ibid.*, 11-C-2850, Report CLDL, March 19, 1921.

100. *Ibid.*, 2-A-1464, T. Sula, Calgary, to McEwen, March 20, 1931; *Ukrainian Labor News*, July 11, 1931.

101. Buck, *Thirty Years*, pp. 75-102.

102. Avakumovic, *Communist Party*, pp. 85-87; *Worker*, August 22, 1931.

103. IB, 513116, Comm. Starnes, RCMP to Supt., IC, November 21, 1931. Avro Vaara was the most controversial member of the group, largely because of the following editorial which appeared in *Vapaus* in 1929, when King George V was on his deathbed: "Will the King die, it does not matter to us. The social order will be equally oppressive to the poor, whoever is king." For his "indiscretion" Vaara was found guilty of seditious libel, and sentenced to six months in jail, and a fine of $1,000. *Debates* 1931, p. 2354.

104. *The Worker*, September 5 and October 5, 1931.

105. Bennett Papers, 927739, Monsignor A.J. Janssen, vicar general, to Bennett, October 1, 1931.

106. Buck, *Thirty Years*, pp. 90-118; Jerry Petryshyn, "Canadian Labor Defence League," pp. 100-42.

107. Avakumovic, *Communist Party*, pp. 91-95; *Parliamentary Guide*, 1935 (Ottawa, 1935), pp. 243-340.

108. Irving Abella, *Nationalism, Communism and Canadian Labour*, pp. 1-22, 66-85, 213-22.

109. Avakumovic, *Communist Party*, pp. 106-37.

110. News of Stalin's "liquidation" of leading Ukrainian Communists, and of the massive deportations to Siberia seriously disrupted the ULFTA between 1933 and 1935. Members of the FOC were also greatly disturbed by reports of these "purges," and by the "disappearance" of those Canadian Finns who had gone to work in Soviet Karelia. In addition, the Russian attack on Finland in 1939 caused many more to leave the party. Marunchak, *Ukrainian Canadian*, pp. 406-9; Avakumovic, *Communist Party*, pp. 120-21.

Conclusion

1. *Report of the Ontario Commission on Unemployment* (Toronto, 1916); W.R. Böhning, *The Migration of Workers in the United Kingdom and the European Community* (London, 1972), pp. 35-36.

2. Alfred Fitzpatrick, *The University in Overalls* (Toronto, 1920); George Emery, "Methodism on the Canadian Prairies, 1896-1914" (unpublished Ph.D. thesis, University of British Columbia, 1970), pp. 340-48; Reports of the Board of Home Missions, *Presbyterian Acts and Proceedings*, 1909, p. 9.

3. Martin Robin, *Radical Politics and Canadian Labour* (Kingston, 1968); *Proceedings of the Trades and Labor Congress* (1901-31); *Canadian Congress Journal* (1922-28).

4. Ivan Avakumovic, *The Communist Party in Canada* (Toronto, 1975); Irving Abella, *Nationalism, Communism and Canadian Labour* (Toronto, 1973).

Note on Sources

A variety of primary and secondary sources were used in the preparation of this book; almost all of them have been cited in the chapter notes. What is offered here is a more general comment on some of the important primary collections examined. The information is divided into two categories, reflecting the major themes of the book.

A   Immigration Patterns and Employment Conditions

The correspondence of Prime Ministers Laurier (PAC), Borden (PAC), Meighen (PAC), and Bennett (PAC) contains a great deal of information both about the general nature of Canadian immigration policy, and about specific events. Their letters cover a great range of subjects and contain memorandums from government officials, letters from Canadian businessmen, petitions from ethnic groups and other relevant material.

The files of the Immigration Branch (PAC) are the single most important source available for the study of Canadian immigration policy and of the adaption of specific European groups. From these files it is possible to assess the factors which shaped immigration policy decisions, most notably the influence exerted by the Canadian business community. Because immigrant workers were regarded as temporary wards of the Immigration Branch the conditions they found in the bush and mining camps were the subject of numerous reports.

The files of the Dominion Department of Labour (PAC), the Department of Agriculture (PAC), and the Royal Canadian Mounted Police (PAC) usefully complement the Immigration Branch records. The Labour files are especially valuable after 1918, when the Employment Service of Canada was established. RCMP files are very useful for understanding the conditions of immigrant workers in Western Canada. Unfortunately, these records are not available after 1921. The papers of the director of Internment Operations (PAC) show how enemy alien prisoners were employed during World War I.

The annual Departmental records of the Interior (Immigration and Colonization after 1918), Labour, Justice, and Agriculture constitute another useful source. These offer concise summaries of contemporary events and a mass of statistical data on immigrant arrivals, employment opportunities, immigrant occupational patterns, wage levels, and homestead entries. In the same vein a number of important studies were conducted by these departments or by Dominion Royal Commissions. Some of the more important are: *Report of the Select Committee to Prohibit the Importation and Immigration of Foreigners and Aliens Under Contract or to Perform Labour in Canada* (Ottawa, 1890), *Royal Commission to Inquire into the Immigration of Italian Labourers to Montreal, and Alleged Fraudulent Practices of Employment Agencies* (Ottawa, 1904), *Select Standing Committee on Agriculture and Colonization: Minutes of Proceedings and Evidence and Report, 1928, Appendix No. 8* (Ottawa, 1928), W. Burton Hurd, "Racial Origins and Nativity of the Canadian People," *Seventh Census of Canada, 1931, vol. xiii, Monographs* (Ottawa, 1942).

Provincial records are an important asset to the historian of Canadian immigration policy. The papers of the provincial premiers, especially those of Ontario and the Western provinces, are of special significance. In periods of economic stress, when federal-provincial relations were strained, the provincial point of view was especially vocal. Provincial departments also dealt with immigration and labour matters. Evidence of this is to be found in departmental correspondence, in annual reports or in special studies. Some of the more notable of these provincial reports are the *Report of the Ontario Commission on Unemployment* (Toronto, 1916), "Report of Labour Conditions in Gold and Silver Mining Districts in Northern Ontario, October, 1920" (PAO), *Report of the Alberta Coal Commission*, 1925 (Edmonton, 1926).

Private records portray yet another dimension of the Canadian migration experience. In the corporate sector the railway, mining and lumbering companies are of central importance. The railway companies, especially, were involved in every phase of immigrant life: recruitment, movement, and placement. Fortunately, some of the records of the Canadian Pacific Railway Company (PAC, Glenbow) and the Canadian National Railway Company (PAC) are now open to the researcher. Although it is not possible to obtain the same degree of information from the mining and lumbering companies, there are at least two useful collections: these are the Western Coal Operators Association (Glenbow), and the BC Loggers' Association (UBC).

The activities and attitudes of organized labour in Canada towards European immigrant workers can be studied in several ways. The least satisfactory is through the files of either specific trade unions or the Trades and Labor Congress. Not only have few union records survived, but also most Canadian craft unions were generally uninterested in unskilled workers, particularly those of non-British background. Major exceptions were the United Mine Workers of America (UMWA) and the Western Federation of Miners (WFM): fortunately, the records of District 18 of the UMWA (Glenbow) and District 6 of the WFM (UBC) are available. The proceedings of the annual conventions of the Trades and Labor Congress make extensive reference to Canadian immigration policy. Most of what is to be found here, however, is rather general in nature or concerned primarily with skilled workers. Somewhat more useful are the labour newspapers such as *The Voice* (Wpg.), the *Western Labor News* (Wpg.), the *One Big Union Bulletin* (Wpg.), the *B.C. Federationist* (Vanc.), the *Industrial Banner* (Hamilton), and the *Fernie Ledger*. Socialist newspapers like *The Clarion* and *The Worker* offer a heady mixture of investigative reporting and ideological discourse.

Other social groups also attempted to influence Canadian immigration policy. Organized farmers sought to advance their collective interest through the *Grain Growers' Guide*, the *Western Producer*, and the *Farmers Sun*; and by lobbying and direct political action. There is also evidence of the lobbying adopted by agricultural groups in collections such as T.A. Crerar Papers (Queen's). The Protestant churches, most notably the Methodists, Presbyterians, and Anglicans, discussed immigration matters at their annual conferences (UCA and AA). The *Christian Guardian*, the *Presbyterian Witness*, and the *Canadian Churchman* reflected their interest. The papers of Frontier College (PAC), a philanthropic organization which worked among European immigrants in the northern bush camps, constitutes another valuable source.

English language newspapers and journals offer a great deal of local information about the adjustment of European workers. They also illustrate a variety of opinions about Canadian immigration policy. Not surprisingly, they were most critical during hard times or prior to an election.

B Immigrant Worker "Radicalism"

Many of the collections already mentioned contain information about the collective action of European immigrant workers. Major strikes and the activities of organizations like the Industrial Workers of the World (IWW), the One Big Union (OBU), and the Communist Party of Canada (CPC) are commented upon in the papers of prime ministers and the provincial premiers. Of even greater value are the records of the Immigration Branch (PAC), the RCMP (PAC), the Department of Justice (PAC), the Department of National Defence (PAC), and the Secretary of State, Chief Press Censor Branch (PAC). Provincial police files, most notably those of Alberta (APP), British Columbia (PABC), and Ontario (PAO), are also relevant. A common characteristic of all these records, however, is the hostility towards the immigrant activist, often on cultural as well as class grounds.

The bias can be partly offset by reference to the record left behind by the radicals themselves. Here the papers of the Communist Party of Canada (PAO) are particularly valuable. These contain extensive references to the activities of Ukrainian, Finnish, and Jewish groups within the broader Communist organization. The records of District 18 of the United Mine Workers (Glenbow), District 6 of the Western Federation of Miners (UBC) and the One Big Union (UBC, PAM) are similarly revealing. Ethnic newspapers such as *Robotchny Narod* ("Working People"), *Vapaus* ("Truth") and the *Ukrainian Labor News* offer a commentary on contemporary events that often differed from those found in English working-class newspapers such as *The Worker*, the *One Big Union*, and the *B.C. Federationist*.

Appendices on
Demographic Data

TABLE A
Components of Population Growth
Canada 1861-1941
(Thousands of Persons)

Decade	Population Start of Decade	Births	Deaths	Natural Increase	Immigration	Emigration*	Net Migration
1861-1971	3,230	1,369	718	651	183	375	− 192
1871-1981	3,689	1,477	754	723	353	440	− 87
1881-1991	4,325	1,538	824	714	903	1,109	− 206
1891-1901	4,833	1,546	828	718	326	506	− 180
1901-1911	5,371	1,931	811	1,120	1,759	1,043	716
1911-1921	7,207	2,338	988**	1,350	1,612	1,381	231
1921-1931	8,788	2,415	1,055	1,360	1,203	974	229
1931-1941	10,377	2,294	1,072	1,222	150	242	− 92

* A residual, calculated by adding natural increase and immigration to the population count at the start of the decade and subtracting the population count at the end of the decade.

** Includes deaths resulting from the two world wars, numbering 120,000 and 36,000 respectively.

SOURCE: "Immigration and Population Statistics": *Canadian Immigration and Population Study* (Ottawa, 1974), p. 8.

TABLE B
Occupational Background of Immigrant Males
Arriving in Canada, 1907-1935

A. 1907-8 to 1913-14: 58% Total Immigration for Entire Period. (59% of all immigrants were male workers.)

	Farmers	General Labourers	Mechanics	Clerks	Miners	Others	Total
Ocean Ports	250,614 (55%)	289,103 (70%)	126,240 (67%)	59,648 (77%)	18,087 (60%)	32,969 (66%)	776,661 (64%)
Via U.S.	205,530 (45%)	129,962 (30%)	61,075 (33%)	17,899 (23%)	12,057 (40%)	16,749 (34%)	443,272 (36%)
TOTAL	456,144	419,065	187,315	77,547	30,144	49,718	1,219,933
% of Total Immigration for Periods	37.4	34.4	15.4	6.4	2.4	4	100

B. 1914-15 to 1918-19: 10% of Total Immigration for Entire Period. (53% of total immigrants were male workers.)

	Farmers	General Labourers	Mechanics	Clerks	Miners	Others	Total
Ocean Ports	13,684 (18%)	26,156 (45%)	6,525 (15%)	3,155 (31%)	907 (28%)	8,328 (40%)	58,755 (28%)
Via U.S.	63,120 (82%)	31,782 (55%)	37,817 (85%)	7,078 (69%)	2,383 (72%)	12,760 (60%)	154,940 (72%)
TOTAL	76,804	57,938	44,342	10,233	3,290	21,088	213,695
% of Total Immigration for Period	35.9	27.1	20.8	4.8	1.5	9.9	100

C. 1919-20 to 1924-25: 11.5% of Total Immigration for Entire Period. (47% of total immigrants were male workers.)

	Farmers	General Labourers	Mechanics	Clerks	Miners	Others	Total
Ocean Ports	71,300 (62%)	22,093 (65%)	26,188 (60%)	9,896 (63%)	4,394 (78%)	15,512 (61%)	150,383 (63%)
Via U.S.	43,310 (38%)	11,756 (35%)	17,398 (40%)	5,829 (37%)	1,263 (22%)	10,102 (39%)	89,658 (37%)
TOTAL	114,610	33,849	43,586	15,725	5,657	25,614	240,041
% of Total Immigration for Period	47.8	14.2	18.3	6.6	2.4	10.7	100

D. 1925-26 to 1929-30: 18% of Total Immigration for Entire Period. (52% of total immigrants were male workers.)

	Farmers	General Labourers	Mechanics	Clerks	Miners	Others	Total
Ocean Ports	248,961	22,241	22,000	11,298	3,006	7,640	315,146
Via U.S.	25,445	8,926	13,412	7,963	803	6,907	63,456
TOTAL	274,406	31,167	35,412	19,261	3,809	14,547	378,602
% of Total Immigration for Period	72	8	9.5	5	1	4	100

E. 1930-31 to 1934-35: 2.5% of Total Immigration for Entire Period. (33% of total immigrants were male workers.)

	Farmers	General Labourers	Mechanics	Clerks	Miners	Others	Total
Ocean Ports	18,340	3,444	4,009	2,438	200	2,027	30,458 (58%)
Via U.S.	6,760	1,541	4,135	4,941	198	4,464	22,039 (42%)
TOTAL	25,100	4,985	8,144	7,379	398	6,491	52,597
% of Total Immigration for Period	48	9	15.6	14	.8	12.6	100

F.

TOTAL NO. OF	Farmers	General Labourers	Mechanics	Clerks	Miners	Others	Total
Ocean Ports	602,899	363,037	184,962	86,435	26,594	66,476	1,331,403
Via U.S.	344,165	183,967	133,837	43,710	16,704	50,982	773,365
TOTAL	947,064	547,004	318,799	130,145	43,298	117,458	2,104,768
% of Total Immigration for Period	45	26	15.1	6.2	2.1	5.6	100

TABLE C
Deportations

By Causes	1902 to 1913-14	1914-15 to 1918-19	1919-20 to 1924-25	1925-26 to 1929-30	1930-31 to 1935-36
Medical	2,866 (33%)	792 (17.5%)	1,920 (21%)	2,649 (24%)	2,488 (10%)
Public Charges	3,568 (41%)	1,779 (39%)	3,341 (36.5%)	3,840 (34.5%)	15,248 (62%)
Criminality	1,459 (16.5%)	1,520 (33.5%)	3,124 (34%)	2,358 (21%)	3,677 (15%)
Other Civil	693 (8%)	375 (8%)	409 (4.5%)	896 (8%)	1,332 (5%)
Accompaniment of Deported Person	155 (1.5%)	97 (2%)	378 (4%)	1,371 (12.5%)	1,999 (8%)
TOTAL	8,741	4,563	9,172	11,114	24,744
% of Total Deportations for Period	15	8	15.6	19	42.4
By Nationalities					
British	5,310 (61%)	1,800 (39%)	4,836 (53%)	4,820 (62%)	14,858 (60%)
American	1,471 (17%)	1,908 (42%)	2,991 (32%)	1,400 (13%)	1,534 (6%)
Other Countries	1,960 (22%)	855 (19%)	1,342 (15%)	2,794 (25%)	8,352 (34%)
TOTAL	8,741	4,563	9,172	11,114	24,744

SOURCE: *Report of the Department of Immigration and Colonization for the Fiscal Year Ending March 30, 1936* (Ottawa, 1932), pp. 76-77.

Acknowledgements

In the writing of this book I have incurred many debts. My first obligation is to the late Dr. D.G.G. Kerr of the University of Western Ontario who supervised my Ph.D. thesis, my first venture into the field of immigration and ethnic history. I am grateful for his sensitive guidance. My second debt is to my wife Janet who always found time in a busy family life to offer intellectual assistance. The support I enjoy from my sons Richard and Bruce has also been an inspiration.

Among the scholars who have helped me in the preparation of "*Dangerous Foreigners*" my colleague and friend Peter Neary heads the list; his stylistic suggestions have been particularly valuable. Michael Cross and Diana Swift greatly facilitated the smooth transition from manuscript to book, while Sam Clark, Jim Rinehart, Michael Bliss, Bryan Palmer, and Wayne Roberts have all offered useful comments.

I am grateful to the Canada Council and the University of Western Ontario for financial support, and to the secretaries in the UWO History Department for their hard work on my behalf.

My research was aided considerably by the co-operation of the staff of the following institutions: the Public Archives of Canada, the University of British Columbia Archives, the Manitoba Archives, the Alberta Archives, the British Columbia Archives, the Ontario Archives and the Glenbow Institute.

Errors of fact, judgment, and interpretation are, of course, my own.

Index